Contents

Preface

The purpose in writing this book is to clarify the many elements that are grouped together under the umbrella of 'good practice' in managing the teaching of mathematics at school and classroom level in nursery and infant schools.

The art of 'good practice' in schools and classrooms has always implicitly included the skills of good management. Good leadership skills, clear planning, strategic organisation and systems analysis are as important to teaching as they are to the world of business. Since the Education Reform Act 1988, schools have been accorded the responsibility of managing themselves as a business or a 'family firm', with all the attendant responsibilities of financial management and accountability. This has resulted in significant changes in the ways schools conduct their affairs. In responding to the need for change, schools have adopted management strategies which, in many respects, mirror those of the business world, through analysing the current situation, establishing long, medium and short-term targets and reviewing the subsequent progress of planned developments. Whilst these principles can be generalised to apply to the management of all schools, the details need to take account of the fact that no two schools are the same. Catchment area, geographical layout of buildings, number of children on roll and the background cultures of staff contribute to the uniqueness of all educational settings. For the classroom teacher, where everything is subject to constant change, the principles of 'good practice' are more difficult to achieve. 'No single moment is like the next, no child is like the next, no teaching or learning episode is an exact replica of any other, and even the content of the curriculum is subject to constant change and review' (Clemson and Clemson, 1994).

This book sets out to explain and give examples of 'good practice', related to recent research and initiatives which identify 'quality indicators' in relation to the management and teaching of mathematics in the early years. Whilst it is inappropriate to offer definitive advice on how to manage the effective teaching of mathematics in schools and classrooms, it is hoped that this book will help students and experienced teachers to formulate a view of mathematics teaching that is informed by current educational and political perspectives. It is hoped that student teachers will be able to gain an understanding of the importance of management skills, at school and classroom level, to assist them in developing and implementing effective mathematics programmes on 'school experience'. For experienced teachers, it is hoped that this book will enable them to reflect on existing practices and formulate plans for development. There are several recurring themes throughout the book, which include:

- the skill of working interactively with children, other staff and adults;
- the process of taking stock of situations as they present themselves;
- the process of formulating realistic and apporpriate plans of action; and
- the process of putting plans into action and evaluating their effectiveness.

Section 1 sets the scene by examining ways in which children learn mathematics and how teachers can create contexts for learning to take place. It represents important background knowledge for any teacher of young children who has to undertake the task of managing the effective planning, teaching and continuous assessment of mathematical work in the early years of schooling.

Chapter 1 considers the ways in which children begin to make sense of mathematics, through early experiences of social interaction with adults and other children and through playful exploration of objects and ideas. The chapter also discusses how quality provision of playful experiences can support mathematical learning throughout the primary school.

Chapter 2 continues the story by presenting ways in which children develop later mathematical knowledge and skills through drawing upon a network of experiences which involve handling objects and articulating ideas, creating representational pictures of mathematical ideas and representing ideas through the mathematical language of number symbols and arithmetical signs. The chapter also looks at differences in children's mathematical learning arising from natural endowment or cultural upbringing.

The final chapter in this section recognises the problem that mathematics is recognised as a difficult subject to learn, and it explores some of the common problems children experience in learning aspects of number, shape and measures at nursery level through to beginning KS2. This is supported by examples of strategies used by teachers to support children in overcoming these problems as they arise.

Section 2 examines the overall management of mathematical provision throughout a school.

Chapter 4 examines the process of formulating a mathematical policy and the importance of active participation by all staff involved in teaching mathematics in a school. It discusses key stages in the process of creating a new policy document, from creating forms for staff discussion to preparing for publication, and concludes with emphasising the process of review and the establishemnt of development plans.

Chapter 5 examines the middle management role of the mathematics co-ordinator in supporting developments in mathematical provision throughout a school, and strategies to support and initiate staff development through in-service training.

Chapter 6 examines the processes involved in the management of mathematical resources at school level, including the financial implications. It discusses the establishment of a resource inventory, arrangements for central storage, and strategies for maintaining and developing a resource base.

Chapter 7 discusses developments in parent partnership initiatives since the 1980s, together with examples of models from recent practice. Strategies are offered for the implementation of new initiatives in schools, and ways are discussed as to how parents and other adults can be involved in supporting mathematical activities in classrooms.

Chapter 8 examines the collective staff approach to creating long and medium-term plans for mathematics in nursery and infant schools. It includes the formulation of schemes of work and topic plans as well as discrete plans, and discusses the issues related to overuse of published maths schemes. Chapter 8 also sets the scene for the management of short-term planning and lesson management discussed in Section 3.

Section 3 discusses the responsibilities of a classroom teacher to manage and deploy the use of resources effectively in relation to teaching mathematics to a class of children. It considers the skills involved and the documentation required for lesson management, and looks at ideas for planning mathematical activities in a variety of contexts.

Chapter 9 examines the process of reviewing the existing provision, the organisation of space, storage of resources and accessibility as well as the establishment of regular routines for maintenance. It considers the role of adult helpers in supporting teachers with resource management and teaching, including the creation of displays.

Chapter 10 discusses the process of lesson planning, giving detailed analysis of the proceedings of a lesson from start to finish, with examples of different lesson plans. it considers common 'hot spots' in control management, together with examples of strategies to reduce problems occurring. It discusses the planning of assessment opportunities in mathematics sessions and examines the process of reflective evaluation to inform subsequent planning.

Chapter 11 reflects the current concern about the teaching of number in primary schools and points to ways in which teachers can plan activities to develop early number skills and increase children's ability to calculate mentally. It focuses on the use of mental arithmetic games and open-ended tasks to develop children's understanding of number patterns and relationships, and includes a section on appropriate use of calculators.

Chapter 12 examines the opportunities for mathematical development and enrichment that can arise from active learning through play, crosscurricular work, mathematics topics and the planning of mathematical events. It also includes a discussion on how work in shape, space, measures and handling data can arise naturally from practical activities related to real-life contexts.

Section 4 takes a look at the different processes involved in assessment, including planning considerations, the use of baseline and continuous assessment, and the procedures involved in administering SATs for mathematics at KS1.

Chapter 13 examines the requirements for a school to establish a mechanism for monitoring the progress and continuity of children's achievements throughout the school in a form that is standardised and easy to manage.

Chapter 14 examines the use of baseline assessment procedures in respect to screening children on entry to school and as a process for guiding planning when teachers receive new children into their class.

Chapter 15 discusses key skills which enable teachers to make accurate judgements about children's mathematical performance. It includes the process of review and target-setting together with examples of the different types of action that might be taken as a result of children's mathematical performance. The importance of evaluation procedures is re-emphasised in relation to the long-term benefits of continuous assessment.

Chapter 16 examines the statutory procedures currently in operation for administering SATs to Year 2 classes, including task, test and teacher assessment, as well as the consideration of special cases and procedures for disapplication.

Section 5 considers some of the more difficult elements of managing the teaching of mathematics including a discussion and examples of strategies for managing a differentiated curriculum for mathematics in the classroom. It examines key factors associated with 'low attainment' and 'giftedness' and gives suggestions on ways to support low attainers and gifted children in mathematics. Strategies are offered for documenting children's mathematical achievements in ways that include the recording of relevant formative and summative information. The final chapter discusses the establishment of formal and informal communication networks to enable the important process of reporting to take place.

Chapter 17 presents a brief historical perspective, followed by a discussion on strategies which support differentiated teaching and ways to plan work for different levels of ability. This includes the use of baseline assessment, open-ended tasks, more flexible use of class time and grouping arrangements, and inviting parents to help their children at home.

Chapter 18 discusses some of the problems associated with learning mathematics and identifies key factors related to low attainment. Strategies for supporting the low-attaining child are presented, including the importance of building on children's strengths as well as supporting weaknesses, and the need for early formal identification of special educational needs where there is evidence of significant concern.

Chapter 19 discusses some of the problems gifted children experience at home and at school and identifies key factors associated with 'giftedness'. Strategies for supporting gifted children with mathematics include the importance of respecting their talents and establishing learning partnerships, where the teacher and child learn together.

Chapter 20 examines the process of record-keeping as a tool for monitoring progress and continuity in children's mathematical achievements throughout a school. It discusses the management of record-keeping at school and classroom level, with examples of strategies that are commonly in use throughout early years education.

Chapter 21 presents the process of reporting in terms of the statutory duties of headteachers and staff to send written reports to parents and to 'following' schools in relation to children's levels of achievement in mathematics, together with examples of arrangements for formal and informal discussions with parents. The importance of giving positive feedback to children is discussed alongside the need to establish communication networks between other members of staff and the headteacher. Finally, the chapter concludes by discussing the requirement to keep the school governors and LEAs regularly informed about the mathematical provision in a school.

Acknowledgements

The author would like to thank the following people: Graham Edwards for his continuous support over the years and his special encouragement and help with the technical production of this book; David (Bud) Winteridge, Dean of Academic Studies, Westhill College of Higher Education, Birmingham, for his professional guidance and encouragement; and Keith Barker, librarian, Westhill College of Higher Education, Birmingham, for his support and informed advice on source material.

Also the following colleagues in schools: Barrie Morris, headteacher, and the staff of Ashton Hayes County Primary School, Ashton, Cheshire; Linda Hopkins, headteacher, and the staff of Weaver County Primary School, Nantwich, Cheshire; Linda Salmon, headteacher, and the staff of Beeches Nursery and Infant School, Frankley Beeches, Birmingham; Sue Bennett, headteacher, and the staff of Brearley Nursery School, Newtown, Birmingham; Angela Freer-Hewish, headteacher, and the staff of Selly Oak Nursery, Selly Oak, Birmingham; and Pat Ninham, nursery manager, and the staff of Smallwood Manor Prepreparatory Department, Uttoxeter, Staffordshire.

Thanks need to be expressed to generations of children and student teachers who, for better or worse, were the subject of my own teaching and enabled the gradual refinement of ideas represented in this book.

Finally, gratitude is due to special guiding lights during my career as a teacher: Mary Cox, Elsie Holdham, Connie Stone, the late Ken Hardcastle and especially Graham Edwards. Without their support and encouragement, this book would not have been written.

We acknowledge permission to reproduce the following copyright material:

Figures 2.6 and 2.7 from S. Atkinson (1992) *Mathematics with Reason*, reprinted by permission of Hodder & Stoughton Educational.

Figures 2.10 from A. Pollard and S. Tann (1993) *Reflective Teaching in the Primary School* 2/e, reprinted by permission of Cassell plc.

Figures 2.11, 2.12 and 2.13 from H. Hughes (1986) *Children and Number:*

Difficulties in Learning Mathematics, reprinted by permission of Blackwell Publishers.

Figure 13.1 from Clemson, D. and Clemson, W. *Mathematics in the Early Years*, (1994) reprinted by permission of Routledge.

SECTION I
The process of learning mathematics in the early years of schooling

1

Learning mathematics through interactive play

For young children, learning is about developing a sense of meaning and understanding of the world around them. It represents, predominantly, a social process where the highest incidence of learning takes place in social settings, in the company of interested adults and other children (Bruner, 1990). Young infants initially learn through watching, imitating actions and speech, handling objects and exploring the space around them in playful situations, which can be initiated by caring adults or older siblings.

It is through playful social interaction and encouragement that young children develop a love for learning. Through interactive play children also develop confidence to explore new experiences to the point where, for example, in mathematical terms, they begin to verbalise their experiences, ask questions, make comparisons, establish generalisations, make predictions and solve problems. Teachers of young children will acknowledge that, when young children are left on their own to play unsupervised, without the stimulus of interested company or interesting activities to do in school, they are more likely to display behaviours associated with boredom and frustration.

Young children characteristically have a natural curiosity and love for learning and respond with enthusiasm to interactive playful experiences which are stimulating, challenging and exciting. The challenge to nursery and infant teachers is not simply to provide repetitive sessions of free-play activities but to establish the provision of a carefully structured, activity-based curriculum, within a well resourced environment, built around high adult involvement and opportunities for children to learn together.

Learning mathematics through play

Purpose

Children (and adults) learn better when they are interested and motivated to learn. This in turn makes learning a purposeful and pleasurable experience. Play activities have a built-in pleasure element. Because they are pressure-free and predominantly active and social activities, the enjoyment factor is often sufficient to encourage children to concentrate and persist on a task for long enough for learning to occur (Griffiths, 1994).

Play as a context for learning

Mathematics is a powerful tool which has its application rooted in the use of mathematical models and symbols to represent and find solutions to problems which occur in everyday life. Mathematics is also acknowledged as a difficult subject to learn because some elements are very abstract. Early mathematical learning occurs when young children interact with adults and other children, through the active exploration of 'concrete' objects and materials (sand, water, etc.) within playful situations in a variety of contexts. As children develop, ways need to be found to help them to see the links between concrete and abstract ideas (this is developed further in Chapter 2). To sustain motivation and interest and avoid children becoming anxious as the mathematics becomes more difficult, the presentation of mathematics in interactive playful contexts can support and inspire learning in ways difficult to achieve through formal didactic teaching, or working in isolation through workbooks or textbooks.

Time for play

Time for mathematical play provides children with valuable opportunities to practise skills and gain mastery of mathematical ideas in pressure-free situations. They can learn with and from other children and ask questions to clarify ideas. This is especially important with those aspects of mathematics which are hierarchical, where the understanding of new knowledge and skills depends on children having understood previous ideas (Griffiths, 1994).

Practical activity

Playful contexts are important in practical activities, where they represent a significant part of the mathematics curriculum that is not pencil and paper driven. Where written recording is required, it should serve to represent evidence of practical work and discussion that has taken place, as well as providing opportunities for practice and mastery.

Play for learning and play for practice

Corinne Hutt's work with young children (1979) resulted in an analysis of play behaviours in relation to learning. This analysis identified *epistemic* and *ludic* behaviours, and *games with rules*.

Epistemic play behaviours

In the context of mathematical learning, epistemic behaviours are principally related to the acquisition of knowledge and skills through use of language, visual experiences and exploratory practical investigations and problem-solving activities with objects and materials (paint, clay/dough, sand/water, etc.). Activities to stimulate epistemic behaviours might include:

- teacher/adult-directed interactive exposition of new concepts and/or skills in number, shape, space and measures;
- individual or collaborative free-play experimentation with unfamiliar objects or materials;
- teacher/adult-directed interactive investigations with familiar objects and/or materials;
- observing and/or participating in collaborative practical activities with other children;
- individual or collaborative problem-solving activities;
- playing a new whole-class, group or individual mathematical game;
- looking at new books/reading new books with a mathematical theme;
- listening to a new mathematical story;
- learning a new number song or rhyme;
- exploring novel presentations of mathematics in a variety of crosscurricular contexts through topic work;
- going on educational visits or having visitors to school;
- watching a mathematical video or television programme;
- playing a new mathematical computer game or known game at a new level of difficulty; and
- acting out real-life mathematical experiences in role-play simulations.

Whilst this list is not exhaustive, the examples given demonstrate that classroom activities designed to stimulate epistemic behaviours are not only for nursery or reception classes but are also relevant throughout the primary age range.

Ludic play behaviours

Ludic behaviour involves the practice or rehearsal of mathematical skills already acquired, through the provision of a variety of contexts, which enable children to develop confidence in applying new learning and to gain mastery of learned skills. Activities which stimulate ludic behaviours might include:

- teacher/adult-directed oral counting, mental arithmetic, and shape or space games;
- playing familiar individual or collaborative maths games with dice, dominoes, board games, etc.;
- free exploration of familiar objects and materials;
- free sorting and classifying activities;
- free play with familiar construction toys, jigsaws, bead threading and junk modelling, etc.;
- free activities involving representational play (farm animals, play people, toy cars, etc.);
- free activities involving fantasy play (dressing up, role-play corner, etc.);
- revisiting well loved mathematical picture books, stories, rhymes and songs;
- replaying a mathematical computer game at the same level of difficulty;
- number writing and number ordering activities (tracing, painting, dot-to-dot, 'staircases', etc.); and
- worksheet, workbook or textbook recording exercises to practise arithmetical skills, reinforce understanding of properties of shapes, etc.

Teachers will be able to identify the different types of activities which can be set up to stimulate epistemic and ludic behaviours for children to learn and achieve mastery of mathematical concepts and skills. It can also be seen that any particular activity may represent epistemic and ludic elements. When an activity is novel it will stimulate epistemic behaviour. As the child develops a sense of familiarity with an activity, the epistemic value will decrease and the ludic value will increase accordingly. It is the role of the teacher to orchestrate a well resourced balance of activities that can stimulate both epistemic and ludic behaviour, whilst recognising that a healthy balance of both elements is important for learning and mastery to take place. A child who is continuously presented with activities which predominantly invoke ludic behaviour is likely to suffer from under-achievement through lack of opportunities to acquire new knowledge and skills. A child who is continuously presented with activities that predominantly invoke epistemic behaviour may well suffer from overload, where learning is superficial and easily forgotten. Without opportunities to practise and apply new knowledge and skills, little depth of understanding is established.

Games with rules

Mathematical games stimulate both epistemic and ludic behaviours depending on the players' level of mastery of a game. Mathematical games also present opportunities for whole-class, group and individual play, at varying levels of difficulty, with nursery, infant and junior children. Games with rules can involve co-operative and/or competitive principles and are ideal for children to learn and practise mental arithmetic skills and to experience games of chance and skill at any age.

Structuring mathematical play through adult involvement

Teachers of young children generally agree that it is much easier to direct individual learning (through asking questions and encouraging children to make decisions) with a small group carrying out a practical activity than when directing a whole class. Whilst there are certain contexts where whole-class interactive work is appropriate, for example a counting game played during 'circle time', interactive group and/or individual activities enable teachers to fine tune outcomes according to the response of individual children.

Hutt *et al.* (1989) state that 'the key to the quality of children's learning experiences is adult participation'. This does not mean that every activity has to be directed by an adult, but that adults are actively involved in a continuous process of analysis and reflection on the relationship between play and learning, in the course of planning and directing learning experiences. According to Wood and Attfield (1996), children can be motivated and challenged through play and can form positive attitudes to learning which can persist in later life if they are actively supported by the provision of:

- an environment which is organised to offer high quality, varied resources which allow for progression and extension;

- experiences which promote self-reliance, co-operation, collaboration, responsibility and interdependence so that children are involved in their own learning;

- educators who have the expertise and take the time to act as partners in children's play so that they can move them forward collaboratively;

- managerial and organisational strategies which empower children as learners and develop their confidence as players and learners;

- contexts which recognise the potential of play as a context for teaching and learning.

(Wood and Attfield, 1996)

Play and the National Curriculum

Learning through play is largely dependent on the social context in which play takes place. It represents the acquisition of knowledge and skills which arise from a spontaneous love of learning as well as from the direct teaching of specific knowledge and cognitive strategies. The discrete subject base of the National Curriculum has given rise to more emphasis on direct teaching in mathematics, particularly with respect to numeracy, and less emphasis on the provision of epistemic stimulation through structured play and crosscurricular work. The play/work divide is a contentious issue. Whilst diligence and playfulness may be acceptable in the preschool sector, the boundaries between work and play become increasingly more evident as children travel through their primary education. Yet there are few teachers who would challenge that children work hard, sustaining high levels of effort, motivation, concentration and outcomes, when rich and meaningful mathematical play situations are offered throughout the primary stage.

The discrete subject model of learning prescribed by the National Curriculum is more in line with the hierarchical pattern of secondary school learning principles, rather than the interdisciplinary network approach common to the early years of schooling. In many respects these approaches represent very different styles of learning. Positively, the advent of the National Curriculum has served to enlighten teachers at primary level to value the direct teaching of specific knowledge and concept strategies in certain contexts. It has also served to initiate critical reflection on early years practice. This in turn has emphasised that quality provision is essential if play is to be used to create a context which energises and inspires children to experience wonder, breadth and balance in learning. Establishing play as a context provides opportunities for children to establish ownership of their learning and to learn with and from other children, in a form that is sometimes spontaneous, sometimes directed but predominantly enjoyable. Janet Moyles (1989) strongly affirms this principle:

> because play is a process rather than a subject, it is really within subjects that one should look to play as a means of teaching and learning rather than as a separate entity. Because of the relevance and motivation of play to children, play must pervade how teachers present learning activities, not set as an uncomfortable and somewhat suspect activity in itself.

Play for life

There should be recognition that play extends beyond childhood into the world of adults, and represents an inherent feature and need throughout life. It serves an important function in satisfying the higher-order intellectual, creative, physical, emotional, social and cultural needs of children, adolescents and adults, beyond the basic needs of survival in any society. One of the most powerful statements about this is presented in the classic work of the Dutch anthropologist Johann Huizinga (1949):

> Play is a social impulse, older than culture itself and pervades all life like a veritable ferment. Ritual grew up in sacred play, poetry was born in play and nourished in play: music and dancing were pure play. Wisdom and philosophy found expression in words and form derived from religious contexts. The rules of warfare, the conventions of noble living were built up on play patterns. We have to conclude therefore that civilization in its earliest phases evolved from play. Play was not an activity that developed as civilization became more sophisticated, rather play was at the heart of civilization.

Children do not outgrow play but their modes of play change as their needs change. In considering changing modes of play, in relation to mathematical learning, there is a gradual shift from play with objects to more sophisticated rule-bound play and representational expression. The following chapter continues the story of how children develop their understanding of mathematics through the learning of specific mathematical knowledge and cognitive strategies.

Summary

This chapter has examined the key issues in relation to the place of play in the nursery and KS1 curriculum. It emphasises that play is a learning process, not a subject in itself, which stimulates natural learning behaviours in childhood and throughout adult life. The involvement of adults in the management and implementation of quality play provision in schools is central to enabling young children to learn effectively. With respect to young children learning mathematics, the process of learning through play should be seen as integral to the acquisition of mathematical knowledge and skills through the stimulation of epistemic and ludic behaviours. If managed well, the process of play can be an energising agent in children's mathematical learning and can support and augment mathematical learning at every stage of primary education.

2

Making connections between concrete mathematical experiences and abstract thinking processes

What is mathematics?

In simple terms mathematics is a group of processes carried out with mathematical objects. According to David Winteridge (1989):

> At the primary level these 'objects' can be generally classified as numbers, measurements and shapes. The child must acquire some knowledge of these 'objects', for example, begin to acquire the concept of number, identify symbols to represent numbers, establish the various relationships between numbers. Much of the knowledge is itself acquired through involvement in mathematical processes.

A model for understanding: making connections

Handling objects

Through handling 'objects', very young children are able to begin to develop mathematical understanding. In the early stages, for example, handling 'objects' enables children to develop their sorting, classifying and counting skills. This will lead to combining and partitioning 'objects' to develop the computation skills of addition and subtraction; grouping sets of 'objects' to develop skills of multiplication, division and fractions; and exchanging 'objects' to develop an understanding of place value.

Prior to coming to school and at nursery level, the handling of familiar everyday 'objects' enables children to learn about their properties and components. Through a range of play activities with different collections of toys, building materials, water, sand, etc., children are able to rationalise their experiences into generalisations through manipulation, sorting and classifying, and by talking to adults and other children.

Language

How to do things with words.

(John Austin)

Language represents the oral or written expression of thought. In simple terms, the process of thinking is carried out by talking in our heads. We create mental pictures and use 'talking' thought processes to interpret these pictures or to communicate meaning to others. Children as young infants learn first to associate spoken words with familiar persons, initially through the use of lullating sounds ('mumumum' 'dadadada'). This is the first step children take in learning to associate 'objects' with the words that represent those objects. As children develop an awareness of the world around them, so their skills of verbal classification of 'objects' increase. Pamela Liebeck (1984) cites the following example of her daughter's early language development:

> At sixteen months, Helen learnt that 'bath' named the object where she sat in water and played. For a while, she called every container of water 'bath'... Later, she learnt that there were other terms (such as 'sink', 'bowl') associated with water containers, and she gradually refined her concept of 'bath' to fit convention.

However, language acquisition does not happen by itself, but requires assistance in the form of interaction with parents, carers and other children. According to Jerome Bruner (1990), 'Language is acquired not in the role of spectator but through use. Being "exposed" to a flow of language is not nearly so important as using it in the midst of "doing"'. It is also important that the child is given the opportunity to explore the use of language in a range of contexts, to develop and refine his or her use of language to establish more precise meaning. For example 'dog' – 'big dog' – 'big white dog'.

By the time children arrive in a nursery school they will normally have a fairly sophisticated command of language. In mathematical terms, many children can classify objects by name ('dog'; 'ball'; 'car', etc.); they can describe objects in terms of simple size and colour ('big'; 'red'). They are aware of simple physical properties such as 'hot' and 'cold', and that a ball 'rolls', and they can understand simple terms of movement and position ('run'; 'walk'; 'up'; 'down'; 'on'; 'under'). Children may have begun to understand the first principles of number through matching, for example, knowing that a shoe is required for each foot, and they may also have started to say numbers and count, through learning counting rhymes, counting toys and counting steps or stairs at home.

The learning of mathematical language, through an interactive activity, is a vital element of children's intellectual development in school. Children should be encouraged to articulate their ideas, ask questions, listen to and follow instructions; and to share challenges in discussion with their friends and teachers at every stage.

In a study of mathematical discussion in primary classrooms, a list of 'competencies' children can acquire through the use of oral strategies in mathematics was drawn up by Tom Brissenden (1988):

- articulating and presenting an idea publicly, in a clear and intelligible way;
- explaining a method;
- arguing logically in support of an idea;
- criticising an argument logically, including one's own;
- evaluating the correctness of an idea, or its potential in attacking a problem;
- speculating, conjecturing, entertaining an idea provisionally;
- accepting an idea provisionally and examining the consequence, keeping track of a discussion, reviewing;
- coping with being stuck, supporting others in difficulty;
- drawing others out, using 'Show me...' or 'How did you get that...?'
- acting as a spokesperson for a group's ideas.

In a small research project investigating children's mathematical talk it was noticed by the author that, at nursery and reception stages, children articulate their mathematical thinking out loud, even when working on their own – for example, counting objects orally, articulating their actions to their peers, trying out ideas and eliciting help and telling others what to do. By Year 2, when children were working on their own, much of their mathematical thinking was carried out in their heads. When working with a partner or in a small group, carrying out a simple arithmagon investigation (see Figure 2.1), they began openly to articulate their thinking processes in much the same way as the younger children.

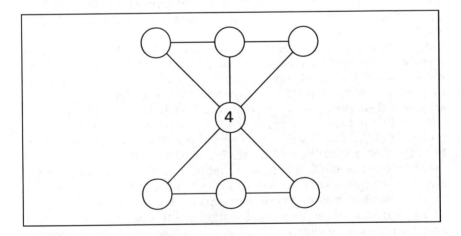

Figure 2.1 Arithmagon activity with Year 2 children (Children were asked to use each of the numbers, 1, 2, 3, 5, 6 and 7 and to write one number in every circle. Three numbers in any straight line had to add up to 12)

At Year 6 the pattern was very different. The children were given a more advanced arithmagon investigation to carry out in pairs or a small group. There was very little cross-talk or discussion except to ask for verification or give approval. The children worked in their heads and processed other children's actions in their heads.

It was difficult to tell whether the Year 6 children were more conditioned to working in relative silence but it serves to indicate that, as children grow older, they perhaps need to be given more encouragement to work with other children, to talk about their work and to discuss ideas. The principles set out in the framework for the National Numeracy Project (1997) recommend that children should be more openly involved in orally expressing their mathematical ideas through whole-class interactive teaching.

Pictures

The making of representational pictures is an important aspect of mathematical development, from the first marks a small child makes on paper to the adult version of a plan of a building drawn to scale. In simple terms, pictures represent the link between objects and numbers or symbolic representation. However, pictures on their own have no meaning without:

- contextual knowledge or experience of the object(s) that a picture represents; and
- an understanding of the oral or written language which defines or describes the object(s) represented by a picture.

Pamela Liebeck (1984) gives the following example by way of explanation:

Sequence for a child's learning about the concept 'ball'

- *Experience with physical objects*

    He sees, feels, tastes, holds, rolls and drops his ball.
    He has 'fun' and learns about many of its properties.

- *Spoken language that describes that experience*

    He associates the sound of the word 'ball' with his toy. This is useful. If he says the word he may be given the ball to play with.
    He will soon associate 'ball' with other objects that have the same rolling property as his ball.

- *Pictures that represent the experience*

    He recognises a picture of a ball. The picture is very different from the ball itself. The picture does not roll, or feel like a ball. But the child sees that it has enough in common with his own ball to be called a 'ball'.

- *Written symbols that generalise the experience*

    Much later, he learns the symbol that we write to represent the sound 'ball'.

This is sophisticated. The symbol has no properties at all in common with a real ball, and it is only artificially associated with the sounds that we utter in saying the word ball.

Liebeck refers to this sequence of abstractions as E–L–P–S (Experience, Language, Pictures, Symbols) and observes that 'a mathematics textbook for children, however carefully prepared, can be concerned only with the last two items of the sequence, pictures and symbols. No book for young children can start where they need to start, namely with experience and spoken language' (*ibid.*).

The use of visual or pictorial representation is important at all levels of mathematical activity. At all stages of learning mathematics, children create their own pictures to represent mathematical ideas. Martin Hughes' work on children's invention of written arithmetic, with children aged 3:4 to 7:9, gives several examples of children's personal interpretations of the question, 'Can you put something on the paper to show how many bricks are on the table?', (Hughes, 1986) as follows:

- *Idiosyncratic*   Scribbles, squiggles, recognisable letters of the alphabet and pictures of irrelevant objects, e.g. Figure 2.2.

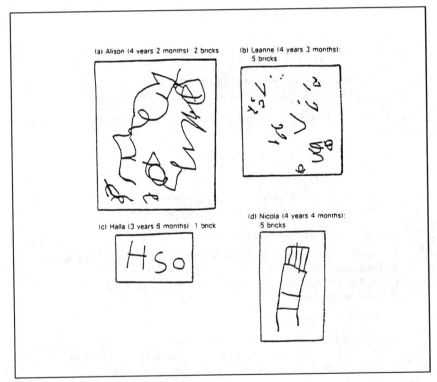

(a) Alison (4 years 2 months): 2 bricks

(b) Leanne (4 years 3 months): 5 bricks

(c) Halla (3 years 6 months) 1 brick

(d) Nicola (4 years 4 months): 5 bricks

Figure 2.2   Examples of idiosyncratic responses
Source: Hughes, 1986, p. 56

● *Pictographic*   A picture representing what they saw on the table, e.g. Figure 2.3.

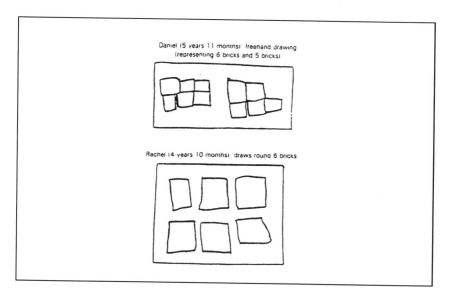

Figure 2.3   Examples of pictographic responses
Source: Hughes, 1984, p. 57

● *Iconic*   Simple tallies or representational marks, e.g. Figure 2.4.

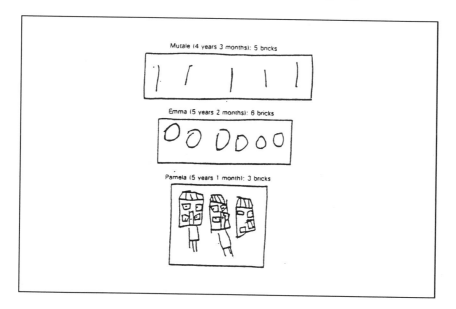

Figure 2.4   Examples of iconic reponses
Source: Hughes, 1984, p. 58

- *Symbolic*   Conventional symbols and words, e.g. Figure 2.5.

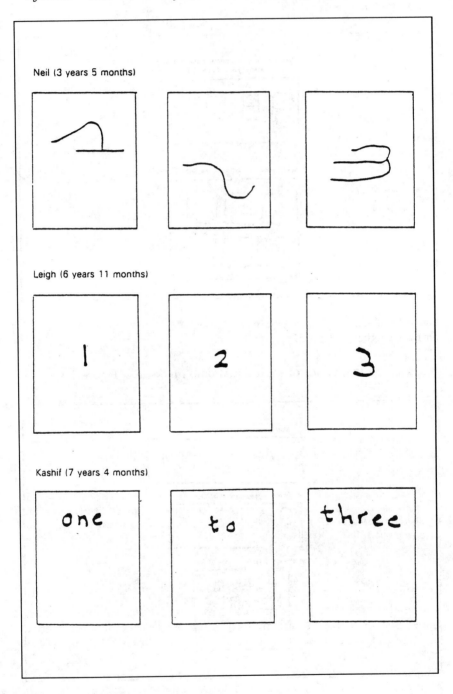

Figure 2.5   Examples of symbolic responses
Source: Hughes, 1984, p. 59

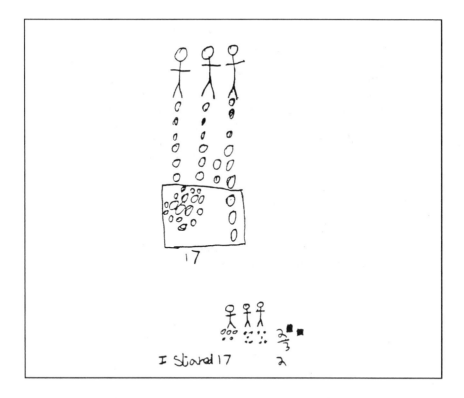

Figure 2.6 A group of 9–11-year-olds' representation of sharing 17 biscuits between three children
Source: Atkinson, 1992, p. 122

An example presented by Sue Atkinson (1992) shows the workings of a group of 9–11-year-olds to find out how to share 17 biscuits between three children (Figure 2.6). According to David Winteridge (1989):

> Models, pictures, diagrams, tables and patterns are needed at all levels of mathematical activity. They may help us to simplify a problem, to understand it, to represent it, to solve it or communicate it to others...Diagrams on paper are also powerful tools. They enable us to portray a situation as a whole rather than sequentially as words must necessarily do.

Symbols

The final component in the process of mathematical development is the translation of mathematical thinking into a conventional written code that allows the processes of mathematical thinking to be easily communicated to, and understood by, others. A similar principle can be seen in the use of musical notation.

In the history of the evolution of number systems, different cultures have developed different methods to convey the meaning of quantity – for example, from tally marks on bones, traced back to 30,000 years ago, to finger-counting systems, to the ciphers of Egyptian hieroglyphics through to the present Hindu–Arabic system of numerals (Flegg, 1984).

The function of number symbols and operator signs in mathematics enables the process of mathematical thinking to be carried out in a special code devised to symbolise quantity and mathematical operations. In this way mathematical calculations can be carried out without the cumbersome requirement to handle objects, especially when numbers are very large.

A further refinement of the symbolic component of mathematics is seen later in the form of algebraic expressions, where conventional number sequences, patterns and solutions are converted into generalised mathematical 'rules' with the use of letter symbols (commonly a, b and c; also x and y) to represent any number the rule can be applied to. For example, the commutative 'rule' of addition:

$4 + 2 = 2 + 4$
represented as a generalised rule in algebraic form as
$a + b = b + a$

Very young children's first experiences with number symbols occur during the course of their daily lives. They hear number names during conversations. They see numbers around them in shops, on buses, on houses and cars, etc. A child's age and birthday create a spotlight for numbers as they appear on birthday cards and are represented by candles on cakes. Even before they start school, some children are starting to count objects orally, write numbers and perform very simple addition and subtraction calculations using objects and their own invented methods (Hughes, 1986).

Research has shown that one of the problems occurring after children commence formal schooling at 5, is the early introduction of written 'sums' using conventional methods. Children are expected to continue to do increasingly more difficult 'sums' as the main thrust of their mathematical work. Doing and talking about mathematics and modelling mathematical processes with objects or in pictorial form can be seriously neglected. Problems arise because young children's understanding of the conventional written methods is very weak compared with their own informal methods. According to Herbert Ginsburgh (1997), they often fail to understand the necessity of rationale for written methods. At a later stage when written methods become more complex, children are starting to struggle badly. Sue Atkinson (1992) presents an example (Figure 2.7) from a group of 8–9-year-olds, described by their teacher as 'a bright lot', who were asked to write down and work out (without looking at anyone else's work) 127 take away 84.

Atkinson (*ibid.*) makes an interesting point about the mental problem, $136 - 54$, given at story time. She reported that when the children were

18 children wote: 127 − 84 = 43 (correct answer)

1 child wrote: 127 − 84 = 53

Out of the remaining children who chose to write it down vertically, as below, only two got it right – 15 got it wrong!

Errors in vertical forms included:

(1)	(2)	(3)	(4)
127	127	127	$\overset{1}{1}27$
− 84	− 84	− 84	84
143	163	727	88

At story time at the end of the session, a similar problem was put to the children to work out *mentally*: 136 − 54.

Figure 2.7 '127 take away 84': responses of a bright group of 7–9-year-olds
Source: Atkinson, 1992, p. 99

presented with the mental problem, even the children who got it wrong in the written form had no problem with the calculation.

A prerequisite to performing conventional written methods for arithmetic effectively seems to be children's ability to translate arithmetical thinking processes from handling objects to conventional symbolic representation. It is suggested by many researchers that practical work, interactive teaching and the development of mental strategies can assist this process. In addition, the process of structuring mathematical learning should not follow a strictly hierarchical sequence but embrace a network approach, where new learning is built on what children already know (Denvir and Brown, 1986).

Building networks of cognitive connections

The nature of mathematical learning is hierarchical in the sense that knowledge of lower-order concepts and skills is a prerequisite to higher-order understanding. For example, the knowledge that a three-sided shape is a triangle leads to the knowledge that triangles can be right-angled, equilateral, isosceles or scalene. However, the way children make sense of mathematical concepts and skills is by building networks of cognitive connections. According to Derek Haylock and Anne Cockburn (1997): 'when we encounter some new experience there is a sense in which we understand it if we can connect it to previous experiences, or better to a network of previously connected experiences. The more strongly connected the experience the more we understand it.'

The growth of mathematical understanding in children, whilst linear in principle, is brought about by children making connections between the four types of experience, handling objects, language, pictures and symbols at every stage, as illustrated by Figure 2.8. Each arrow represents a possible connection between experiences that may shed light on a mathematical concept and bring about understanding.

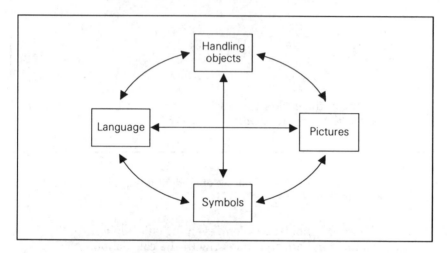

Figure 2.8 The development of mathematical understanding: making connections between handling objects, language, pictures and symbols

It can be seen that the exclusive use of workbooks or textbooks as a means of learning mathematics cannot provide children with the full range of experiences required for them to make strong connections between previous knowledge and new knowledge, as only pictures and written and numerical symbols are provided (Liebeck, 1984).

How theories of learning mathematics correspond to these principles

Jerome Bruner

The central theme of Jerome Bruner's work (1967) represents the definition of three modes of thinking: *enactive* – represented in action or by the direct manipulation of objects; *iconic* – visual or perceptual organisation of knowledge communicated by pictures, patterns and mental images; and *symbolic* – use of symbols for easy transmittal of knowledge at a higher level of thought. From Bruner's perspective, a leap from actions to symbols too early is unlikely to establish healthy foundations for developing mathematical understanding. Rather, it is necessary to allow children to make use of all modes of representation during the process of learning, depending on what is being learnt at the time. Bruner also recognised teaching as a important component in the process of learning, in that concept and skill acquisition in children is moved along by effective interaction and intervention from teachers, parents and/or carers (Bruner, 1990).

Robert Gagne

The work of Robert Gagne (1970) differs from Bruner in that his work focuses on the steps which must be mastered in order for an individual to acquire a given skill through task analysis, to establish 'instructional hierarchies'. The processes involved in compiling an instructional hierarchy are:

- 'Establishing the terminal goal' – stating what the pupil is expected to be able to do at the end of a sequence of activities.
- 'Outlining the enabling skills and related intact skills' – establish what needs to be taught in relation to previous knowledge and experience of the pupil.
- 'Sequencing the intact, enabling and terminal behaviours' – creating a teaching plan.

(Gagne, 1970)

In many respects Gagne's work represents the basis for lesson-planning strategies of today, where a pupil's needs are assessed in relation to his or her previous experience. Learning outcomes are then defined in terms of concepts and skills and a series of activities are planned to direct children towards achieving the defined 'goals'.

Lev Vygotsky

The Russian psychologist Lev Vygotsky (1962; 1978) provided a framework for teaching and learning which led to the development of the theories of social constructivism in the 1980s. Vygotsky proposed that learning occurs on two levels. The first level he names as 'intermental' – the social level, where pupils experience the language and handling of objects in the company of others. The second level he names as 'intramental' – the individual or personal level where each learner tries to make sense of new knowledge and connect it clearly to what is already known. According to Vygotsky, at the second level the support and guidance of the teacher in 'scaffolding' children's learning are critical to the process, where high involvement is required at the beginning with a gradually decreasing dependence on the teacher until learning mastery is achieved. Vygotsky emphasises the relationship between language and concept acquisition, the active engagement of the learner and the shifting role of the teacher throughout the process of learning. Vygotsky's theory can be seen to closely mirror Corinne Hutt's theory (1979) on the stimulation of epistemic and ludic behaviours.

Vygotsky also proposed that a learner is more likely to receive new knowledge more easily if there is an association between the new knowledge to be learnt and previous knowledge learnt which he defined as learning within the 'zone of proximal development' (or ZPD), which is 'the distance between the actual development [of the child] as determined through problem-solving and the level of potential development as determined through problem-solving under adult guidance or in collaboration with more capable peers' (Vygotsky, 1978).

Anne Edwards and Peter Knight (1994) present a useful diagram which demonstrates Vygotsky's principles (Figure 2.9). They also point out that Vygotsky's ZPD relates to the current thinking on the process of assessment, where new learning is planned from a teacher's diagnosis of a child's need, instead of what a teacher thinks a child should learn.

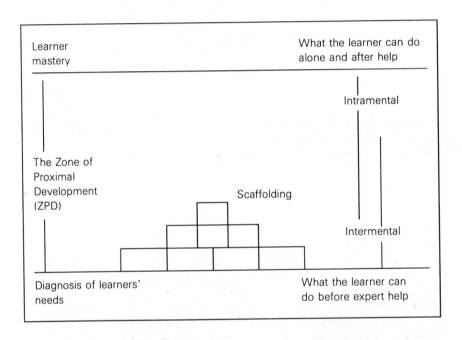

Figure 2.9 A Vygotskian framework for teaching and learning
Source: Edwards and Knight, 1994, p. 32

Social constructivism

The theories of social constructivism have significantly influenced practice in primary education since the 1980s. The principles emphasise interaction with others and the importance of learning in a social context, as well as the need for the learner to construct his or her own meaning and understanding of knowledge through continuously 'reflecting' on his or her experiences (Wood, 1988). The social and cultural upbringing of a child is seen to have a significant influence on learning, which continues throughout life (Rogoff and Lave, 1984). Learning is therefore social as well as individual.

The theories also recognise the importance of the role of the teacher as an interactionist and an interventionist in the learning process, where the teacher acts as a 'reflective agent', offering supportive challenge and creating a theatre for refining thinking processes until a level of mastery is achieved (Figure 2.10).

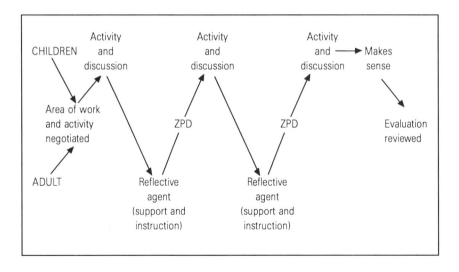

Figure 2.10   A social constructivist model of roles in the teaching–learning process
Source: Pollard and Tann, 1993, p. 112

Connectionism

Recent work on connectionism (Bechtel and Abrahamsen, 1991), which takes brain activity during the learning process as one of its focuses, supports Vygotsky's principles. The theory is complex, but in simple terms the brain is a web of neural networks that become more intensely active in a learning situation. If the new knowledge to be learnt can connect easily to previous knowledge stored in the brain through association, then the learning will take place much more easily. One of the experiments, carried out in America, used a sample of children who had difficulty with learning to read. The researchers used word families such as *at, fat, cat, hat,* etc., where there is a clear association between the words, and found that brain activity became more intense when there were clear associations or 'connections' between knowledge stored and knowledge to be learnt than when a child was presented with a random set of words, for example *at, hit, put, get, man.*

The notion of pattern can be used to establish connections between knowledge previously understood and new knowledge to be learnt. For example, developing children's understanding of number patterns and sequences enables children to predict and generalise 'rules' more easily and to develop mental arithmetic skills. The notion of pattern creating associations or connections in the brain enables the learning to take place more easily.

Factors that cause differences in the ways children learn mathematics

Different learning styles: grasshoppers, caterpillars and snails

Research by Bath *et al.* (1986) identified two different learning styles in children: *grasshoppers* (high fliers) and *inchworms* or *caterpillars* (steady plodders). Grasshoppers are able to make leaps in learning development and are quick to recognise associated connections between one concept and another (see Chapter 19). Caterpillars, on the other hand, are more cautious in their strategies, requiring affirmation of the ground they have covered before proceeding to new work.

To explain these principles, the following example is used:

$$37 + 19 + 43 =$$

Caterpillar

The 'caterpillar' will rewrite the sum in vertical form and will work in the order in which the numbers are given, starting with the units followed by the tens. Addition may be carried out with tallies to mark progress and help to keep the count as the child moves up or down the numbers. The child is unlikely to use a pre-estimate or check.

Grasshopper

The 'grasshopper' is likely to cluster tens together first – 30 (+10) → 40 (+40) → 80 then look for pairs or clusters to make 10 (7 + 3), making 90 and then adding the final 9 to get 99. The 'grasshopper' will also estimate that the answer will be about 100.

The caterpillar/grasshopper notion is similar to the serialist/holist

Table 2.1   Cognitive styles of the caterpillar and grasshopper

	Caterpillar	Grasshopper
Analysing and identifying the problem	1) Focuses on parts, attends to detail and separates 2) Objective of looking at facts to determine useful formula	1) Holistic, forms concepts and puts together 2) Objective of looking at facts to determine an estimate of answer or range of answers
Methods of solving the problem	3) Formula-recipe orientated 4) Constrained focus using a single method or serially ordered steps along one route – generally in one direction 5) Uses numbers exactly as given 6) Tending to add and multiply, resists subtraction and division 7) Tending to use pencil and paper to compute	3) Controlled exploration 4) Flexible focusing using multimethods or paths, frequently occurring simultaneously. Generally reversing or working back from answer and trying new routes 5) Adjusts, breaks down/builds up numbers to make an easier calculation 6) Tending to subtract 7) Tending to perform all computation mentally
Verification	8) Verification unlikely; if done, uses same procedure or method	8) Likely to verify; probably uses alternative procedure or method

Source: Adapted from Bath *et al.* 1986

theory of Pask and Scott (1975), where the serialist uses a step-by-step approach to solving problems whilst the holist will look at the whole problem and see if there is an easy way of tackling it. It is suggested by John Backhouse *et al.* (1992) that serialists should be given specific teaching in holist strategies, and opportunities to work in an holistic way should be presented through:

- activities involving mental arithmetic;
- directing children towards quick methods;
- providing activities which encourage holistic methods; and
- encouraging learners to describe their methods.

Snail

In addition to grasshoppers and caterpillars, teachers will acknowledge another type of learner – which can be likened to a snail climbing a wall, where it climbs so far and then slips back a bit. It is this type of learner who has significant difficulty with learning mathematics and requires special learning support if he or she is not to fall by the wayside (see Chapter 18).

High and low achievers

There are differences in the rates of learning of high and low achievers. A high-achieving child who is proactive and driven by natural curiosity and enthusiasm will be highly motivated to learn new mathematical knowledge and skills. A more passive, uninterested child is not likely to seek the same level of satisfaction from learning something new, and would be identified as a low achiever. These children are often more difficult to teach than children with learning difficulties. A factor that can exacerbate low mathematical achievement in children is persistent failure and negative criticism at school, although sometimes excessive parental expectations can lead to a child seeking relief by 'switching off' in school. It is often very difficult to restore a child's interest and confidence in learning mathematics once he or she has become disaffected and many children leave school declaring a hatred or phobia of mathematics because their low achievement has remained unresolved for a significant part of their time in school.

Different ways of working

Young children will devise their own strategies to solve arithmetical calculations. The examples given in Figures 2.11–2.13 present different strategies children used to solve problems in the 1996 SATs mathematics test for 7-year-olds (SCAA, 1997C). Sue Atkinson (1992) presents evidence to show that the methods shown in Figures 2.11–2.13 are to be found throughout the primary school, in particular when children are asked to solve 'real problems', such as the sharing biscuits problem mentioned earlier. In many cases children do not apply the 'book-taught maths' to a 'real problem' because they do not fully understand how it works. Instead they use methods which have some personal meaning for them so that they can tackle a problem in a way they understand. This shows how important it is for mathematics to be taught practically and interactively and not driven by 'book-taught maths'.

Figure 2.11 A child representing a problem with tally marks
Source: SCAA, 1997d, p. 19

Figure 2.12 A child representing a problem with a picture
Source: SCAA, 1997d, p. 20

How many children are in the class altogether?

$$14 + 1 = 15$$
$$15 + 6 = 21$$
$$21 + 8 = 29$$

Figure 2.13 A child creating his or her own calculating method
Source: SCAA, 1997d, p. 20

Nature/nurture differences

Difficulties may arise from differences due to gender, ethnicity, socioeconomic circumstances and relationships. However, it is difficult to distinguish between nature/nurture differences as there is a strong inter-relationship between them. For example, girls can behave or be treated differently from boys because of cultural circumstances. Friends and teachers may create stereotypical expectations for girls to behave differently from boys.

Management considerations

With respect to nature/nurture differences, it is important for teachers to regard all learners as developing individuals and not to have expectations of potential restricted by stereotypical perceptions of race, gender or class differences. Strategies should be established to provide equal opportunities for all children to achieve their potential in all areas of the curriculum. It is important that girls and boys are encouraged equally, to achieve their potential in mathematics. Equal access should be provided to boys and girls in all areas of the mathematics curriculum and greater emphasis placed on discussion, group work and investigative work. Teachers should also be alert to the possibility that subtle inferences can be drawn by children from classroom interactions which give messages that there are different expectations for boys and girls, particularly in relation to their performance in mathematics and their attitude to the subject (Backhouse *et al.*, 1992).

Summary

The ways in which children learn mathematics cannot be generalised into a universal formula. Whilst there are common principles, the active process of learning is dynamic and idiosyncratic. The teacher has two key roles to play in the process, to inspire children to learn through the stimulation of epistemic and ludic learning behaviours (Hutt, 1979), and to facilitate intermental and intramental learning through direct teaching strategies (Vygotsky, 1962; 1978). Through continuously identifying the needs of individual children, teachers are able to 'scaffold' new learning and support children's endeavours to make sense of mathematics at every stage of their development. For children to develop an understanding of mathematics they need to have opportunities to construct meaning for themselves, through various combinations of handling objects, talking about their mathematical experiences, creating and interpreting pictures and representing their experiences in the language of mathematical symbols.

3

Common difficulties children experience in learning mathematics

Number: counting and writing numbers

Early counting and number recognition

There is considerable evidence to suggest that very young children can identify the number of items in a series when the size of the series is relatively small (Gelman and Gallistel, 1978; Hughes, 1986). However there are children who arrive in school at 5 with very little understanding of counting and number recognition. As early as 1921, Descoeudres identified a phenomenon in very small children starting to verbalise counting, which she defined as the 'un, deux, trois, beaucoup phenomenon', where a breakdown appears in the counting process between the numbers two and five. Empirical evidence supports that this phenomenon exists in school-age children whose early experiences have been severely limited (see Figure 3.1). For example:

> Victor (5 years 2 months, second term in school) was unable to sort objects by colour. He counted orally, 'one, two, five'.
> Given a line of three beads, he was unable to point to the beads with his finger and count. Asked to draw a set containing one object, he was unable to respond.
>
> (Edwards and Edwards, 1992)

Problems also arise in children if the 'learning to count' process has been taught purely by rote, where children are taught to recite numbers, out of the context of handling objects. Such children may arrive in school able to chant numbers but not having any understanding that the last number in the series represents the quantity of a counted set. Additionally, learning counting purely by rote offers no opportunity for children to relate number names to their associated quantity and place value (Edwards and Edwards, 1992).

Research carried out in Geneva by Anne and Hermine Sinclair (1984) found that about one fifth of a sample of 45 children aged 4–6 years were unable to identify numbers just as numbers, and required an associated context to establish recognition. For example, a child was able to state,

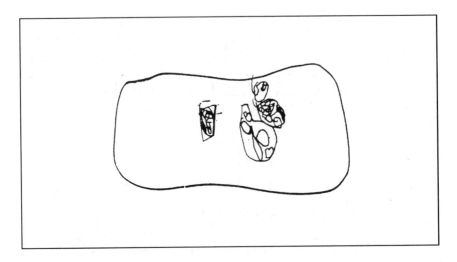

Figure 3.1   Victor (5;2) – second term in school

that 'somebody was just 5 years old' when shown a picture of a birthday cake with five candles. Some children are able to count a small number of objects but with no recognition of number symbols and the quantity they represent, beyond the number one. An example of this is shown from the result of a baseline assessment activity carried out with Stephen, aged 5;1, in his first term at school (see Figure 3.2):

- Can recite numbers to five.
- Can count objects using tag-counting to five.
- Can recognise two objects by sight and say the number 'two'; uses tag-counting for three to five objects.
- Can match the number 1 to one object.
- Could not match the number 2 to two objects or 3 to three objects; same with 4 and 5.
- Can only write the number 1 on demand.
- Can copy the number 1 with evidence of emergent attempts to represent other numbers.

Planning considerations   Children who demonstrate that their experiences of counting, number recognition and matching numbers to objects are limited require a great deal of individual help and support. This is provided by letting them handle objects to develop counting skills and by using flash-card and matching games in an interactive teaching situation. The use of published scheme material is inappropriate in this situation. If problems persist, this may indicate that the child could be in need of special learning support (see Chapter 17).

Figure 3.2   Stephen (5;1) – first term in school

Number reversals

Many number reversals will be noted during the experimental or emergent stages of children's attempts to write numbers. In the very early stages this is a normal part of children's first experiments with writing numbers. If the problem persists, however, sensitive vigilance together with a little 'on the spot' guidance will help to prevent the child perceiving reversals as the 'norm' (number reversals are much more difficult to correct when the 'habit' of reversal has formed). Some children will inadvertently reverse numbers (predominantly threes, sevens and nines) when they record arithmetical computations because they concentrate on the process of computation rather than the skills of recording. A gentle 'on the spot' discussion – with a rubber to hand – is a useful form of direct teaching when monitoring work in progress in the classroom (see Chapter 14).

Planning considerations   Common problems with number reversals can become the focus of a formal number-writing lesson with a whole class or group of infants. (Squared paper is very useful for this purpose, as it helps the children to space, write or copy numbers more easily.) If the problems persist, they must be considered alongside the child's reading and writing skills as they may be early evidence of dyslexia.

Numerical computation: counting-on more than one

When children begin to combine two sets of more than one object, they frequently count the first set in ones and then follow this by counting the second set in ones. They then put these together and proceed to count the combined set in ones yet again. If the process of 'counting on' from the first set is not introduced to the children, this may cause significant problems later when the children are working with harder computations. The following example demonstrates this problem:

> Claire is calculating 23 + 15. She collects and counts out 23 cubes in ones, followed by counting out 15 cubes in ones. She puts them together and proceeds to count the total in ones. She has difficulty keeping track of the count and has to keep starting again.

Planning considerations Once children understand the principle of combining sets, it is important to introduce the strategy of counting on. Counting-on patterns with sets of objects or pictures can be helpful (see Figure 3.3).

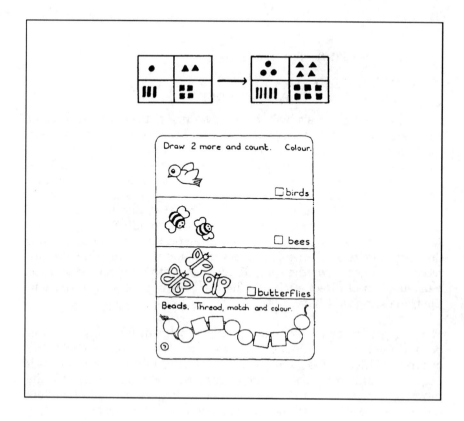

Figure 3.3 Count-on 2 activities

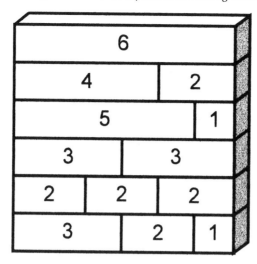

Figure 3.4   Ways to make 6 with Cuisenaire rods

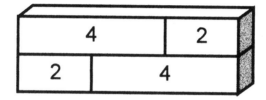

Figure 3.5   Commutative law demonstrated by Cuisenaire rods

Cuisenaire rods

Cuisenaire apparatus is very useful for developing the concept of counting-on, providing the children are familiar with the colours and the number/size relationships of the rods. For example, they can help a child understand two as a 'whole two' and not as the last number in a count of ones.

Cuisenaire rods are also self-correcting by design in that, for example, the 'four rod' added to the 'two rod' will only match the 'six rod' or any other combination of rods that adds to six (see Figure 3.4). They also make it much easier for children to see that, for example, 4 + 2 gives the same answer as 2 + 4 – the commutative law (see Figure 3.5).

Numberlines

When children are familiar with counting, writing and operating simple addition using objects with numbers to ten, a numberline can help to develop children's skills of counting-on, using addition and early multiplication through repeated addition sequences. This also applies to counting-back using subtraction and repeated subtraction sequences. Work can be extended by the use of a 'tens' or a 'hundreds' numberline.

Planning considerations When first introduced to working with numberlines, children often have difficulty because they begin the count from the number they start on rather than the next number on the line. Help with 'finger tracing' along the line is useful. Some teachers invent simple jingles, for example 'Whizz-Bang!' (*whizz* over one number and land *bang* on the next!') for counting in twos (see Figure 3.6).

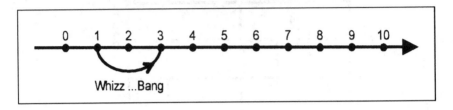

Figure 3.6 Counting on 2 on a numberline using 'Whizz-Bang'

Dice, spinners and playing cards

To increase children's confidence with counting-on and counting-back mentally, games with dice, spinners or playing cards can be introduced – for example, the 'Add 2 Game' where the child adds two to the number thrown on a die, or drawn on a card, and records the 'sums' on paper.

Games like the 'Add 2 Game' can be played orally with a group or with the whole class to develop children's mental arithmetic skills with counting-on. For example:

Teacher: My number is 4. Jane, what is your number?
Jane: 6.
Teacher: Good ... My number is 7. Ramu, what is your number?

Missing number equations

Children often find first work with missing number equations difficult. For example:

$$(\ ) + 4 = 5 \quad or \quad 5 - (\ ) = 4$$

Planning considerations Cuisenaire rods are helpful in assisting children with understanding these calculations because the 'missing number' is physically represented by the correct amount of space when two different number rods are placed side by side (see Figure 3.7). Missing number equations can also be calculated by the partitioning of objects or pictures (Figure 3.8).

Difference

Children find first work with difference subtraction difficult, particularly if they have not developed confident 'counting-on' or 'counting-back' skills.

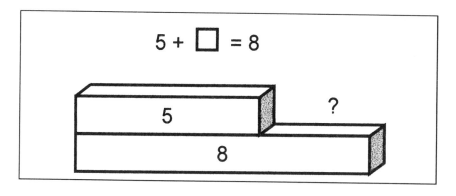

Figure 3.7   Missing number equation represented by Cuisenaire rods

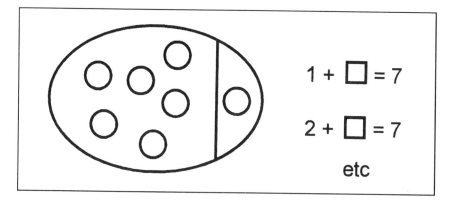

Figure 3.8   Solving missing number equations by partitioning sets

Planning considerations   For children who have difficulties in under-standing this concept, it is initially useful to demonstrate representations in linking cubes of two numbers that are the 'same', or have 'no difference'. It is then easier for children to recognise and calculate the 'difference' between two numbers that are not the same (see Figure 3.9).

Cuisenaire rods are also helpful when making comparisons between two numbers because, when the rods are laid side by side, the 'space' represents the 'difference', which can be matched with the correct number rod that fits the 'space'.

Equivalent values (money)

Children generally do not have a lot of difficulty in understanding how to arrive at equivalent values with respect to number. With experience, they are also normally quite happy with the process of creating bonds of

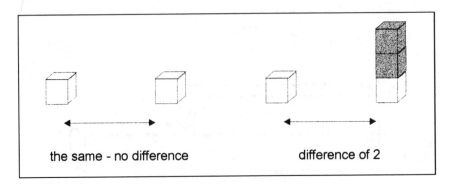

Figure 3.9   Introducing difference comparisons by first recognising 'similarity'

two numbers to ten. The principle of equivalent values often becomes difficult for children when they are first introduced to working with money, especially if they have had no experience of handling money.

Planning considerations   Before children are introduced to 'Stories of 5p', for example, it is important that children have a good understanding of addition of numbers to 5 and experience of different ways to make 5 or 'Patterns of 5'. To introduce equivalent values in money it is helpful to demonstrate the process to children by starting off with the amount in 1p coins (see Figure 3.10).

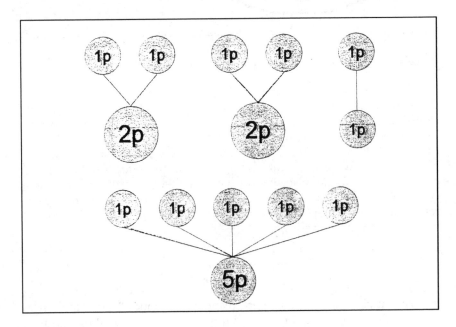

Figure 3.10   Exchanging coins to make 5p

The physical process of exchanging 2 × 1p coins for a 2p coin or 5 × 1p coins for a 5p coin is a very useful strategy in helping children towards understanding equivalence in money. A real shop in the school, that sells drinks or cakes can help children to experience handling money within a 'real' context.

Place value

The problem of equivalent values can become a difficulty for some children when they are first introduced to the concept of place value and grouping tens and units.

Planning considerations   Cuisenaire rods or Dienes apparatus can help children understand this principle more easily because ten 'one' rods, when laid side by side, are exactly equivalent in size to a 'ten rod'. (For younger children, Cuisenaire rods are easier to recognise because of the distinctive colours of each number rod whereas Dienes apparatus is made of natural wood.) Building patterns of tens and units with apparatus or on squared paper makes understanding easier (see Figure 3.11).

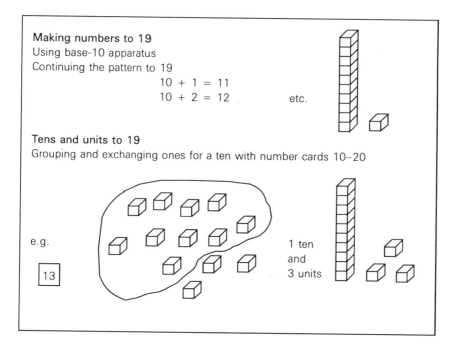

Making numbers to 19
Using base-10 apparatus
Continuing the pattern to 19

10 + 1 = 11
10 + 2 = 12 .   etc.

Tens and units to 19
Grouping and exchanging ones for a ten with number cards 10–20

e.g.

13

1 ten
and
3 units

Figure 3.11   Apparatus work with tens and units

Exchange games with a die can be played with Cuisenaire rods or money – for example, first to 50 or 50p, where each time ten ones are gained they must be changed for a 'ten'. The winner is the first with five 'tens' or a 50p coin.

Number rectangles and squares

To support later understanding of place value, children can be encouraged to write the numbers 0–99; 100–199; 200–299, etc., in stages in number rectangle or square configurations on squared paper. A number square can provide many challenging activities and games to develop mental arithmetic skills in computation and place value. For example, in the 'Add 10 Game' a child throws a cube on to the square, adds 10 to the number he or she lands on and records the answer on paper. Variations of this game can be as simple as 'Add or Take One' to 'Take 10' or 'Add 20'; at later stages, 'Multiply by 20' or 'Divide by 20'. Number square games can provide challenging activities for children up to Year 6 and beyond. A useful resource is *Zero to Ninety-Nine* (Graham and Blinko, 1989) (see Chapter 11).

Spike abaci

Spike abaci are particularly suitable in helping children to understand the principles of place value, hundreds, tens and units because the position of the 'noughts' is represented by 'empty' spikes. Activities with spike abaci develop children's ability to add and subtract in tens and hundreds mentally (see Figure 3.12).

Algorithmic methods

One of the biggest difficulties in numerical computation skills, especially for the less able child, is the use of algorithmic methods for vertical notation for addition, using the principle of exchange. Subtraction using decomposition presents even greater problems. Many children experience difficulties with these methods because their knowledge and understanding of place value is very tenuous. They are unsure where to put 'carrying figures' and often do not fully understand what is happening in the process. This is often compounded by weak arithmetical skills with larger numbers. For example:

$$8 + 9 \text{ and } 17 - 8$$

For many children this is where they start to experience significant failure and loss of confidence in learning mathematics.

Planning considerations Children need to be able to demonstrate confident understanding of the principles of place value before being introduced to addition and subtraction using vertical notation. They need

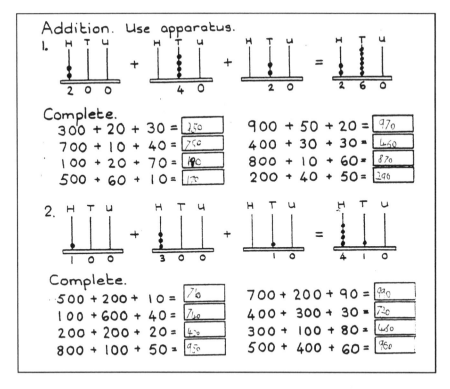

Figure 3.12   Activity involving addition of tens and hundreds using a spike abacus carried out by a Year 3 child

to be confident with addition and subtraction patterns through ten with larger numbers such as

$$6 + 7 \qquad 6 + 8 \qquad 6 + 9, \text{ etc.}$$
$$17 - 7 \qquad 17 - 8 \qquad 17 - 9, \text{ etc.}$$

(see Chapter 11).

When working with addition (using more than two numbers), children should be encouraged to look for pairs of numbers that make ten, doubles or near doubles, which make the calculation easier (see Chapter 2). Children should also be able to understand what happens when tens are added to or subtracted from a number and similarly with hundreds. Home-made HTU baseboards with Dienes apparatus are useful for this purpose (see Figure 3.13).

The games and activities described for use with number squares and spike abaci are very useful in helping children to develop arithmetic skills with addition and subtraction of tens and hundreds. Children can add 1, 10, 100 to a number and, it is hoped, they will start to generalise 'rules' which will assist them in performing these calculations mentally (see Figure 3.14).

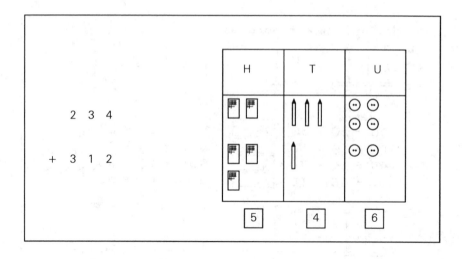

Figure 3.13   Using HTU baseboard for addition

A key problem with algorithmic methods

Too often children are rushed through these important background experiences in the haste to get them on to 'proper sums'. The computational work that follows at KS2 draws principally upon the assumption that children have a good understanding of these foundation processes. Without these skills children will start to experience significant difficulties with computational work at KS2. It is principally children's difficulties with arithmetical computation at KS2 that have been highlighted in the SATs results (SCAA, 1996). Whilst the problems are overtly apparent at KS2, it is important that the work in early years represents a careful grounding for children, to prepare them for an easier passage into later, more difficult arithmetical knowledge and skills.

Written arithmetical problems

Research has shown that written arithmetical problems cause major difficulties for many children at all ages, from infant to the secondary stage. At the infant stage many of the problems stem, first, from children's inability to read written problems and, secondly, from children's inability to translate the problem into conventional arithmetical form as discussed in Chapter 2. The following observation of a Year 2 child demonstrates this:

> Daniel is very proficient with handling money and change, yet he progresses so slowly with his maths cards because of his inability to read the 'problem-solving' type questions which are of a very simple level, e.g. Joe bought an apple for 4p and a sweet for 2p. How much did it cost altogether? Yet Daniel

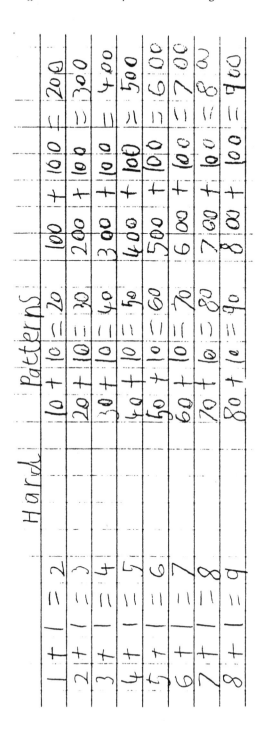

Figure 3.14   Add 1, 10 and 100 patterns by a Year 2 child

can calculate what he has spent and what change he needs from 50p in his head when he spends, for example 36p, at the school tuck shop.

Helping children to overcome difficulties with written problems can be challenging for teachers. The suggestions offered below are some strategies teachers have tried with a measure of success but they in no way offer a universal panacea.

Starting with objects in the context of play

Teachers can use objects in the classroom that are in use in a play situation to devise simple arithmetical problems for children whilst they are working. For example: 'Here are two teddies playing together. Another teddy joins in. How many teddies now?'

'Let's pretend' mental problems

Teachers can help children to start to work out simple arithmetical problems mentally by presenting them within a 'let's pretend' context. For example:

Let's pretend there are four cars in a car park. One drives away, how many left? (If children cannot solve the problem mentally, they should be encouraged to solve it with 'real' cars or by drawing a picture to represent the problem.)

Mental arithmetic picture puzzles

Mental arithmetic puzzles, such as arithmagons or magic squares, encourage children to solve numerical problems mentally and give children opportunities to use 'trial and refine' methods in solving problems. Arithmetical puzzles also provide good opportunities for children to work together and to discuss their ideas (Figure 3.15).

To carry out the work in Figure 3.15, the children needed a lot of help to get started. It was suggested that they first found three different numbers that made 9. After several attempts they came up with the solution to the 9 square and decided that the rule was that the middle number had to be put in three diagonal squares. When they tried this with the 12 square they realised another rule was needed. The numbers needed to be 'next to each other'. They were then able to complete the 15 square easily and went on to create an 18 square (5, 6, 7), a 21 square and a 24 square. One of the children was able to predict that the next square would be a 27 square: 'it's three more each time and the numbers jump up one.'

Solving oral and written problems with pictures

Children commonly represent arithmetical problems with pictures because this helps them to construct meaning (see Chapter 2, Figures 2.6 and 2.12). This is a valuable strategy in developing children's

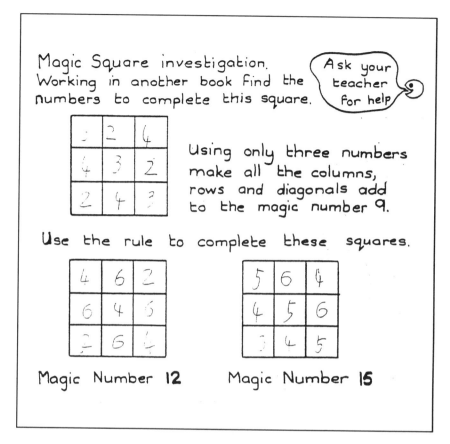

Figure 3.15   Magic Square work by two Year 3 children

confidence in tackling problems, and also presents a useful focus for mathematical discussion and diagnosis. Children are generally more articulate about their own pictorial methods than conventional algorithmic methods.

In the early stages of trying to solve written problems, children may combine pictures with conventional forms of representation. At a later stage, when children may appear to solve problems competently with conventional representation, they should always be encouraged to use other methods if they are 'stuck'.

Use of decoding charts

When children begin to solve word problems using forms of conventional arithmetical representation, assistance with decoding key words can be given through direct teaching combined with a visual aid displayed in the classroom (see Figure 3.16).

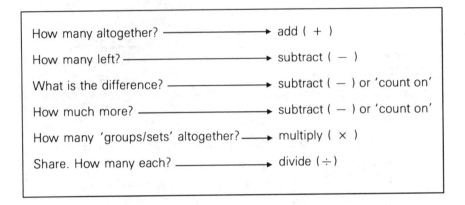

Figure 3.16 A chart that translates the key language in word problems into arithmetical operations

Problems with shape and measures (including data handling)

Shape

There is a belief that 2D shape needs to be taught before 3D shape because 3D work is 'more difficult' – even though young children have been making sense of a 3D world since birth! Additionally, there are teachers who consider the names of 3D shapes are difficult for children to learn. When we consider that a young child can identify an aeroplane by its name, then the words cube, cuboid and prism cannot be more difficult. There are, however, some problems with the word 'sphere'. To the young child a 'sphere' is a 'ball'. Until they become comfortable with connecting the word 'ball' with 'sphere', there is no reason why they should not use the word 'ball'. There is no substitute for children handling 2D shapes alongside 3D shapes to gain experience of the related properties of shapes. Pictures on paper alone cannot generate any depth of understanding. When pictures of 2D shapes are used, teachers should include drawings of different 'orientations' of triangles, squares and rectangles as well as the recognised 'regular' configurations.

Measures

Children need to have practical experience of working with weight/ mass, linear measurement and capacity if the life skills of estimation and accuracy when using standard measures are to be learnt effectively. Working with pictures on a page alone, such as 'colour the longest ribbon red', cannot offer children the physical mathematical experience of comparing lengths (for example, the provision of a box of coloured ribbons of different lengths for children to find the longest ribbon and draw a representational picture).

Conservation of measure

Work on conservation of measure is often considered difficult. However, when carefully directed by a teacher, many young children are able to understand the principle. The following describes a lesson on the conservation of mass with a group of Year 1 children:

Group: 6 children
Resources: Plasticine, 3 balancing scales

A directed lesson involving the understanding of conservation of mass with a group of six mixed-ability Year 1 children took place in the autumn term. The children were each asked to make a ball of Plasticine and then make a second ball of Plasticine to balance the first, by adding or removing Plasticine from the second ball.

The children were then asked to take the second ball and make it into a sausage. They were asked what would happen when the sausage was balanced against the ball. Four children were able to say that the sausage would balance the ball because 'it was the same Plasticine', one child did not know and the other child said it would not balance because 'it's different'.

After the 'test' the children were asked to take the sausage and make it into an animal. Before they started to make the animal one of the first four children remarked 'it's gonna balance the ball' and another said: 'yeh...peasy, it's the same bi'ov Plasticine!' Three other children questioned after making their animal said the animal would balance the ball, giving valid explanations and the final child who said the sausage would not balance did not really know and clearly had not understood the concept.

A similar principle applies when dealing with capacity, where children need to understand that different-shaped containers may hold the same amount of liquid. A teacher directing the activity with instructions and questions can lead children to recognise the principle of conservation. Repeated sessions of undirected pouring and filling of containers are more likely to generate the required result by accident rather than design – if at all – and it may take a long time for the child to recognise and understand the principle of conservation.

Counting frame

Work on measures involving counting and number work should be planned to match the children's repertoire of number and counting experiences or 'counting frame'. For example, if a child's counting frame is composed of numbers to 20, then measuring activities involving counting should not exceed 20. Children learning about 'half past' in telling the time should have some understanding of a half. Children learning about 'minutes past' in five-minute intervals should be able to count confidently in fives to at least 60.

Handling data

Common mistakes are found in the representation of data in pictorial or graphical form where no attention has been paid to establishing a clear axis and where the representation is not to scale or positioned accurately. Any pictorial representation of data has to be carefully planned and designed beforehand by the teacher to avoid representations which may be misleading. Making comparisons in interpreting pictorial data is difficult for children if the principles of accurate matching and the use of a clear axis are not observed in the construction of the graph (Figure 3.17).

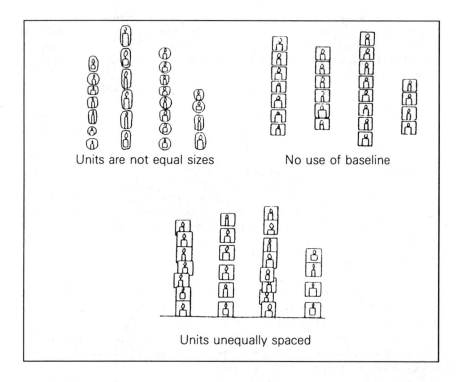

Figure 3.17   Examples of misrepresentation of data

Problems with numerical comparisons in interpreting data

Once children have understood the concept of 'difference', they should be encouraged to develop their skills in making numerical 'difference comparisons' when interpreting pictorial and graphical data. In the research carried out by the Assessment of Performance Unit in 1978–82, (DES, 1985a) into mathematical achievement in primary school children, there was clear evidence to suggest that children find this aspect of interpreting data difficult or have had little experience of the process. For example, children can easily calculate the number of each variable investigated – the number of dogs, cats, fish, etc., on a 'pets graph'. They can state there are more dogs than fish but find it difficult to calculate 'how many more dogs than fish?'

Children need lots of experience of difference problems, by making comparisons with sets of objects, work with Cuisenaire rods, etc., before being taught how to interpret them on graphs. This should be followed up with subsequent work on handling data that is planned to include difference problems. These problems can be taken as a focus for discussion during classwork.

Summary

This chapter has presented some of the common problems that young children experience when learning mathematics, and some tried and tested strategies which help children overcome these problems. Many of the problems stem from children's weak knowledge and understanding of conventional arithmetical processes.

Difficulties are often compounded by teachers' lack of confidence in their own ability in mathematics. Teachers frequently adopt methods they experienced when they were at school, because these are their only frame of reference. This can result in mathematics teaching becoming little more than getting children into the habit of doing 'sums' (using conventional arithmetical methods) and progressing on to workbooks or textbooks as quickly as possible. The results of KS2 SATs clearly show that this approach is not working. It is time to redefine the teaching of mathematics by examining more closely the ways in which children make sense of mathematical understanding and by reframing teaching strategies within this context. Of course, along the way, children are bound to stumble occasionally. If teachers are aware of common difficulties they are able to anticipate them and plan accordingly.

The strategies to help children with common problems presented in this chapter represent a personal repertoire built up over time. Teachers will have their own ideas which can be at least as effective as those suggested. It is important that teachers devise and use strategies that work well for them. In some schools, the issue of common problems children experience with learning mathematics is openly discussed at staff meetings or on training days, where perceptions are shared, strategies formulated and guidelines created.

Section 2
Mathematics: management at school level

4

Formulating a school policy for mathematics

Policy-making: a whole-school responsibility

In recent years there has been a dramatic shift from schools being managed within the support structures of LEAs to becoming autonomous organisations. Schools are now responsible for managing their own finances, have direct control over how curriculum is delivered and assessed by teachers, and are more directly accountable to parents. The structure of school organisation today requires all teachers to adopt 'whole-school' responsibilities as part of a staff team. In order to establish any form of cohesive practice in a school within the nursery/ infant sector, it has been recognised that the adoption of collegiate or democratic management principles is conducive to better organisational health. In accordance with these principles, all members of staff need to be involved in decision-making processes that lead to the formulation of policies and procedures to be adopted throughout a school. There is evidence to support the view that positive educational developments are almost impossible without teamwork and coherent planning at an institutional level (Nias *et al.*, 1992).

With respect to mathematics, Ofsted (1995) reported:

> There is a strong correlation between the *quality of subject management* in the school given by the mathematics co-ordinator or head of department and the standards achieved. The schools which achieve consistently good standards are invariably well managed and provide clear guidance to teachers.

It is recognised nowadays that a curriculum policy should be formulated

47

which presents an explicit philosophy and clear guidelines, including procedures for teaching and assessing mathematics throughout the school.

Who are mathematics policy documents written for?

- *Teachers* To present agreed guidelines and procedures in relation to managing the teaching of mathematics, assessment, recording and reporting mathematical achievement.
- *Parents* To inform parents of children's statutory entitlement, in terms of the mathematics curriculum, methods used to assess children's progress and achievement, and procedures for reporting to parents. There should also be information on the codes of practice which operate in a school – for example, the support for SEN and equal opportunities in relation to mathematics. Where partnership is encouraged, information on policies should be included.
- *Governors* To inform governors of the mathematical provision throughout the school and the procedures for reporting to parents. Governors will also need to be informed about the financial management of the mathematics curriculum, in terms of staffing, resources, indoor and outdoor space, in-service training for staff and plans for curriculum development.
- *LEAs* For the purpose of accountability, LEAs require schools to compile formal documentation, which presents a full account of the mathematical provision in the school that can be consulted for the purposes of monitoring standards between schools at a local level.
- *Ofsted inspectors* The process of inspection is centred around the assessment of a school's effectiveness in providing a good standard of education for the children who attend. This is carried out through a rigorous process of examining 'evidence of practice' during an inspection visit. School policies form a significant part of the documentary evidence used to make judgements on the effectiveness of a school.

What are the benefits for a school?

A curriculum policy provides guidance for new staff and sets out a framework for continuity and progression throughout the school. It assists the headteacher and staff in evaluating the teaching and learning of mathematics throughout the school and, by providing a systematic overview of practice, it can help in establishing priorities and targets for development (Richardson, 1996).

What makes a good policy for mathematics?

A good policy will offer:

- an explanation of the school's overall philosophy on the teaching and

learning of mathematics and the ethos it seeks to achieve;
- helpful guidelines to teaching staff to assist them with planning and managing the teaching of mathematics in their classroom;
- information on mathematical resources available and their location in the school;
- guidelines on the achievement of consistency throughout the school in the planning and assessment of mathematical work;
- guidelines on record-keeping, reporting and partnership arrangements with parents;
- guidelines for supporting equal opportunities and children with special educational needs; and
- a 'handbook' written in a clear, user-friendly style that is easy to read and is not too lengthy.

Formulating a curriculum policy for mathematics

The responsibility for formulating a curriculum policy for mathematics is normally undertaken by the mathematics co-ordinator or the head-teacher. It requires staff to meet together, to share views and establish a common understanding, before a policy can be generally approved and formally drafted.

Getting started

Initially, it is helpful to establish a number of headings for discussion and to draw up a timetable for meetings at times when all staff can attend. The co-ordinator will need to circulate an agenda and any relevant articles/documents to staff, ensuring they have time to read the documentation beforehand. Documentation should be kept as brief as possible and meetings should be planned within a set time limit. It is helpful if key issues for discussion are listed so that the meeting has a detailed structure. During the meeting it is important that notes are taken on points staff have raised. A flipchart is useful as it helps to move discussion along, whilst presenting a visual record of the discussion to the group as it develops. In conclusion it is helpful to summarise the points that have been agreed. After the meeting notes should be written up into a draft statement to be circulated to staff for approval or amendment at the next meeting.

With some issues it may be difficult to achieve agreement and some form of compromise will need to be sought. It is important however that different views are respected. Creating a statement of intention which does not reflect the general values of the staff will create situations where the policy bears little relationship to the actual practice in the school. For example, some staff may feel strongly that it is important to use published mathematics materials as a core scheme, whilst other staff may prefer a school-devised scheme of work. In this case, it would be important to identify the staff's views on the advantages and disadvantages of each method before formulating a policy statement which represents an agreed plan of action.

Most infant and nursery schools already have some form of policy document relating to the management of teaching mathematics throughout the school. However, if a school wishes to create a new mathematics policy, it is very important that the 'first edition' represents an *audit of the existing practice* and not a plan of action for radical change. The initiation and management of change is a more complex process and is dealt with more fully in Chapter 5.

What should be included in a mathematics policy?

There are no set rules about what should be included in policy documents, but many LEAs have formulated guidelines for schools. The following represent key headings with some explanation about each one, supported by examples.

The school philosophy

Most policy documents contain a brief opening statement which outlines the philosophy and commitment of the school to the teaching of mathematics and why it is important for children to learn mathematics. For example:

——School believes that it is important that children develop a good understanding of mathematics which will provide firm foundations for confident use of mathematics in their adult life. The schools aims to:

- encourage a positive attitude to mathematics by presenting it in an interesting, meaningful and enjoyable way;
- create a sense of achievement in the learning of mathematics at each stage to promote confidence and enjoyment in the subject;
- ensure that all children are given equality of access and entitlement to the National Curriculum for mathematics;
- lay foundations for mastering and consolidating basic arithmetic skills with an emphasis on developing mental arithmetic skills;
- enable children to understand the principles of measurement and the properties of shapes through practical experiences and to develop confident use of a computer in a mathematical context;
- develop children's understanding of the importance of mathematics in the world today through the provision of a wide range of mathematical activities in different contexts; and
- encourage parents to support their children at home as an integral part of their child's mathematical education.

Entitlement

An important central element in all curriculum policies is the principle of entitlement in all areas of learning. Mathematics as a core subject has a central place within the school curriculum.

Time allocation for mathematics

One of the first elements of entitlement is the time allocation for mathematics within the school's timetable. Recent national guidelines have recommended that a minimum of 5 hours per week should be spent on the study of mathematics in primary schools, with most of that time being used to focus on the development of numeracy skills. The National Numeracy Project (1997) recommends daily lessons of 45 minutes on numeracy at KS1, and 50 minutes at KS2.

Content of the mathematics curriculum

The entitlement, in terms of the content of the mathematics curriculum, is established through the Desirable Outcomes at nursery level and the Programmes of Study for the National Curriculum for mathematics at KS1.

Using and applying mathematics

Desirable Outcomes: Mathematics
Attainment Target 1: Using and applying mathematics

This element of the mathematics curriculum emphasises entitlement in the use and application of mathematical skills that are prescribed in Attainment Targets 1 and 2. To enable readers to identify where these apply, the key elements of Attainment Target 1 have been incorporated within the content frameworks for Attainment Targets 1 and 2 in **bold**.

Number

Desirable Outcomes for nursery: Mathematics
KS1 Attainment Target 2: Number

Entitlement places a high emphasis on numeracy, where children should be given opportunities to develop their skills of handling numbers confidently in all subjects of the curriculum and in situations they encounter outside school. The key elements of number emphasised at nursery, progressing to KS1 and KS2 are:

- numbers and the number system;
- calculations; and
- making sense of numerical problems (see Figure 4.1).

The framework of the content to be taught, in terms of knowledge, skills and understanding, should include:

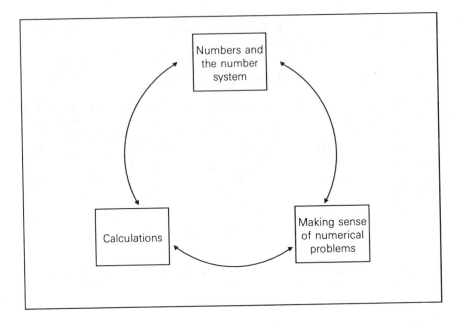

Figure 4.1 Key elements of number

- *Numbers and the number system*:
    — sorting, matching and classifying objects
    — patterns and sequences
    — counting and ordering objects and numbers
    — recognising, writing and reading numbers in symbols and words
    — properties of numbers and place value
    — estimation.

- *Calculations*:
    — appropriate use of objects, language, pictures or symbols to develop understanding and use of number operations; addition, subtraction, multiplication and division
    — mental recall of number facts
    — mental calculation strategies
    — checking strategies for accuracy.

- *Making sense of numerical problems*:
    — appropriate use of objects, language, pictures and mental images, or symbols to solve numerical problems set in familiar everyday contexts
    — trial and refine strategies
    — sharing ideas with others
    — collecting, presenting and interpreting numerical data.

Shape, space and measures

Desirable Outcomes: Mathematics
Attainment Target 3: Shape, space and measures.

The framework of the content to be taught, in terms of knowledge, skills and understanding, is:

- *use of mathematical language to describe shape, position, size or quantity;*
- construction, properties and measurement of shapes;
- *use of appropriate systems of measurement in practical contexts;*
- *visual sizing and estimation in practical contexts;*
- *collecting, representing and interpreting shape, space and measures data; and*
- *solving shape, space and measures problems within a familiar context, with the appropriate use of objects, language, pictures or mental images, or symbols.*

Equality of opportunity

In addition to the content framework for mathematics, the curriculum also contains elements that are not defined within the Programmes of Study. These include provision of equal opportunities for children with special educational needs, mathematically gifted children, boys and girls, and children from different ethnic and cultural backgrounds. Statements should be formulated and presented within a policy document. For example:

> At —— School we recognise that all children are individuals with varying needs and competencies. We use baseline assessment when the children first come to school as an aid to early identification of any special learning support required. This may simply be through extra help from the teacher but help from outside agencies will be sought if the school has any serious concerns about a child's work, or a child's physical or emotional health. Parents will always be consulted if a child requires special learning support and we value the support of parents helping their children at home through our Parent Partnership Scheme.
>
> Children will not be withdrawn from their classes unless it is thought that this offers a child more than it could gain from a class activity. For the mathematically able child there is provision throughout the school for challenging work at their own level within the school mathematics programme and an after-school Maths Club is available for children with a keen interest in the subject.
>
> All children will be assessed on a continuous basis. Any problems will be quickly identified and support given. We aim to build on success and encourage all children to participate as active, equal and valued members of our school community.

Managing equal opportunities and special needs in relation to mathematics is discussed more fully in Chapters 18 and 19.

Crosscurricular skills

Many aspects of mathematical knowledge and skills are not discrete, and opportunities should be given to children to develop and use mathematical skills in the context of other areas of the curriculum. At nursery level the Desirable Outcomes are designed to promote understanding in the six areas of learning:

- personal and social development;
- language and literacy;
- mathematics;
- knowledge and understanding of the world;
- physical development; and
- creative development.

The guiding principle of nursery work is to create meaningful contexts for learning, through structured play and practical activities, which promote skill acquisition in one or more of the different areas of learning.

At the infant stage, there is more emphasis on discrete mathematical learning. However, the use and application of mathematical skills, within the context of other subject areas and 'topic work', provide meaningful practical contexts for enriching mathematical learning and promoting understanding. For example, opportunities to develop mathematical skills across the curriculum occur frequently in science, geography, art and technology.

The following is an example of a nursery policy statement for mathematics:

> In the nursery, mathematical activities are planned within a framework of structured play and topic work. We offer opportunities for children to explore and investigate materials which have been selected by an adult who leads and guides them towards the development of mathematical concepts and skills. We encourage children to experience materials and equipment of their own choice with the active participation of an adult. Children are also encouraged to explore materials independently. The order of activities will be flexible as mathematical concepts form a network through which there are many different paths.
>
> In the early years, the main emphasis in children's learning is generally placed on language development and we aim to ensure that mathematical activities in the nursery reflect this emphasis. The development of accurate, everyday mathematical language should go hand in hand with first-hand experience of exploring mathematics in a variety of practical contexts.

Crosscurricular work in the context of mathematics is discussed more fully in Chapter 12.

Curriculum planning

The process of curriculum planning is central to the management of teaching and learning mathematics in all schools. For planning to be effective it needs to be underpinned by an agreed set of principles in order to establish a whole-school approach. This can ensure that there is a high level of consistency and continuity throughout the school.

Long, medium and short-term planning

Schools operate different strategies for long, medium and short-term planning. Some schools plan a term or a year in advance, where others plan a curriculum framework for mathematics covering the age range of the children in the school, representing a framework for three or four years' work. A useful text in this area is *Developing a Scheme of Work for Primary Mathematics* (Atkinson, 1996).

Points for whole-staff discussion:

- What arrangements are in place for long and short-term planning for mathematics throughout the school? Are there any planning proformas that have been designed for use throughout the school?
- How much time is allocated for the teaching and learning of mathematics during the course of a week? How much time is allocated for number work; shape, space and measures; topic work?
- Are any specific approaches emphasised in the teaching of mathematics, such as whole-class work, investigational practical work in small groups?
- Is there a scheme of work or an overview of the aspects of mathematics to be taught each term?

The following is an example of an infant school policy statement on planning for mathematics:

> Mathematics is planned termly for topics and on a weekly basis as a discrete subject with reference to the overall scheme developed for mathematics. When planning topics, mathematical possibilities will be identified, with an emphasis on investigation and problem-solving. This will allow our pupils to explore mathematics in a variety of contexts and gain confidence in using and applying mathematics in different situations. Teachers are expected to plan a minimum of five hours work on mathematics per week with three hours for developing skills in number and arithmetic through whole-class work, mental arithmetic activities and practical work in small groups directed by a teacher or adult helper. A photocopiable form has been devised for topic planning and lesson planning throughout the school. Copies are kept in the planning drawer in the filing cabinet in the staffroom.

Long and medium-term planning is further discussed in Chapter 8.

Progression and continuity

Agreed guidelines should be established on how progression and continuity in mathematical learning can be sustained throughout the school. This may take the form of a school scheme of work for mathematics, which may include use of published scheme material. Assessment, record-keeping and regular review should also represent an important feature of this process. For example:

> Our school curriculum for mathematics is based on the school scheme of work supported by additional materials from —— published scheme. Children's work is continuously assessed and records of progress are maintained by all teachers on individual record cards which are used throughout the school. Regular phase group meetings are held twice a term to examine all areas of the curriculum. At one of these meetings, ideas and good practice are shared by teachers to make sure there is progression within the mathematics curriculum. Year-group teachers meet termly to plan topic work and areas for inclusion relating to mathematics are worked out to ensure continuity within the year group.

The process of monitoring progress and continuity in children's learning is discussed in more detail in Chapters 15 and 20.

Teaching styles

To teach mathematics effectively it is recognised that different teaching styles are appropriate for different types of mathematical work. Some work is best carried out using a whole-class teaching approach – for example, introductions, expositions and reviewing work at the end of lessons. Practical work is best managed through group work, which will also involve some individual teaching. Individual work may also be needed for children with learning difficulties or with exceptional ability, where individualised learning programmes may have to be planned.

A curriculum policy will normally include a statement on teaching styles. For example:

> Teachers use a variety of teaching styles including opportunities for pupils to work as individuals and in pairs, as groups both large and small and as a whole class. Different groupings are decided on for a variety of purposes and tasks, matched to pupils' needs. Tasks are planned as mainly practical activities which are balanced between investigations, problem-solving activities, oral and mental mathematics, consolidation and practice.

Teaching styles are discussed in more detail in Chapter 10.

Class organisation

The ways in which children are organised for teaching purposes will vary according to the size of school and the age of the children. In nursery schools, where a lot of emphasis is placed on children's personal and social development, teaching is mainly carried out in mixed-ability groups. In infant schools, it is not unusual to find a variety of organisational strategies in operation for teaching mathematics within one school. For example, in a large infant school with more than one class in a year group, the school may operate mixed-ability teaching in the reception year, ability grouping in Year 1 and setting across the year group in Year 2. The following example represents an infant school policy statement on class organisation for mathematics:

> All children are assessed on entry and then informally assessed at the beginning of each year so that they can be grouped according to their needs and ability for mathematics and English. We operate a system of flexible grouping throughout the school which allows for children's different rates of progress in mathematics. Group membership is reviewed on a regular basis by the class teachers to ensure that children are maintaining progress at a level appropriate to their needs and aptitude for mathematics. Group work will also include opportunities for children to work in pairs to encourage collaborative work and mathematical discussion. When mathematics is taught as part of a class topic, some activities will offer opportunities for children to work in mixed-ability groups and with friends.

Class organisation is discussed in more detail in Chapter 17.

Assessment

This should include information on a school's established strategies and procedures for continuous assessment that are in operation throughout the school. Infant schools will also need to include information on National Baseline Assessment on entry and the assessment procedures for SATs for Year 2.

For example:

> All children are assessed on entry during the first half-term to find out their previous knowledge and experience in mathematics so that teachers can plan work to meet individual needs. There is a programme of continuous assessment which operates throughout the school, where individual children's work is continuously reviewed through teachers observing ways in which children work, marking and discussing work with children. Mid-year review and target-setting conferences with individual children are used by Year 3 teachers.
>
> Arrangements for completion of KS1 SATs with Year 2 children commence at the beginning of the Spring term with the administration of the level 1 mathematics task. Teacher assessments are completed by the second week of the Summer term with the administration of the mathematics test normally carried out in the week before the Summer half-term. Tests are marked and moderated by teachers at a marking meeting held in the Summer half-term. For any child absent during the time of testing and for any child recommended to take the KS2 test, the tests will be administered during the first week after the Summer half-term. KS2 tests are sent for external marking. All results of English and mathematics SATs are normally sent to ——— in the first week in July. A staff meeting is held annually to review all assessment arrangements during the Autumn term.

Managing assessment in relation to mathematics is discussed in more detail in Chapters 13–16.

Record-keeping

Records of achievement represent documentary evidence of how the school monitors individual children's progress over time and provide a means to ensure continuity in children's mathematical development from year to year. Since the Education Reform Act 1988, parents have been entitled by law to access their child's official school records. Information recorded by members of staff on official records should be written with this in mind. If a school operates a computerised record system, this should be done in accordance with the Data Protection Act 1985. The following represents an example of a school policy statement on record-keeping for mathematics:

> As part of a whole-school policy on record-keeping, all staff are expected to complete the school record for mathematics annually for each child, to monitor their progress throughout the school. In addition, staff are expected to select a representative piece of mathematical work at the end of each year to include in each child's portfolio together with an explanatory note. Individual teachers have their own system of records for recording children's mathematical progress on a continuous basis.

Record-keeping is discussed in more detail in Chapter 20.

Resources

Information on the availability and storage arrangements for mathematical resources is particularly useful for new members of staff and supply teachers. As well as a policy statement, schools often compile a list of available mathematical equipment and where it is located, so that staff know where it can be found (theoretically!). The principle of resource management is discussed more fully in Chapter 6.

The following represents an example of a school policy statement on mathematical resource management:

> All classrooms are stocked with a collection of basic mathematical equipment, according to the needs of the age group, for number work and work with shape, space and measures. All other equipment is stored centrally. For small pieces, such as stopwatches and spring balances, these are stored on a trolley in the corridor outside the hall. For larger pieces, such as the height measure and trundle wheels, these are stored in the large stockroom behind the hall. The key to this stockroom is kept in the office. When using small or large equipment stored centrally, staff are expected to sign in the book on the trolley or in the office to signify when the equipment was taken out and when it was returned. A list of all equipment in each class and items stored centrally is reviewed annually and circulated to members of staff.

Use of IT and calculators

The use of information technology forms part of the educational entitlement that every child should be offered in school. In most nursery and infant schools computers are now familiar pieces of equipment in use on a daily basis. Smaller nursery settings such as those run as local playgroups may not have a computer because of limited funds. Also, playgroups often operate in premises that are shared by other organisations which restrict the installation and secure storage of a computer. The following is an example of an infant school policy statement on the use of IT for supporting mathematical development:

> There is a PC computer on a trolley in every classroom and we use a range of Windows educational software throughout the school to extend children's mathematical knowledge and skills. We use a Roamer programmable toy for children to explore computer control, leading on to using early LOGO and a turtle at Year 2. At present we only have one printer unit located on the computer trolley in the library which can be moved into classrooms for use when required. The IT co-ordinator is responsible for reviewing, installing and supporting staff in the use of software. Staff are expected to lock all computers away each night in their classroom stockcupboards.

The use of calculators in schools remains a sensitive issue. There is tension between the concern that children should develop quick and accurate arithmetical skills and not become 'calculator dependent' and the concern that children should become familiar with using calculators because of their everyday use in domestic, commercial and industrial settings. It is important that a policy is established on the use of calculators throughout the school so that all staff can operate from a position of shared understanding. For example:

> Calculators are available for use in classrooms from Year 1. We aim to ensure that children are familiar with basic operations in using a calculator but only encourage children to use them in practical investigations and problem-solving situations when calculations involving large numbers are required. For routine arithmetic, children are encouraged to use mental skills and/or appropriate pencil and paper methods with the support of structured number apparatus if required.

A discussion of the use of computers and calculators can be found in Chapters 11 and 12.

Display

Creating mathematical displays in classrooms and around the school is an important aspect of valuing and sharing children's mathematical work. It also contributes to visual evidence of the school's ethos for parents and other visitors to the school. Creating displays, whilst they take a lot of preparation and hard work to assemble, also contributes to a sense of personal satisfaction and ownership on the part of the teacher and the children concerned. The following represents an example of a nursery school policy statement of the use of display and mathematics:

> We aim to incorporate a display of children's mathematical work each half-term in the nursery. This will include work with number, shape, measures and

graphs. Children are invited to bring objects from home to add to displays and we try to include photographs of children working whenever possible. There is also a permanent display of a number frieze in the maths and science area. Mathematical work also forms part of regular displays in art and craft work in the nursery. It is planned to reflect current work in a form that is visually attractive, and an example of each child's efforts should be included somewhere in displays around the nursery.

The use of display in relation to mathematics is discussed more fully in Chapter 9.

Partnership with parents or carers

Many schools nowadays have established arrangements for parents and families to help children at home with mathematics. The following is an example of a nursery school policy statement on parent and community partnership in mathematics:

> We operate a parent partnership scheme for mathematics where parents are invited to help their children with learning mathematics at home. This is carried out under the guidance of the nursery staff, where different groups of children are encouraged to choose a maths game, from the home boxes in the family room each Friday, to play with their parents at home. All games that are borrowed must be signed out in the home book and should be returned on Monday morning. Guidelines on how parents can help their child at home with learning maths are included in our 'Information for Parents' booklet. We also invite parents to help us with our work in school. A few parents assist on a regular basis, taking small groups for baking and helping children with practical maths activities in the Red Room. We also have occasional visits from workers in the local community and arrange visits to the local supermarket.

Setting up a parent partnership scheme for mathematics is discussed in detail in Chapter 7.

Information for parents

As seen in the above statement, information is included on the teaching of mathematics in a general booklet written for parents about the school. Schools try to write these documents in a form of friendly 'parent speak', which gives brief details of what the school offers the child in terms of curriculum provision, as well as the rules and procedures parents need to know. This document may need translation into first languages other than English.

Arrangements for reporting to parents

Schools are required by law to make arrangements for regular reports to be given to parents on their child's progress and achievement. For Year 2 children this must include the results of standard attainment tasks and tests in English and mathematics (SATs). To ensure consistency and reliability, schools will need to decide on how the process of reporting will be managed throughout the school. For example:

> It is our legal obligation to produce annual reports for the parents/guardians of our pupils. The format of our reports are guided by the requirements of DfEE Circular 1/97 and include:
>
> - comments on general progress;
> - details of arrangements for parent/teacher discussion;
> - comment on every NC foundation subject;
> - a record of pupils' attendance; and
> - results of statutory assessments.
>
> We also provide reports for other audiences, including:
>
> - other schools (for transferring pupils);
> - educational psychologists;
> - social workers in education; and
> - the school governors.
>
> Parents evenings are scheduled to take place in the Autumn and Summer term of each year but we welcome parents to discuss informally matters relating to their child with their class teacher any evening after school between 3.00 and 3.30 pm.

Full details of statutory reporting procedures for mathematics are included in Chapter 21.

Provision for evaluation and review

As part of good practice, all policies and procedures should be reviewed on a regular basis. Teachers should also spend time together examining recent reports and recommendations published by the DfEE and Ofsted, to consider these against existing practice in the school so that agreed strategies for action can be established. This may involve updating policy documentation where changes are agreed.

Strategies for action

In the process of school development, agreed targets should be set for refining and improving elements of practice in the management of teaching and learning of mathematics. This could be a simple refinement of the way resources are managed, to a more complex change, for example, where the staff wish to change the published mathematics scheme they are using. As evidence of ongoing development a policy document for mathematics should contain a separate page which outlines an action plan for each academic year. As part of the process of the management of change, it is important that new initiatives in an action plan are not written into the main body of a policy document until they have been trialled and reviewed. Sometimes new ideas do not work out as they were planned.

Provision for professional development of staff

This will normally be the responsibility of the person nominated as the mathematics co-ordinator, discussed more fully in Chapter 5.

In a policy document it is important to include a statement which presents information and evidence about arrangements that are in place for the support and development of staff in the teaching of mathematics in the school. For example:

> The maths co-ordinator together with the headteacher will endeavour to support and develop the maths teaching skills of the staff through various INSET programmes within the school and at other venues. At an informal level, staff are invited to share any concerns or good ideas with the co-ordinator that could be used as a focus for discussion at INSET meetings.

Publishing a mathematics policy document

With the advent of sophisticated computer software and reprographic equipment, schools are now able to pay considerable attention to the professional presentation of official documents. A suggested format is as follows:

- *Front Cover* School name. Title of document and publishing date. Name of the maths co-ordinator and other contributors. A picture, school logo or design added for illustration.
- *Page 1* A brief statement from the maths co-ordinator giving an introduction to the document and explaining his or her role in supporting the staff in teaching mathematics throughout the school.

  Names of other key staff who may need to be consulted, for example, co-ordinators for special needs, IT, assessment.
- *Page 2* Index of contents with page numbers.
- *Page 3 – ?* Title followed by subtitled policy statements in order of considered priority.
- *Final page* Strategies for action.
- *Appendix* The school scheme of work for mathematics. A copy of any agreed proformas used by the whole school for planning and record keeping, etc. A list of mathematical resources and their location in the school, including computer software available for mathematics and any other documentation that is required by all members of staff to manage the teaching of mathematics throughout the school.

For ease of reference, regular updating and revision, schools are finding it better if each member of staff is given copies of all policy documents in a ring binder file, so that only relevant pages requiring updating need to be revised.

Rome was not built in a day!

As a final note it is important to emphasise that the process of developing a policy for mathematics is not an end in itself but a continuous process that reflects the culture of a developing school. In compiling a 'first edition', it is more important that the policy reflects the existing practice than a perceived 'state of the art' document which bears no relationship to the practice in the school. In principle, it is through the process of regular whole-staff evaluation and review that changes should be initiated. However in reality, there are often changes that staff have to respond to 'on the hoof' – for example, schools selected to pilot KS1 SATs or more recently, the National Numeracy Project.

From the perspective of internal management of a particular school, it is important that the culture of a developing school is encouraged through a recognition of change for good reason. Changes in the strategies for managing the teaching of mathematics should represent a refinement and development of shared ideas over a period of time. Decisions which result in modification or change should be informed by the review of existing practice. This may arise internally or be considered because of recommendations from the DfEE or an Ofsted inspection.

The process of effective change is highly complex and needs to be viewed as a long-term process rather than short term (Day *et al.*, 1990). It is natural for schools to feel anxious in the run-up to an Ofsted inspection, where the need may be felt to produce exemplary documentation. However, inspectors are more likely to be impressed by evidence that the policy documentation represents an agreed reality by all the staff, with indications of plans for development, than documentation which bears no relationship to the practice observed and discussed during the inspection visit. Even worse – there is no documentation at all!

Finally, the process of policy-making requires individual members of staff to become actively involved. In relation to curricular policies for mathematics the DES (1989c) reported:

> Where the [mathematics] work was good in the majority of classes, the school had a clear curricular policy for mathematics...The more satisfactory guidelines had been worked out collectively by staff and were the product of discussion and shared understanding. This degree of involvement appeared to be a major factor in determining whether the curriculum document had a significant impact on the work in classrooms.

Summary

This chapter has discussed the main strategies and procedures that guide the process of formulating a policy document for mathematics in nursery and infant schools. The participation of all staff involved in the teaching of mathematics is central to the process. The creation of a new policy document initially involves an audit of current practice and clarification of agreed values and procedures in the form of clearly written statements of intent. This is normally initiated by the person nominated as the maths co-ordinator through a series of staff meetings.

5

The role of the maths co-ordinator
1. Supporting developments in mathematical provision

Responsibilities of a mathematics co-ordinator

The post of maths co-ordinator is a position of middle management in a school. The person in this post has the responsibility for the administration of all aspects of mathematics throughout a school. According to the Cockroft Report (1982, para. 354–8), this will include:

- preparing a scheme of work for the school in consultation with the head and staff;
- providing guidance and support to other members of staff, by meetings and working alongside individual teachers;
- organising and purchasing teaching resources, maintaining an up-to-date inventory and ensuring that staff are familiar with how to use the resources available;
- monitoring mathematical work throughout the school, including methods of assessment and record-keeping;
- assisting with the diagnosis of children's learning difficulties and providing courses of action;
- arranging school-based in-service training for members of staff as appropriate;
- maintaining liaison with schools from which children come and to which they go, and also with LEA advisory staff;
- keeping up to date with current developments in mathematics education;
- helping young teachers and colleagues who lack confidence in maths.

More recently, the writing of policy documents has been added to the responsibilities of the co-ordinator.

Getting started

A person newly appointed as a mathematics co-ordinator may find it difficult to know how or where to begin. As a starting point it is useful to consider the tenancy of the position. Has the post been newly created or is it replacing someone who has left? Is the appointment as a result of promotion within the school or a career move from another school? Each of these will have a bearing on how a new co-ordinator starts to tackle the job. Whatever the legacy of the appointment, it is important to commence by making a systematic audit of the school situation, to see what is already happening and identify the school's stage of development. This will include finding out the following:

- Does the school have an existing policy document for mathematics? What does it contain? Are there any existing development plans for mathematics?
- Is there a scheme of work in use throughout the school? Has it been devised by members of staff or delivered through a published scheme?
- What are the arrangements for long and short-term planning, assessment and record-keeping?
- How is progression and continuity in mathematical learning monitored throughout the school?
- How much time is allocated to the teaching of mathematics throughout the school?
- How are classes organised for mathematics? Ability or mixed-ability groups?
- What use is made of whole-class, group and individual teaching in mathematics lessons?
- Is mathematics taught as a discrete subject or within the context of topic work?
- Are the staff actively involved in developing mental, investigational and problem-solving skills with their pupils?
- What is the provision for children with special educational needs and equal opportunities in mathematics? Is there a special needs co-ordinator (SENCO)?
- Are parents encouraged to help with the teaching of mathematics in classrooms and at home?
- What are the resources available for teaching mathematics? Which resources are located in classrooms? Stored centrally – where?
- What does the school own in the way of computers, printers, control technology (roamers, turtles), mathematical software and repro-graphic equipment – where is it located? Is there an IT co-ordinator?
- Are there mathematical displays in classrooms, corridors, etc., throughout the school?
- What are the arrangements for reporting to parents and following schools?
- Do the staff meet regularly to discuss mathematics?
- Are there arrangements in place for regular school-based in-service training?
- Who are the LEA advisers/inspectors responsible for Nursery and KS1 mathematics?

- What are the feeder/following schools and the names of the headteachers, maths co-ordinators?

This will require the co-ordinator to talk to the headteacher and the staff. As a new member of staff, this presents a useful opportunity to get to know everybody and to establish a 'feel' for the job. In the course of discussion it is important to find out what individual staff feel about teaching mathematics and their views on what is needed at a personal level as well as at a school level. There should also be some consideration of the perceived personal needs of the appointed co-ordinator, to enable them to carry out the job effectively, which should be discussed with the headteacher.

Working with the headteacher

To perform the job effectively, the co-ordinator will require supportive leadership from the headteacher (assuming that the headteacher is not the co-ordinator!). A headteacher's style of management will largely dictate the level of support offered. A headteacher operating an *autocratic* or dictatorial style of management is less likely to invite staff to participate in decision-making processes and offer support to curriculum development initiatives generated by the staff than a headteacher operating a *collegiate* or democratic style of management (Bush, 1995). In practical terms, a good working relationship with the headteacher will involve:

- partnership in planning and evaluating curriculum developments;
- a two-way exchange of advice, ideas and experience;
- shared discussion of issues; and
- mutual professional respect and support.

If the headteacher indicates an unwillingness to participate in this way, it is often better to maintain a low profile and work constructively with other colleagues.

Working with other teachers

Establishing a good working relationship with other members of staff involves the same principles as working with the headteacher. However, because of the core status of mathematics in the National Curriculum, everybody is expected to teach it well. Consequently, there may be a variety of strong views held by different members of staff about the teaching of mathematics. This may cause tensions, even conflict, and achieving consensus can be fraught with difficulties. The co-ordinator requires good interpersonal skills and the ability to negotiate agreement where possible. It is also recognised that realistically, teachers get on better with some colleagues than others. It is often better to focus on those colleagues where a good relationship has been established, as they are more likely to respond positively to any support:

Working with those who are keen to develop their approach to mathematics can be an exciting and fruitful experience for both parties and the results of the collaboration can be seen by other teachers and thus generate interest. It may even sway those who were initially sceptical and reluctant to change.

(ATM, 1987)

However, it is important to avoid the establishment of cliques which actively exclude certain members of staff and create ill feeling. A useful text in this area is *Managing Mathematics in the Primary School* by Marion Stow (1989). A positive starting point is to establish a programme of support that can be offered to new members of staff, newly qualified teachers, supply teachers, student teachers and NNEB students working in the school.

Initiating strategies for change

There are a number of acknowledged ways in which developments are initiated in schools. Amongst these are:

- staff meetings;
- workshops;
- displays of work;
- visits to other schools;
- visits from LEA advisory staff or other teachers with specific skills;
- setting up working parties;
- working with colleagues in their classrooms;
- school-based in-service training programmes.

(ATM, 1987)

The method chosen will depend on the nature of the development and the willingness of staff to participate. Bringing about development and change in schools is never straightforward and can be a very slow process. One of the chief inhibitors of change may be the disposition of the staff towards change. Martin Skilbeck (1982) compiled a list of factors related to staff that may cause difficulties in initiating school-based curriculum development:

- a sense of low esteem and inadequacy in staff and the lack of relevant skills;
- lack of conviction in staff, particularly in sustaining change;
- conflicting priorities on the part of the teacher e.g. planning, teaching, domestic commitments, leisure interests etc.;
- rapid staff turnover;
- inadequacy of exemplar models (teachers tend to reject what they cannot easily relate to);
- tendency of staff to revert to earlier practice if impetus is not sustained;
- readiness of staff to abandon new practices before they have been fully implemented and reviewed;
- reactive attitudes of staff that are obstructive to change.

(Adapted from Skilbeck, 1982)

Setting the climate for change

Having identified an area of concern through analysis of the needs of the school (see Figure 5.1), the co-ordinator will need to inform the headteacher, deputy head, staff colleagues and other involved parties, for example, ancillary helpers or parents, and create an opportunity to clarify any issues and invite discussion of ideas.

A plan of action should be agreed (see Figure 5.2), including time and resources required and ways of monitoring the implementation of the plan. After a plan of action has been implemented and trialled for a period, the innovation should be collectively reviewed and modified if necessary. A period of consolidation of the new 'pattern' should follow, combined with the consideration of 'long-term after-care support and evaluation' (Day *et al.*, 1990). In the busy life of teachers, it is often the weekly staff meeting that becomes the only regular forum for initiating and following through procedures required for the management of change and where collective impetus for the process can be sustained. However, it is important not to assume that because something has been discussed and agreed in a staff meeting it will automatically become part of everyone's practice. It will be the job of the co-ordinator to initiate support in whichever way is deemed appropriate to ensure that the plan of action gets off the starting grid, and to follow it through with after-care support to ensure that 'teething problems' are sorted out.

Being realistic about the process of change

It is important that targets for change are set within realistic and manageable parameters, which the staff feel able to cope with, are reasonably confident of achieving in the time available and recognise the value of the change as leading to improvement. It is also important to remember that implementing change takes emotional as well as intellectual energy. Teachers of young children invariably have a variety of important life roles to play in their family life outside school as well as carrying out their job, which may include, for example, the role of home manager, parent, partner or care assistant to an ageing relative. It is important to recognise that additional demands on their time may add to the stress of their daily lives. Any plan of action for change should be clearly thought through beforehand to avoid placing colleagues under undue pressure as a result of the changes to be made. Michael Fullan (1982) offers the following useful points to be considered in the process of initiating and implementing change in schools:

1. Do not assume that your version of what the change should be is the one that should or could be implemented... Assume that successful implementation consists of... continual development of the initial idea.

2. Assume that any significant innovation, if it is to result in change, requires individual implementers to work out their own meaning. Significant

Curriculum/Responsibility Review
MATHEMATICS

Strengths	Weaknesses	Opportunities	Threats
Specific, identifiable	Specific, identifiable	Specific, manageable, achievable, realistic	Specific, identifiable
1. Improved opportunities for classroom support by co-ordinator.	1. Poor mental/arithmetic skills.	> Start of National Numeracy Project. Use of Circle time.	1. Time.
2. Inclusion of school in next phase of National Numeracy Project.	2. Standards of numeracy low.	> Review of set number of lessons per week etc., through staff discussion, workshops, and INSET days.	
3 Piloting of new record scheme by Reception/ Nursery.	3. Insufficient differentiation.	> Review planning – Staff meetings etc.	
4. Completion of maths profile by end of July 97.	4. Inconsistent recording.	> Staff discussion/referral to school policy etc.	
	5. Topics only covered once – need regular practice. Also need more direct teaching.	> Review of half-terms plans – Year groups and staff meetings. Also consider Year group 'team teaching' and 'Maths Enrichment' (A. Maguire)	
	6. Insufficient experience of reading scales, digital clocks, etc.	> Review of half-term plans (and equipment).	
	7. Low priority of mathematical language.	> Yr. group planning to include key words in half-term (weekly plans). More maths displays/words for children to see and use.	
	8. IMPACT not reviewed last year.	> Review in staff meeting at start of new year.	

Figure 5.1 Curriculum responsibility review

Action Plan Monitored by:		1 of 2	MATHEMATICS		
What	How	When	Success Criteria	Project Cost	
Specific, achievable, realistic	Manageable, realistic, specific	Specific, realistic timescale	Identifiable, specific, achievable	Realistic, manageable	
Start National Numeracy Project.	• Use of framework • Staff training day • 5 day course for head, co-ordinator and one other	September for 2 years	Improved SATs results 1998, 1999	?	
Review half-term plans to improve • differentiation • regular practice of shape, space & measure • maths language (key words, etc.)	• Year group meetings • Staff training day • Staff meetings	January 1998	Improved SATS		
Review recording in books – leading to consistent approach.	• Year group meetings • Staff meetings	September 1997 Term	Consistent approach in school by July 1998		
Review of published scheme – especially how it supports teaching of shape, space and measure.	• Staff meetings				

Figure 5.2   Action plan for mathematics

change involves a certain amount of ambiguity, ambivalence, and uncertainty for the individual about the meaning of change. Thus, effective implementation is a process of clarification.

3. Assume that conflict and disagreement are not only inevitable but fundamental to successful change.

4. Assume that people need pressure to change (even in a direction which they desire), but will only be effective under conditions which allow them to react, to form their own position, to interact with other implementers and to obtain technical assistance.

5. Assume that effective change takes time... Expect significant change to take a minimum of two to three years.

6. Do not assume that the reason for lack of implementation is outright rejection of the values embodied in the change or hard-core resistance to all change. Assume there are a number of possible reasons: value rejection, inadequate resources to support implementation, insufficient time elapsed.

7. Do not expect all or even most people or groups to change. The complexity of change is such that it is totally impossible to bring about widespread reform in any large social system. Progress occurs when we take steps which increase the number of people affected... Instead of being discouraged by all that remains to be done, be encouraged by what has been accomplished.

8. Assume that you will need a plan which is based on the above assumptions and which addresses the factors known to affect the implementation... Knowledge of the change process is essential.

9. Assume that no amount of knowledge will ever make it totally clear what action should be taken. Action decisions are a combination of valid knowledge, political consideration, on-the-spot decisions and intuition.

10. Assume that change is a frustrating, discouraging business. If all or some of the above assumptions cannot be made, do not expect significant change as far as implementation is concerned.

Monitoring work in mathematics throughout the school

A key role of the co-ordinator is to monitor the work in mathematics throughout the school. This can be seen as perhaps one of the most difficult aspects of the job because it requires the establishment of strategies which are seen as constructive and non-threatening to colleagues. There are many teachers of young children who lack confidence in their own mathematical abilities and may consider it a threatening experience to have their work put under a spotlight. The co-ordinator will need to work at building the confidence and trust of colleagues, through reassurance and being forthcoming with praise (for example praising wall displays, class assemblies); inviting colleagues to share any new ideas and examples of good work from children; and encouraging them to share any personal concerns about any child or elements of teaching. Chatting to staff informally over a cup of tea in the staffroom in an atmosphere of relaxed openness can help in the establishment of good relationships.

One of the most successful strategies for monitoring the mathematics work throughout the school is by working alongside colleagues in their classrooms, providing they are happy about the arrangement. This enables the co-ordinator to gain first-hand experience of other teachers' work, and can provide opportunities for supporting new ideas that the class teacher has initiated or wants to try out. It makes it possible for the teacher to observe or work with the co-ordinator to see the results of working in different ways with the class, for example, whole-class mental arithmetic games, or children working with a new piece of mathematical equipment. It also gives the co-ordinator an opportunity to evaluate the personal strengths and needs of individual colleagues and offer appropriate support. One of the main advantages of this approach compared with others is that it involves first-hand experiences of working with children in actual teaching situations rather than from theoretical models.

One of the problems in setting this up, even if staff are in agreement, is securing time for this work. All co-ordinators generally have their own classes and therefore require cover. This may need some discussion with the headteacher to establish timetabling for this work to take place. ATM (1987) presents the following advice to co-ordinators on securing time to work with colleagues:

> Whatever the arrangement made, it is essential that the time is granted on a regular and reliable basis and that the importance of the work is recognised. Working with other teachers can be a sensitive matter and to turn up spasmodically and at short notice in other people's classrooms can do substantial damage.

Another strategy, perhaps more commonly in use, is the process of regular review carried out as part of year group meetings or full staff meetings, where work in different areas of mathematics is monitored and evaluated in terms of levels of consistency and continuity throughout the school. For example:

- reviewing planning documents in relation to the scheme of work;
- discussing examples of children's work;
- a review of mathematical resources;
- a review of methods of assessment and record-keeping,
- a review and analysis of SATs results;
- use of adult help in the classroom;
- discussion of problems encountered in teaching and in children's learning; and
- sharing new ideas that teachers have tried out.

Implementing school-based in-service training

Perhaps the hardest task of all for the co-ordinator is the implementation of a programme of school-based in-service training for staff. Apart from staff having different needs, they also have different attitudes towards the principle of in-service training, ranging from 'any experience that inspires professional development is worth while' to 'a complete waste of time'.

One of the most successful strategies is working alongside other colleagues in their classrooms, as discussed earlier. In this way the co-ordinator is able to match training/support to individual needs. Whole-staff, school-based in-service training sessions require the identification of a few agreed priorities year by year. To be of value, the INSET plan must be of sufficient strength and quality to enable it to have a decisive impact on the mathematical work of the school in the areas targeted (Alexander *et al.*, 1992). Capturing the interest of the staff requires the planning of a varied and stimulating programme which may include, for example:

- a visit from an outside speaker;
- use of an educational video, such as those produced by the Open University or television documentary programmes on education, followed by discussion;
- a visit to another school, followed by discussion;
- a visit to an educational exhibition, for example 'The Education Show' at the NEC in Birmingham;
- a forum for staff debate and discussion related to a particular issue, followed by the establishment of an agreed plan of action;
- a practical workshop for staff to familiarise themselves with new resources or equipment and design activities;
- opportunities for members of staff in turn to inform other members of staff of the content and ways in which mathematics is taught in their classroom and to share the successes and difficulties they experience;
- inviting members of staff to present innovations that have proved to be successful in their classrooms; and
- planning a school maths event or a maths trail.

The most important considerations in setting up a whole-staff in-service programme is cost and time. This has to be considered realistically in terms of the annual financial budgeting of the school for staff development and against priorities for developments in other areas of the curriculum, which require the approval of the headteacher and governors.

It is the responsibility of the maths co-ordinator to communicate the need for 'windows of opportunity' for whole-staff in-service training during the school year to the head and present a planned programme of events, together with proposed costs. Realistically, there may only be time for one or two sessions that can be allocated for maths during the year and it is important that needs are prioritised.

Professional development of the co-ordinator

One of the responsibilities of co-ordinators is to ensure that they are aware of current developments in mathematical education so that they can communicate them effectively to colleagues. This will involve reading guidelines and reports sent to schools by the DfEE and Ofsted. It is also useful to keep an eye on the press, particularly *The Times Educational Supplement*, which usually prints articles on newly published research papers, has a regular early years/primary section and periodically presents a special feature on mathematics. Professional journals, such as *Child Education*, run regular features on early years education and present good mathematical ideas that have been tried out in classrooms by practising teachers. Membership of a national professional body, for example, AMET (Association of Mathematics Education Teachers) and ATM (Association of Teachers of Mathematics), is also helpful. Both AMET and ATM produce a professional journal and ATM also produces a variety of helpful publications. They offer programmes of conferences and workshops which enable teachers to attend lectures given by prominent specialists in mathematics education, to share and discuss mathematical issues with other teachers and to attend presentations on new initiatives. There are also regional organisations, for example, NORMAC (Northern Region Mathematics Council) and international organisations such as OMEP (World Organisation for Early Childhood Education) which offer similar programmes. A feature of attending educational conferences is the opportunity to meet other teachers who share a common professional interest, to exchange ideas and establish professional networks with colleagues from other schools.

Liaison with other schools

Establishing links with feeder and/or following schools or departments is an important strategy in sustaining continuity in children's mathematical education throughout their school career. Even where children do not change schools, the culture of the different sectors may be markedly different. Styles of teaching, organisation and methods of teaching mathematics can change very dramatically as children transfer from one sector to another within the same school. It is important to arrange reciprocal meetings with other schools' maths co-ordinators or inter-department meetings within schools. According to David Winteridge (1989),

> the greater the co-operation and understanding of teachers across the whole of the educational system the more mathematics teaching will benefit... Much of the dissatisfaction that occurs over the transfer of children from one school to another is due to lack of communication and understanding between staff in the different areas.

The times of necessary communication between schools or departments are around the transfer period, when records on children who are leaving one sector are passed to the receiving sector. It is a common complaint of receiving teachers in all sectors, from infant to secondary schools, that the information from feeder schools is not particularly helpful. Conversely, it is a common source of frustration in teachers from feeder schools, who spend a lot of time compiling transfer documentation, that their records and reports are largely ignored by receiving schools.

Through the establishment of communication networks between schools and departments, teachers are able to understand how each sector works and create strategies which will enable smoother transitions to take place. Some schools interchange staff for a morning or afternoon session and some join together for combined sessions of in-service training. It is the responsibility of the co-ordinator to initiate and maintain links with other schools. Through regular meetings, good working relationships can be established where staff from the different sectors can work together to create a development plan specifically related to improving continuity from one sector to another.

Summary

This chapter has set out the main roles and responsibilities of the maths co-ordinator in a school, with regard to offering support to staff, monitoring the work in mathematics throughout the school, establishing links with other schools or departments and acting as an agent for development and change within a school. The process of the management of change has been discussed in terms of situation analysis, prioritising targets, timescale, planning and supporting implementation and evaluation. Central to the effective implementation of change is the principle of democratic management, where all staff are encouraged to be actively involved in the decision-making processes at every stage. Another key consideration is the establishment of realistic targets within a realistic timescale. It is emphasised that the process of change is complex and often fraught with difficulties. These may include lack of support from the headteacher, resistance to change from staff as well as the physical constraints of time and money. The co-ordinator will need to bring to the job subject expertise, skills of rational analysis, good leadership and interpersonal skills; an ability to communicate ideas well and negotiate agreement; and the ability to establish good working relationships with all colleagues involved in mathematics education inside and outside the school.

6

The role of the maths co-ordinator
2. Management of mathematical resources

Working within a school budget

Since the Education Reform Act 1988, the overall responsibility for the financial management of a school has been the domain of the governing body and the headteacher. It is at this level that decisions are made regarding the allocation of money for resource provision throughout a school.

The planning of financial budgets at management level is a complex process and warrants more study than can be offered within this book. However, in simple terms, the financial aspect of resource management in the primary sector represents the process of 'programme budgeting', where decisions are made on the basis of perceived needs and priorities in relation to other programmes – for example, mathematics *vis-à-vis* language and literacy or science (Lévacic, 1989). Additionally, most schools operate a budget plan where a basic annual 'maintenance' budget is allocated to different areas of the curriculum to sustain a reasonably stable resource base. Where larger amounts of money are required, for example, investment in mathematical games for use throughout the school, a costed proposal or 'capital bid' will need to be prepared by the maths co-ordinator to be approved for funding by the headteacher and governors.

In a small school it is often quite easy to identify priorities in relation to areas of the curriculum which require targeting for development. However, in a large school where priorities may be viewed differently, for example, between infant and junior departments, conflicting priorities may occasionally arise between departments. It is for this reason that it is important for schools to establish long-term development plans where different areas can be targeted for budget allocation over a period of years. In this way schools are able to plan for a stable and efficient deployment of resources within the context of overall curriculum development.

Management of mathematical resources

One of the responsibilities of the co-ordinator is to manage and develop the resource base supporting mathematical work throughout the school. To carry this out effectively, the co-ordinator will need to take stock of the existing resource provision in every classroom and items that are stored centrally within the school. If this process has not been carried out before, it can represent an arduous task. An effective strategy is to focus on one area at a time. To make the job easier for members of staff, an inventory can be provided (see Figure 6.1).

Class_____ Age group_____

Number apparatus	None/limited/adequate/a lot
Real objects for sorting/counting	
Sorting hoops	
Multilink cubes	
Pegboards and pegs	
Coloured beads and laces	
Multisided and blank dice, spinners	
Number cards/playing cards	
Dominoes	
Board games and counters	
Cuisenaire rods	
Numberlines in ones and tens	
100 number squares (grid trays, numbered and blank cards)	
HTU spike abaci, tray abaci, base-ten boards	
ThHTU base-ten equipment (Dienes)	
All denominations of up-to-date currency in plastic coins and fake notes	
Calculators	
A range of different-sized squared paper (1 cm, 1.5 cm and 2 cm sq)	
Computer number software	

Figure 6.1. An example of a resource inventory for number apparatus in classrooms

This will establish a picture of the resource base throughout the school. Gaps can be identified and resources redistributed where necessary.

Supporting the use of specialised mathematical equipment

Teachers often inherit equipment in classrooms they have little knowledge or experience of using, with the result that resources such as Cuisenaire rods and Dienes apparatus can be consigned to the back of the stock cupboard. One of the ways the co-ordinator can initiate development in this area is to organise a meeting where members of staff are invited to bring a favourite piece of equipment and give a brief demonstration of its value to other staff. Conversely, members of staff can be invited to bring a piece of equipment they are not sure about using, and the mathematical possibilities can be discussed and shared by everyone. It remains a source of amusement to the author that as a new teacher to a school, it took several months before I discovered the function of foldaway sorting hoops. It had been wrongly assumed that they were contraptions bought to create angel's wings for nativity plays!

Storing maths equipment centrally

Many pieces of mathematical equipment are too expensive, bulky or used too infrequently to be allocated as a piece of standard equipment in every classroom, for example programmable toys, electronic maths games, Quadro construction kits, Polydrons, precision stopwatches, thermometers, etc. Arrangements are generally made to establish a central location for storing these specialist items.

One of the problems in managing resources stored centrally is the establishment of an effective system for borrowing and returning items. Even with carefully considered systems in place, items can be borrowed and not returned. Alternatively, tension may be created because more than one member of staff wishes to use a piece of equipment at the same time.

Topic boxes

One of the most successful strategies appears to be the compilation of mathematical topic or concept boxes together with an inventory of contents. Whilst these involve considerable time and effort to set up, it enables individual teachers to secure time to use the available resource base for a particular mathematical topic at the planning stage. In this way topic boxes can be viewed as a 'unit' and individual items are less likely to become dispersed or squirreled away in different classrooms. For large specialist items such as Quadro or Polydrons, these can be shared on a rota basis.

One of the advantages of topic boxes is that the contents can be built up over time. They can include picture and reference books for children, games, a folder of ideas for activities and assessment materials, as well as a collection of equipment and artefacts. For example, in a time resource box there could be a collection of different timepieces, clocks and watches. However, because topic boxes are compiled for use throughout a school, some consideration needs to be paid to establishing some form of structure and progression to their use to avoid unnecessary repetition of work. This may be through referencing the contents of topic boxes to the school scheme of work or, in larger schools, there may be the facilities to create a set of graded topic boxes for each of the mathematical areas.

Developing a resource bank of published resources

Another way of building up a collection of centrally stored resources is to establish a resource bank or library of published resources which offers ideas for activities, investigations, display, etc. Published teachers' manuals and photocopiable publications are expensive items to buy. Establishing a centrally stored collection is a good way to provide a reasonably sound selection of these resources for all staff to use that can be built up over time. Again, it is useful to catalogue and store these resources under topic headings, which may include topics such as 'play and maths' or 'maths across the curriculum', as well as discrete subject areas. Books that contain a compendium of ideas can be cut up, sorted and stored in folders or boxes.

Reviewing resources and making purchasing decisions

Making provision for wear and tear

The mathematical resource base within a school requires to be regularly and systematically reviewed in terms of necessary updating, wear and tear replacement and repair (see Chapter 5, Figure 5.1). An admirable culture exists among early years teachers, where many would openly admit that they subsidise the provision of resources from their own pocket in order to do their job as well as they can. They are renowned for scouring markets and jumble sales for lengths of material, games and educational toys, etc., for their classrooms. They persuade friends to save egg cartons, milktops, toilet roll centres, etc., and are seen on holiday collecting shells from beaches. Underpinning this culture is a generic philosophy of teachers having to improvise and make do. This can result in equipment that has seen better days, and essential resources past their effective best still being used in classrooms. New materials are added to the resource base from allocated financial budgets but established resources tend to get overlooked in terms of renewal or replacement – for example, tape measures with frayed ends, cardboard clocks without hands or balances without equalisers.

It is important that the maths co-ordinator ensures that the financial budget allocated for buying mathematical resources is used to maintain a stable and effective resource base, as well as seeking to promote curriculum development through the addition of new materials. A useful strategy is for co-ordinators to target an area of mathematics annually and encourage teachers to withdraw equipment from use that is no longer effective, giving it to the co-ordinator rather than storing it in stock cupboards. The co-ordinator will then be able to make a more accurate assessment of how much of the annual budget should be allocated for general wear and tear.

Buying new resources

Money is never freely in abundance within school budgets. In making decisions about the purchase of additional new resources, the school or individual classroom needs should be identified in collaboration with other members of staff to ensure money is spent as wisely and fairly as possible. Some headteachers or co-ordinators may consider that it is fairer to offer equal amounts of money to individual teachers. However, it is important to recognise that unless some discussion takes place between staff there is a possibility that resources may be wasted or duplicated. For example, a member of staff may order an expensive piece of equipment for personal use which may become redundant if the member of staff leaves or changes age group. Equally, items may be ordered on the basis of their attractive appeal rather than mathematical value. Also, because the amount of money is necessarily small, staff may be tempted to opt for the cheapest versions rather than consider the quality or durability of resource items.

Working outside the budget

There may be rare occasions when a mathematical resource priority can exceed the normal budget. Funds available for capital bids may have been allocated to other curriculum areas targeted for development within the school's long-term budget plan. It is on these occasions that the co-ordinator may wish to enlist the support of the head and other members of staff to organise a one-off fund-raising event to raise some additional cash (for example, to purchase a range of teacher and classroom resources to implement a programme of mental arithmetic activities throughout a school). It is important that the staff are committed to the need for the additional funding and that these events are sensitively planned. It is unrealistic to expect parents continually to put their hands in their pockets, for example, to raise money for science resources this term, English next term, maths the following term, etc. On the other hand, the decision to hold a one-off fund-raising event to purchase specific resources may represent the collective wishes of the staff and parents to make a prompt response to national recommendations in the interests of the children.

Spending money wisely

Investment in published schemes

Decisions about what to spend an annual budget on can be very difficult beyond maintaining the bread and butter needs of essential classroom resources, including pencils, paper, etc. Priorities will need to be established, for example, in the situation where staff have agreed on the investment in a published scheme; the purchase of these materials should be considered carefully. Recently published schemes are marketed as comprehensive resource packages comprising workbooks, workcards, photocopiables, games packs, assessment materials, record sheets, management guides and resource handbooks for teachers. There is strong persuasion, through glossy advertising, for schools to buy the entire compendium which can represent a very expensive investment. Schools which take this decision often find themselves with a lot of the resource materials rarely or infrequently in use and a feeling that money has been wasted. Realistically, it is impossible to evaluate how effectively the materials work as a resource base in supporting the needs of the pupils and the staff throughout a school until a published scheme has been implemented and running for some time.

The most effective use of published scheme materials in schools is when they have been implemented gradually over time and effectively service the resource needs of the staff and pupils who use them. It is also a commonly misplaced assumption that resources cannot be mixed from different published schemes. Recent published materials are specifically designed to support the delivery of the National Curriculum for mathematics, as prescribed in the Programmes of Study and Attainment Targets, and contain generic principles. However, different schemes have different strengths, for example, the teachers' resource manual may be an outstanding feature in one scheme, the games pack in another, the teachers' cards in another, etc. Where a school has established its own structured scheme of work for mathematics, teachers are more able to make a discerning choice from the wide range of published materials, according to the resource needs of the school. The effective use of published mathematics schemes is discussed in Chapter 8.

Investing in mathematical equipment

When considering the purchase of mathematical equipment, whilst quality and durability should be taken into account, it is not always the attractive and specialised pieces of equipment that are the most useful mathematical resources in the classroom but often the simplest – for example, having a wide range of objects that can easily be collected through teacher initiative or appeals to parents, costing nothing except the time to initiate collection (corks, bottletops, buttons, cones, conkers, cotton reels, etc.). These provide a flexible resource for counting, sorting, shape recognition, building patterns and sequences, early computation, balancing and measuring length with arbitrary units, science and artwork. Sets of dominoes, numbered cards and collections of different-sided dice can form the basis for a wide range of number games, and computational work extending through nursery to KS1 and 2. On the other hand it is well worth investing in, for example, well designed large pieces of equipment for sand and water play, quality construction materials and outdoor play equipment that will give good service for many years.

Summary

This chapter has discussed the principles of mathematical resource management at school level and the important role of the co-ordinator in ensuring a stable, cost-effective deployment and use of resources throughout a school. Establishing an effective resource base and priorities for development is not an easy task. It is often constrained by limited finances and needs within other areas of the curriculum that may be seen to have greater priority in the context of a whole-school development plan. In addition, the process of rationalising the existing resource base can unearth equipment that is redundant, in a poor state of repair or unused because staff do not know how to use it. In establishing a development plan the co-ordinator will need to consider strategies which involve the staff in:

- creating inventories of mathematical equipment in their classrooms;
- making decisions about establishing an effective system for storage and retrieval of centrally stored resources;
- systematic regular review of the resource base;
- establishing priorities for purchasing resources and equipment in relation to the school's maintenance budget for mathematics;
- preparing costings for priority developments to be included in the school's development plan; and
- implementing sessions of in-service training for staff on the use of new and unfamiliar resources.

7

Developing and managing partnerships with parents

Developments in the 1980s

One of the most widely known schemes is the IMPACT programme (Inventing Maths for Parents and Children and Teachers). In the late 1980s, Ruth Merttens and Jeff Vass were responsible for developing a national initiative in twenty local education authorities for parent partnership in mathematics. The impetus for this initiative came at a time when a lot of political attention was being given to the relationship between parents and schools (Merttens and Vass, 1990). For example, in the Thomas Report, *Improving Primary Schools* (1985, para 4.2), within the section on 'Agreement between teachers, parents and government' it is stated that:

> None can suppose that all parents and all teachers can see eye to eye all the time...what is necessary is that children sense that their parents and their schools are in broad agreement about their education...and are prepared to work together in its interest.

Paragraph 4.25 goes on to say:

> The view has grown that parental involvement with schools should be increased to the point where parents share in the activities of the school both with respect to their own children and more generally. We are persuaded that this trend is right partly because there is convincing evidence in favour going back over twenty years.

Developments in the 1990s

Since the development of the IMPACT programme, many schools have either adopted the IMPACT model or established their own to suit the needs of their school. A description of some different models follows to give readers an idea of the diversity of interpretations.

The IMPACT programme

The IMPACT model is described as an 'activity cycle' representing an on-going aspect of classwork comprising three phases:

Phase 1: Preparation in the classroom

Teachers use ongoing classwork as a focus for planning a home task which may include work on a maths topic or work integrated with other areas of the curriculum. Children are briefed about the task as a whole class, described as 'the rug session'.

Phase 2: The home task

Children carry out the home task with the support of their family. A key principle of the IMPACT model is that children act as tutors to explain the task to their parents. According to Merttens and Vass (1990), this may involve collecting data for subsequent use in class, problem-solving or investigational work, carrying out experiments (such as finding and predicting what objects found in the home will float and which will sink) or playing mathematical board games.

Phase 3: The follow-up

Further classwork, which includes responding to the outcomes of the work at home, incorporates any content or material arising from the home task into classwork, mounting displays and developing cross-curricular activities that arise from the outcomes of the home task. Feedback is requested from home about the task which can be used to inform future planning and for refining task design.

(IMPACT packs of materials for the nursery are available from the University of North London; photocopiable books of materials for KS1 and 2 are now published by Scholastic.)

Maths Games Library

The following is a summary of an initiative set up in an inner-city primary school with a high proportion of children who do not speak English, and many one-parent families:

A Maths Games Library was set up with the help of parents. An INSET evening was organised where a person came with loads of wrapping paper and ideas. A crèche was organised and about thirty parents came. Parents set about the task of making games and money was also spent on buying manufactured games. Initially the games were used in classes with parents coming in to play them with the children. A system was then set up where all the games were put in plastic wallets by parents. Each game has a borrower's card and each wallet had a sticker on it saying what it contains, for example, number of dice, counters, name of the playing board and a set of rules. A copy of the rules is also stuck to the outside of the wallet. Parents run the Maths Games Library each week on a Friday afternoon. The games are graded in terms of suitability for an age group and stored in large plastic boxes. Each class is given a box of games for children to select from and take home, providing the parent signs the game out for the child. Children can keep the game for a week, or two if they want. Parents who run the library take on the responsibility for checking that everything is returned and chasing up missing items. Children have to return a game before they are allowed another one and there is caution about allowing children, who persistently lose pieces, to borrow further games. A copy of the rules of each game is kept in a folder in school. The scheme was developed over a long period of time with gradual refinements added to the process, particularly the setting up of the system to ensure that games are returned in a complete state wherever possible.

Maths games session from 11.30 to 12.00 one morning per week

The following is a summary of an initiative set up in a suburban primary school:

> Ten maths games are planned at the beginning of each term. Children are grouped into ten groups (approx. 4–5 children per group). Each group comprises children from Year R to Year 2 and includes a range of abilities. The children play a different game each week. Each game is supervised by a teacher or parent helper, whose role is to encourage understanding of the game and ensure fair play whilst developing maths skills. This is an example of the games planned for one term:

> *Board games*: Aladdin, Incey Wincey Spider, Snakes and Ladders.
> *Games without dice*: Ladybirds, Scaredy Cats.
> *Money games*: Money dominoes, Shopping game.
> *Pattern games*: Cuisenaire, Connect 4.
> *Dice games*: Clowns.

An informal system of 'homework'

The following is a summary of an initiative set up in a small rural primary school in an infant class of 4–7-year-olds

> The initiative was started by the teacher suggesting to individual children that they might, occasionally like to take unfinished maths work home to complete. This led to children asking for work to be set for them to do at home. A bank of activities on laminated cards was devised for the purpose and integrated into the scheme of work. Children were given a 'Homework Book' and when they arrived at certain points in the scheme, they were invited to carry out a related piece of 'homework'. A set of published mathematical games for children to play with their parents at home was also introduced. Before the scheme was officially launched, a parents meeting was held, with the support of the headteacher. The scheme was discussed and it was agreed that the amount of work to be carried out at home should be flexible and negotiable, since parents were already spending time helping their children with reading. Weekends were considered the best time for 'homework cards' and games, and parents were happy for children to finish off work or do work on their own at any time when there were no prior commitments to activities during the week, such as swimming. The scheme was implemented by operating an informal arrangement between the teacher and the child during the week, and on Friday afternoon parents were invited into the classroom to collect a homework card or a game (or both) if they wished. Most parents were enthusiastic participants in

the scheme and said they really enjoyed doing the cards with the children and playing the games. They also said that they valued the flexibility of not being placed under pressure at times when they had other commitments. As the scheme developed children were asking if they could take home a game or a 'homework card' during the week and, providing the parents were happy, this took place. Care was taken to emphasise to parents that the impetus should be through mutual agreement between the child, parent and teacher and not imposed on the child by the parent (or the teacher!). An unexpected development to the scheme was that parents started to offer ideas for different activities they had tried out at home.

Baking sessions two afternoons per week

This initiative was set up in a reception class in a village primary school:

> One of the mums said she had a Baby Belling cooker and asked if she could bring it to school to do some baking with the children. She set up a baking area in the corridor and money was found out of school funds for baking equipment. She made simple recipe cards and the children were chosen to bake on a rota basis, four at a time, twice a week. The 'bakers' were allowed one cake to eat. The next day the children sold the rest of the cakes at morning break time and the money was used by the mum to buy more ingredients. Soon there were more mums who said they were willing to do baking with the children so a termly rota was set up and pasted on the noticeboard in the entrance hall. Mums contributed new recipe cards and the recipes were put into a book for parents to buy so they could bake with their children at home. The money from the sale of the books was put towards developing the baking area.

Maths guidelines for parents

The following is a summary of an initiative in an inner-city nursery school:

> A booklet, *How to Help your Child at Home*, included a list of maths activities that parents could do with their child, together with a picture record chart to be coloured in. When the chart was complete it could be taken to school and a blue 'smiley-face' badge was given to the child. The idea started with a parents' booklet for language and reading (red badge). After a while, a list of physical skills was added to the programme (yellow badge) and later, maths was added to the booklet.

Setting up a parent partnership programme for mathematics

Before any programme is initiated, staff discussion is necessary to consider the principle and the implications of involving parents in a partnership for mathematics in relation to the school situation.

How do parents and teachers feel about it?

One of the first considerations is the people who will be involved –

parents and teachers. Schools may like to start by making a list of advantages and disadvantages for the parents and for teachers, as suggested in Table 7.1.

Table 7.1 Examples of advantages and disadvantages of establishing a parent partnership programme for mathematics

Advantages	Disadvantages
Parents feel they are doing something positive to help their child	Some parents may not feel confident in helping their child with maths
Encourages parents to help their child with maths on a regular basis	Some parents, particularly those with large families, may find it difficult to find the time to become regularly involved
Teachers and parents will be able to work together	Parents may feel under pressure from teachers to help their child
Enables children to spend more time doing maths	Some parents may put their child off maths because of pressure to do lots of maths work at home
The work will help to improve home-school relationships	Some teachers may be reluctant to take on an extra workload

Will all the staff be involved?

One of the key factors for the success of the IMPACT project was the enthusiasm of the teachers to be involved in the project and it is suggested by Merttens and Vass (1990) that it is best to start with only those teachers who are keen on the idea. This could mean that in some schools only a few staff and a few classes are involved at the outset, with the hope that other staff may join in on the basis of evidence of the programme's success. In implementing a new initiative, there are bound to be teething problems. It does not help to have reluctant members of the crew on board in these situations. It is important to establish who the 'team' will be before any decisions are made about the content of the programme and how it will be implemented and managed.

What will the programme contain?

Teachers who have agreed to become involved in the programme should decide what is the most suitable approach. They will need to consider the implications for the staff in terms of management and the selection of materials in relation to the age of the children, balanced against what they feel the parents can realistically cope with. They may choose to use one or more elements of the approaches given as examples above, or devise their own approach. It is important that whatever is decided, it should not be too ambitious to start with. A modest beginning is much easier to implement and developments can be added gradually over time. It is far better that staff 'grow' with the programme than take on too much at once and find they are unable to cope. Each of the examples above evolved through a gradual process of development, which was a key factor in achieving success.

Getting started

All necessary materials will need to be prepared beforehand. A meeting with parents should be held to explain the details of the programme (offering crèche facilities is likely to encourage more parents to come). For the benefit of parents who are unable to attend the meeting, it is useful to circulate details in a letter, with a tear-off slip for parents to send back saying whether or not they are prepared to become involved.

It is important to try to identify a group of enthusiastic parents who would be prepared to trial or pilot the programme for a few weeks so that any teething problems can be sorted out before the programme is fully implemented. A further meeting will need to be held for the 'pilot' group to explain the process and the value of their input, before the programme can commence. A timetable of meetings needs to be agreed with the parents throughout the pilot period, where the group is able to meet at regular intervals to share findings and discuss ideas for improvement. It is useful to pilot the programme during the summer term where there is the long break to change or refine anything before starting the full programme at the beginning of the autumn term. In this way existing parents have plenty of notice and new parents can be informed at induction time.

Implementation and review

At the start, it is important that the programme is supported by parents who are interested and that pressure or coercion is not used to persuade reluctant or unwilling parents to become involved. Selling it to the children is perhaps more important in the beginning stages. Very often reluctant parents are persuaded by the enthusiasm of their children to join in. To support the management of the programme, it is important to set up a monitoring group of parents and teachers. Initially, this may be through the pilot group continuing to play an evaluative role. The programme should be regularly reviewed, including the response of the users, through discussion of feedback reports from parents, children and teachers.

Inviting parents to take an interest in the mathematics work in school

For any partnership programme to be fully effective it is important that parents are encouraged to take an interest in the mathematics that happens in school as well as taking part in any home maths initiative.

This helps parents to have a better understanding of what the school offers in the way of mathematical education and also helps to build up parents' interest and confidence in the subject. It is common practice in nursery and infant schools for parents to help in classrooms and, more recently, teachers have begun to value the help of parents in assisting with mathematical activities (see Chapters 9 and 10).

Valuable ways of involving parents in directing mathematical activities in the classroom are represented in the examples of parent partnership initiatives, through playing mathematical games with children and directing baking activities. Other examples include helping with practical measuring activities, directing mathematical artwork and the exploration of mathematics – in role-play situations – where a parent can involve him or herself in the 'play'. Other strategies include inviting parents to attend a maths event which might include, for example, an assembly on a mathematical theme; a mathematics fair (toys, books, games, etc.); and an open day where parents are able to see children working, view displays of mathematical work and visit informal workshops, for example, trying out computer programs for mathematics or watching a maths television programme used in school.

Communicating information to parents

To improve communication links between school and home with respect to mathematics, some schools have created a handbook for parents which sets out, for example:

- what the school offers in the way of maths education;
- how parents can help in school and at home;
- recommended commercial resources for parents to buy (books, games, etc.);
- 'do's and don'ts' (for example, guidance on number formation);
- what to do if a child is having difficulties;
- arrangements for parents to discuss children's progress informally with teachers; and
- formal arrangements for reporting to parents (written reports at KS1).

In addition, some schools have a maths noticeboard and/or send out newsletters to parents offering suggestions on how parents can support the work happening in school, for example:

Year-2 News

Our topics this term is WEATHER. We will learn about different types of weather and the climates of other countries. The role-play area will be a TV weather studio full of maps, charts, etc.

Can you help your child to learn the names of the days, months and seasons? Can you draw their attention to weather reports on the television and in newspapers?

GAMES. Is anyone willing to come into school and play a maths game with the children on Friday afternoons? Please see Mrs ———— if you are able to do so.

SUPERMARKET TOKENS. Thank you to all parents who have started to collect them for us. So far we have 200 tokens. Please keep up the good work.

FAMILY READING GROUP. January 28th at 2.30 pm.

BOOK FAIR: Begins January 28th – details to follow.

Informing governors

Finally, an equally important aspect of communication is ensuring that the governors of the school are informed of initiatives the school is taking to work in partnership with parents in the teaching of mathematics. It is the governors' responsibility to ensure that the school is delivering the entitlement for mathematics to each child, set out in the Desirable Outcomes and/or the National Curriculum. They will be particularly concerned that staff do not embark on anything that might adversely affect this delivery or cause undue pressure on staff who already have a heavy workload. In addition, as they are responsible for the financial management of the school, they will need to be informed of the resource implications and any funding that may be required.

Summary

This chapter has presented a discussion of the processes involved in establishing and developing parent partnerships in the teaching of mathematics at home and in school. It gives a brief outline of developments since the 1980s and some examples of different initiatives in schools. Strategies for setting up partnership programmes are discussed, including how staff need to analyse the implications for the school, staff, children and parents before any initiative is established. The building of a team of people who are enthusiastic to become involved and starting from modest beginnings are key factors in establishing success. Finally, the establishment of any new initiative is a long-term process where the staff, children and parents involved 'grow' with developments, through a process of regular review and the establishment of good communication networks between home and school.

8

The management of long and medium-term planning for mathematics

---

Progress and continuity

One of the principle reasons given by the Conservative government for the introduction of the National Curriculum (see Figure 8.1) was to ensure continuity and progression in children's education between classes and schools (DES, 1988). In the *Non-Statutory Guidance for Mathematics* (NCC, 1991, para. 3.1) it is stated that:

> Progression requires that individual teachers plan for a coherent and progressive experience of mathematics for pupils in their class. Different teachers and different schools who have responsibility for the same pupils over a period of time, need to work together to ensure a continuity of experience for pupils.

KS1 (infant) Programmes of Study and Attainment Targets levels 1–3	KS2 (junior) Programmes of Study and Attainment Targets levels 4–6	KS3/4 (secondary) Programmes of Study and Attainment Targets levels 7–8
AT1 Using and applying mathematics	AT1 Using and applying mathematics	AT1 Using and applying mathematics
AT2 Number	AT2 Number and algebra	AT2 Number and algebra
AT3 Shape, space and measures	AT3 Shape, space and measures	AT3 Shape, space and measures
	AT4 Handling data	AT4 Handling data
Expected range in pupils' performance in mathematics: • KS1: between Attainment Target Levels 1 and 3 • KS2: between Attainment Target levels 2 and 5 • KS3/4: between Attainment Target levels 3 and 7 with level 8 available for able students		

Figure 8.1 Structure of the National Curriculum for Mathematics 5–16
Source: DFE, 1995a; 1995b

The National Curriculum for mathematics (DFE, 1995a) presents an explicit structure of the scope and sequence of mathematics to be taught in primary schools within Programmes of Study for KS1 and 2 and through the Attainment Target Levels 1–6. However, the documentation is viewed by teachers as being very thin in resourcing the planning for mathematical learning throughout a school. Whilst broad recommendations are made in relation to the development of crosscurricular links, the documentation presents a view of mathematical learning as predominantly discrete and linear in principle. This principle may be viewed as appropriate at secondary level, but teachers of young children feel that it does not sufficiently embrace the principle of breadth and depth and balance emphasised as the bedrock of early mathematical learning. The responsibility, therefore, lies with individual nursery and infant schools to formulate a structured scheme of work that reflects the culture of their school, whilst at the same time ensuring that provision matches the entitlement prescribed by the Desirable Outcomes for nursery education (SCAA, 1996) and/or the National Curriculum Programmes of Study for mathematics (DFE, 1995a). According to Alexander *et al.* (1992), the way in which schools manage the process of planning in the long, medium and short-term is seen as a key indicator in their ability to provide a cohesive curriculum framework for mathematics throughout the school.

Long-term planning: developing a scheme of work for the whole school

Developing a scheme of work for the whole school represents part of the policy-making process where the maths co-ordinator, in consultation with the headteacher and other members of staff, plans the mathematical content children will cover in each year, in relation to the Desirable Outcomes for nursery schools (SCAA, 1996) and the National Curriculum Programmes of Study for KS1 and 2 (DFE, 1995a) in infant/primary schools.

Breadth, balance and depth

For the mathematical content to sustain breadth, balance and depth throughout the school, it is recognised that mathematics needs to be planned within a long-term framework so that different areas are revisited at different times, and also, where areas are revisited, that a sense of progression is built into the programme to avoid unnecessary repetition.

In addition to establishing a general long-term framework, infant/primary schools are now beginning to break these frameworks down into sequences of small units of progression in relation to the Attainment Target levels within the National Curriculum. This principle has been adopted in mathematics frameworks published by LEAs and in curriculum materials published by the National Numeracy Project. Some nursery schools also create long-term frameworks for mathematics (see Figure 8.2).

Autumn	Spring	Summer
Practical number work – trays, comparing sizes – children, toys. Counting objects. Home corner – sets, 1 to 1. Oral counting to 5, 10.	Number books 1 and 2. Threading patterns. Counting objects and writing numbers to at least 5. Comparing more or less. Laying tables 1 to 1 sets. Oral counting 10 to 20.	Matching 'odd one out' sets (book). Building sequence patterns. Counting objects and writing numbers to at least 10. Laying tables counting beakers and cutlery. Addition and subtraction with objects. Oral counting to 100.
Number games – ladybirds, counting games, computer.	Number games – paper plate games, lotto, ladybirds, computer.	Number games – dominoes, board games, computer.
Number songs and rhymes.	Number songs and rhymes.	Number songs and rhymes.
Table activities, water and sand – number, shape, matching, weighing, measuring, comparison.	Table activities, water and sand – number, shape, matching, weighing, measuring, comparison.	Table activities, water and sand – number, shape, matching, weighing, measuring, comparison.
Building with shapes. Describing shapes.	Practical 2D and 3D shape work. Printing and building.	Practical sets work with objects – toys, etc. Sets book. Graph work – set diagrams for sorting and counting.
Matching shapes and pictures of shapes.	Shape books.	Making shape pictures.
Maths about 'ourselves' and 'colour'.	*Maths about 'toys' and 'spring'.*	*Maths about 'pets' and 'boxes'.*

Figure 8.2 Long-term planning for mathematics in a nursery

Long-term planning within a crosscurricular context

Many schools create long-term plans which give an outline framework of the mathematical content to be taught within the context of crosscurricular topic work throughout the school. This is to ensure that aspects are not unnecessarily repeated and that the planned programme offers continuous opportunities for mathematical enrichment, alongside discrete programmes taught within sessions timetabled specifically for mathematics throughout a year. Figure 8.3 shows an example of a year topic plan in relation to the areas of mathematics to be included for children in reception classes through to Year 3.

Long-term planning and published maths schemes

Concerns

The use of published schemes to teach mathematics in schools has represented a major issue for many years. Before discussing strategies for long-term planning involving the use of published schemes, it is important to consider the issue in some depth so that readers can understand the reasons behind the concerns. In 1992 it was reported by HMI that commercial mathematics schemes were the dominant influence on the work done in each key stage in mathematics, and this removed the need, according to many teachers, for the school to undertake detailed planning of the curriculum (HMI, 1992). In the following year Ofsted (1993) reported that:

> In over a third of (primary) classes there was an over-reliance upon a particular published scheme which usually led to pupils spending prolonged periods of time in which they worked at a slow pace, often on repetitive, undemanding exercises, which did little to advance their skills or understanding of number, much less their interest and enthusiasm for mathematics.

The issue was pushed further into the spotlight by the recent national concerns over low standards of numeracy in primary school children in the UK compared with similar aged children in other countries, in particular countries identified as the 'Pacific Rim'. As a result of research by Reynolds and Farrell (1996), it was reported that one of the key differences was teaching methods. Pacific Rim primary teachers use predominantly whole-class interactive teaching for most of the time during maths lessons. In comparison, the majority of lesson time in UK primary schools is used for group work or children working individually through books of mathematical exercises. In the light of this research, and the evidence of primary pupils' low achievement in the results of KS2 SATs for mathematics in 1996 (SCAA, 1997e), Ofsted and the Teacher Training Agency, together with primary educationalists and practitioners, have been challenged to re-examine the ways in which mathematics should be taught in primary schools. One of the principal recommendations is a greater emphasis on whole-class interactive

Mathematics Curriculum

Term	Autumn 1	Autumn 2	Spring 1	Spring 2	Summer 1	Summer 2
Topic	OURSELVES	COMMUNICATION	TIME	NATURAL WORLD	MOVEMENT	HOW WE LIVE past & present
Rec	Me/Us Investigations Algebra Numerals Length	Senses Block charts	Seasons/Weather Time Venn Diagrams	Pets Logic Tree	Wheels Addition Shapes Caroll Diagrams	Parks Weight/balancing Capacity/Volume Intersecting sets
Yr 1	Food Sorting Number 1 to 5 Shape	Light/Colour/Sound Matching Number 5 to 10	Growing Up/Families Size Sorting and Sequencing Comparatives	Farms Estimation Bar charts Position Number 10 to 20	Toys Capacity Money Number revision	School Clocks and Time
Yr 2	People who help Number 1 to 20 (ongoing) Shapes 2D, 3D Tessellations Symmetry	Post Office Shape - size, rotation & position Roma Repeating patterns Money Odd/Even Area Sorting	New Year/Beginnings Calculators Measure Time Temperature Graphs Birthdays	Wild Animals Measuring Symmetry Sorting/classifying Surveys	Travel Roma Money Investigations Balancing Capacity Time/Distance Shape/Position	Homes Sequencing Odds/Evens Area Shapes Symmetry Position Graph work
Yr 3	Our locality Number to 100 (ongoing) Computation Calculators Roma Shape & Patterns Co-ordinates. Map refs. Handling Data. Graphs	Television/Radio Length	Ancient Egypt Number sequences Shape Right angles Roma	Earth/Landscapes Weight Probability	Fairgrounds Time Symmetry	Romans Volume Tessellations/Shape
All	Hygiene/Health Care	Electricity		Air	Safety	Water

Figure 8.3 A first school long-term 'topic' plan for mathematics

teaching and a reduction in reliance on published mathematics schemes. However, it must be emphasised that proposed changes do not represent an attack on the schemes themselves, as many of the recently published materials have much to recommend them. The problem is seen where teachers rely almost exclusively on published scheme materials, in particular consumable workbooks and textbooks, which suggests that they do not feel sufficiently confident to undertake the process of planning and teaching mathematical work themselves.

Lack of teacher confidence

One of the main reasons given by teachers for their reliance on a published scheme is lack of confidence in their own ability 'to do maths'. Many teachers feel that a published scheme represents a programme written by experts which provides a reliable means by which mathematics can be taught competently and, that by using it, children will make the right sort of progress. Unfortunately, exclusive adherence to a published scheme does very little to develop teachers' personal expertise in teaching maths. Because the planning and progression of a scheme are preordained, teachers who rely heavily on a scheme are less likely to be involved in collective long and medium-planning discussions with colleagues, where ideas can be shared or clarified. They are also less likely to take decisions in the course of their teaching to depart from the scheme. If they do so, this is likely to result in mirroring the scheme by providing more of the same. Teachers who are more confident, with experience of planning for mathematical learning, combined with an adequate level of subject knowledge, are likely to be more flexible in seeking to match work appropriately to the needs and interests of the children.

Subject knowledge of teachers

There is a general concern that teachers' over-reliance on published schemes is related to their lack of subject knowledge. There are many teachers who would admit that mathematics is not their best subject and rely on published schemes, felt to be written by experts, to compensate. Also, many teachers of young children would admit to expressing apprehension about the prospect of teaching mathematics beyond KS1, because they would feel 'out of their depth'. Knowledge of the ways in which children learn mathematics and knowledge and understanding of a range of conceptual strategies and mathematical processes which can be introduced appropriately, according to children's level of mathematical development, are considered key factors in a teacher's ability to plan and teach mathematics effectively. If teachers are unfamiliar with, or uncertain about, mathematical principles they are expected to teach, then they are unlikely to be able to 'cope securely with questions pupils raise' (Ofsted, 1996). They are also less likely to encourage children to explore a range of strategies in solving mathematical problems. They are also more likely to miss key conceptual stages required in enabling children to achieve understanding of a particular concept. At worst, teachers can present concepts in inappropriate or inaccurate forms, which generate confusion rather than understanding in children.

In-service and preservice training

Changing the way in which teachers view the teaching of mathematics is recognised as a difficult task. The problem of teachers' lack of confidence in their ability to teach mathematics is well documented (Walden and Walkerdine, 1982; Desforges and Cockburn, 1987; Ernest, 1989), and is likely to be exacerbated by the national anxiety about low standards of numeracy. The government's response to this has been to initiate an extensive programme of in-service training in infant and junior schools throughout the country, co-ordinated by Anita Straker as the Director of the National Numeracy Project. Teachers are supported in departing from published schemes and emphasis is placed on the development of whole-class interactive teaching skills, including the direction of mental arithmetic activities. This is an issue which teacher training establishments are also having to address. Under the regulations set down by the DfEE (1997b), for primary teacher training, the exit competencies required for newly qualified teachers are evidence that their mathematical knowledge and understanding matches a minimum of level 8 of the National Curriculum (GCSE Grade C is the equivalent of level 7). They must also be familiar with the National Curriculum Programmes of Study for KS1 *and* KS2, and the range of pedagogical principles required for teaching mathematics in relation to the full primary age range. This is expected of all students training to be teachers in the primary phase including students who elect to take courses which specialise in nursery/KS1 or KS2 (DfEE, 1997b).

Is there a place for published mathematics schemes?

As emphasised earlier, the concern lies more in the way published schemes are managed and used in schools than the schemes themselves. If used selectively according to children's needs, the use of published scheme materials can serve effectively to support and enrich the day-to-day teaching of mathematics in the classroom. They can also serve as a useful practice tool and support the process of continuous assessment. As most teachers of young children will readily admit, no single scheme matches the needs of every child in the school. There are often gaps and omissions in the progression structure, in particular coverage of AT1 – 'Using and applying mathematics' (Johnson and Millett, 1996). The following presents the main advantages and disadvantages of using a published scheme for mathematics.

Advantages

- Offers a variety of ready-made resources within the framework of the programme, for example workbooks, workcards, photocopiable masters, games, mathematical resources and assessment materials.
- Includes a comprehensive teachers' manual on the management of the programme and ideas for activities that teachers can carry out in the classroom to support the work taught through the scheme, including links to other areas of the curriculum.
- Workbooks present a variety of mathematical tasks within a highly structured developmental progression. They allow for children to progress at their own pace and provide evidence of individual children's achievements in an easily stored format.
- The print layout, artwork and resources are professionally designed and provide a good model of presentation for children.

Disadvantages

- Published mathematics schemes are expensive items in terms of the school budget. Many of the non-consumable resource components are frequently underused or not used at all, with most use made of the consumable elements which represent a continuous cost to the school.
- Workbook/photocopiables task design, although covering different areas of mathematics, represents mainly closed pencil and paper exercises with little or no scope for 'hands-on' practical work or differentiated outcomes.
- Workbooks/photocopiables predominantly comprise solitary activities and offer little scope for collaborative work or discussion with other children.
- Work throughout a published scheme is often designed for children to use a specified range of structural apparatus and equipment leaving little scope for diversity within and between classes.
- Some early mathematical work within schemes can be laboured and unimaginative. As the scheme progresses, important later work can be insufficiently dealt with.
- Children are mostly at different stages in the scheme and it is often difficult to cluster children to teach new work.
- Children experience difficulties at different times; teachers can spend a lot of time repeatedly helping children overcome the same problems.
- Children associate success or failure with the 'number' of the book they are on in relation to other children in the class.
- Children adopt the view that 'doing maths' is associated with scheme workbooks; that practical investigations, games and puzzles, etc., are not seen as 'proper maths'.

Scheme-driven planning

The case for planning and teaching mathematics in primary schools to be teacher-driven rather than scheme-driven is strongly endorsed by all agencies committed to improving the quality of children's mathematical achievements within the primary sector. However, it is important to recognise that scheme-driven planning exists and, even if schools wished to change, this is something that cannot be done overnight. Where a core published scheme is in use, it is important that staff collectively analyse the scheme in relation to the National Curriculum Programmes of Study and the Attainment Target levels to ensure that the scheme offers coverage of the specified entitlement. Infant schools, where a core scheme is in use, often write a scheme of work which indicates where each aspect can be found in the core material – for example, book and page numbers of workbooks are listed alongside ideas for activities and resources. Most published scheme handbooks go a long way in doing this job for the school. However, what a published scheme cannot do is create a programme of work that reflects the school's view of mathematics and how it should be taught. Nor can it reflect the extent of the resource provision, the arrangements for assessment and record-keeping and the provision for SEN and equal opportunities that should underpin the use of any published scheme. This makes the process of planning using a core scheme more difficult than it first looks. First, it requires a dissection of the scheme and an analysis of its component parts to create a rational basis for planning according to the needs of the children. Secondly, decisions will need to be made about where, when and what supplementary work is needed because of poor coverage in the materials. Conversely, where elements are laboured, some 'pruning' may be required. Additionally, the programme planned by the school should include ideas for activities to consolidate and enrich learning experiences at every stage. Realistically, this process cannot be carried out until staff are fully familiar with the workings of a published scheme. With the adoption of a new scheme, it can take a long time to establish the 'warts' and the 'stars' of the material.

Scheme-assisted planning

An example of this model is where a school uses the content, sequence and progression of a published scheme as a framework for planning, and integrates this into its own programme to form a scheme of work. Children are mainly taught in ability groups through teacher-led practical activities, where teachers use a variety of resources for planning ideas, including the 'Handbook' for the scheme. Decisions about 'what next' in relation to the scheme of work are generated from continuous assessment of children's needs at every stage. Published scheme 'workbooks' are used for practice, consolidation and additional evidence of assessment of core work.

Low-scheme planning

An example of this model is where a school plans its own structured scheme of work in relation to the Programmes of Study for KS1. The scheme of work is implemented throughout the school, principally through teacher-planned and teacher-led activities, with children grouped by ability. Continuous assessment informs planning at every stage. A selected range of materials, chosen by the staff from different published schemes and other published resources, are available for use throughout the school. Recommendations are made throughout the scheme of work on the use of published resources but not prescribed; the choice is left to individual teachers to use as appropriate.

Medium-term planning

Long-term planning documents form the basis for medium-term planning. This involves a more in-depth consideration of the mathematical content to be taught over the period of a term or, in some cases, a half-term. This process may be carried out collectively by staff or by individual teachers, depending on the size of the school. Some schools develop proformas for teachers to use, which help to reduce the workload and maintain consistency throughout the school. Medium-term planning for mathematics can involve discrete subject planning and/or crosscurricular topic planning. This will depend on the educational setting. In nursery schools, where topic work creates a focus for opportunities for children to develop learning in all the six areas of learning defined in the Desirable Outcomes for nursery education (SCAA, 1996), medium-term planning is centred on crosscurricular topic planning (see Figure 8.4).

With the emphasis on early literacy and numeracy skills within the Desirable Outcomes, some nursery schools are carrying out discrete medium-term planning for these areas (see Figure 8.5)

At KS1, medium-term planning for mathematics is more likely to be in discrete form for *core skills* and activities for enrichment embodied in topic work. One of the advantages of long and medium-term topic planning is that teachers do not feel that they have to 'milk' every topic. What does not arise naturally from one topic can easily be planned elsewhere. Long and medium-term planning enables teachers to work within this broader context.

Summary

The processes of long and medium-term planning for mathematics have been discussed in relation to the formulation of whole-school schemes of work, yearly and termly plans for discrete core skills and cross-curricular topic work. The uses and abuses of published scheme-driven planning have been discussed in relation to concerns about standards of

THEME: *This is me*

Area of Learning		Experiences and Development
Language and Literacy	Speaking and Listening	Opportunities for the children to talk about themselves, feelings, senses, body parts, likes/dislikes, sharing experiences and listening to others. Encouraging the children to join in familiar rhymes progressing to songs about the topic. Recall and relating events during the nursery day. Encouraging children to sue the audio cassette correctly and independently. Identifying sound and voices on a tape from a sound walk. Encouraging taking turns in conversation. Stories related to the topic e.g. Me, too, I don't eat toothpaste anymore won't go there again.
	Writing	Provide a variety of writing materials encouraging children to express themselves through pictures and writing. Opportunities for book-making - sound book, Sutton Park. Add own picture to months of the year to show d.o.b. Write music symbolically and on manuscript paper. Recognition of own name in a variety of situations, juice cards etc. Encouraging the correct use of books in the reading area; holding the book right way up etc. Introduction of book language - title etc. Sharing books. Reading notices around the room. Exploring letters/numbers in different situations
	Reading	
Mathematics		One to one matching e.g. coat on peg, cutlery on mat. Sorting for colour, size, shape. Sizes of ourselves - small, medium, large. Colour display - green. Calendar of the months of the year. Children to draw themselves on their day of birth. Introduction to number in the classroom e.g. calculators in the office, display. Symmetry of the face, body - rangoli patterns. Introduction to larger number. Number in the family - sisters, brothers → graphs. Age of children. Footprints/handprints - looking at size. Weighing ourselves - heavy, light, heavier, lighter. Measuring ourselves using standard and non-standard measure. String collage showing children's height. Body parts labelled. Venn diagram of eye colour.
Knowledge and Understanding of the World	Science	Comparing ourselves with each other - magnifying glasses/mirrors. Variety of experiments/activities linked to the senses e.g. pot pourri collage, autumn texture board. Introduction to the correct use of lenses, kaleidoscopes, magnets, mirrors, colour paddles etc. Observing seasonal change. Difference between living and non-living things; liquids, solids. Changes of food and colours - mixing paint and cooking. Autumn interest table. Photographs to record activities. Bulb planting. Healthy eating.
	Technology	Introduce woodwork as a regular activity - appropriate use of tools, safety aspects of this. Introducing the computer and the Internet. Look at what I can make using construction toys. Encouraging appropriate use of wheels, windows, doors. 3D modelling → ourselves. Making musical instruments, jointed moveable puppets.
	History	How we've changed babies → children → adults. Bring in photo of ourselves as babies. Have we/how we have changed? Recalling the nursery day/routine. What do we do before/after we come to nursery. Making a bulb book. Recording sequence of bulb growing.
	Geography	Taping a sound walk - recording the walk with photographs. Layout of the nursery classroom.

Figure 8.4   Sample page from a nursery topic plan

Nursery School
Subject: Mathematics   **Year:** Nursery

Half-term plan
Term: Autumn 1

Key issues, skills and concepts from POS	Teaching and Learning Activities	Relevant Resources	Time
Reorganising basic shapes - 2D and 3D	• Weekly free play - jigsaws, sorting trays, threading • Look-at tables - circle, triangle, square shapes with/without corners • Through daily routine e.g. sitting as a class in book corner, PE	Variety of equipment	Daily/on-going
Identification of position e.g. up, down, in front of... Copying patterns	• Creative activities - pasting, painting linked to specific topics e.g. Autumn, orange, general introduction to nursery • Threading, peg boards → free play	Material, paint, printing things etc. Beads, pegs etc.	Daily Every two weeks or so
Number songs and rhymes	• Start level of sessions, discussion times, music activities etc.	Various	Daily/on-going
Enjoyment of stories involving number	• Story time • Free play use of books • After milk use of books	Wide range some limited to specific topics	Daily
Understanding number games and activities involving counting and matching	• Playing box games in small groups e.g. match the balloon, cake game •	Various games stuff	When extra adult help available
Sorting and matching everyday objects	• Directed activities linked to topics e.g. orange, autumn, harvest • Free play/look-at table activities	Buttons, fruit and veg, cutlery, cups and saucers e.g. pairs	Weekly
Counting	• Part of directed activities e.g. candles on cake, conkers, fingers, parts of body, leaves, sorting sets... • Informal times e.g. How many legs on your table? etc. • Cookery/creative activities	Wide variety	Daily
Start to become familiar with number in the environment	• Numbers on tables, windows, stairs, toilets etc. • Number trails in main school • House numbers etc. e.g. visit to post box	Number labels where appropriate	On-going
Begin to solve problems	• Developing strategies to complete jigsaws, use construction equipment • Free play, adult directed	Variety of resources Adult help	Daily When designated
Begin to estimate quantities	• Part of counting activities e.g. Guess how many conkers are in the bag?	Linked to counting (see above)	Weekly

Fig 8.5   Half-termly plan for mathematics in a nursery school

teaching. It is clear that the process of long and medium-term planning for mathematics has significant benefits for all staff involved. It enables them to know what is happening in other classes and understand the overall pattern of mathematics teaching throughout the school. It also helps teachers to fine tune progression and continuity and creates a forum for sharing and clarifying ideas.

SECTION 3
Mathematics: management at classroom level

9

Resource management in the classroom

Mathematical equipment and resources audit

When a teacher starts to work in a new classroom it is important that he or she is familiar with the extent and appropriateness of the resource base available. As there is normally a lot of maths equipment in classrooms, this process is likely to take a few hours to complete. It would be unrealistic to expect that the previous teacher's system of storage and classification will match the new teacher's needs. At best, the inherited resource base will be carefully classified and labelled and accompanied by an up-to-date inventory. At the other end of the spectrum, the inherited resource base can represent an Aladdin's cave where a collection of 'archive' materials coexists with state-of-the-art resources for maths and other areas of the curriculum in cupboards, drawers or on shelves around the room. Fortunately nowadays the latter is uncommon. However, if this situation arises, it is useful to enlist the support of the co-ordinator to carry out a systematic rationalisation process with the help of a few dustbin sacks!

A framework for compiling a maths equipment inventory

(The content will vary according to the age of the children.)

Number/algebra

- Assorted sets of 'real' countable objects.

- Sorting and matching apparatus.
- A range of well illustrated counting books including number rhymes.
- Pattern apparatus – beads and laces, pegs and pegboards.
- Appropriate range of structured number apparatus for age group.
- Number friezes, numberlines, assorted number rectangles and squares.
- Dice, dominoes, spinners and sets of numbered cards.
- Place value equipment, spike abaci, base-ten apparatus.
- Sets of up-to date currency in play money, coin stamps, shop materials.
- Published and home-made number games.
- Calculators.

Shape and space

- A range of 'real' 3D boxes and natural objects.
- A range of well illustrated 'shape' books.
- Plasticine and/or clay.
- Shape posting boxes.
- Place and position apparatus.
- A range of floor and table construction equipment.
- Floor and/or table jigsaw puzzles.
- Sets of regular and irregular 2D and regular 3D shapes including Logiblocs and pattern blocks and Poleidoblocs.
- Carrel, Venn, tree and matrix diagrams for sorting.
- Published and home-made shape and position games.
- Multilink cubes.
- Geoboards and elastic bands.
- Plastic area grids.
- Tangram puzzles.
- Plastic mirrors.
- Directional compasses.

Measures

Linear measurement:

- Collections of real objects for comparison, e.g. ribbons of different length; and for use as arbitrary measures (cube sized to cane sized).
- A range of well illustrated books dealing with 'comparisons' (tall/short, etc.).
- Clearly marked centimetre rulers (preferably wooden with no 'dead end').
- Clearly marked 100 cm tape measures; metre, half-metre and decimetre (10 cm) sticks.
- Trundle wheel, height measure, surveyors tape.
- Dipsticks, depth gauge.

- String and paper strips.
- Programmable toys (Roamer, Pip or Pixie).

Weight/Mass

- Collections of sets of real objects representing a range of heavy and light materials (milk tops to bricks).
- A range of well illustrated books dealing with comparisons (heavy/ light, etc.).
- Apparatus for cooking, kitchen scales and recipe cards.
- Mystery parcels – same size, different weights; different sizes, same weight.
- Plasticine or playdough.
- Pan balances (NES-Arnold primary balance – good quality wet and dry balance suitable for all ages); range of plastic and metal metric weights (1 g–1 kg).
- Digital letter balance (for weighing very small objects); bathroom scales.

Capacity, water and sand:

- Sand and water troughs.
- Mop and bucket; dustpan and brush.
- A range of water and sand toys.
- Floating and sinking equipment.
- A collection of well illustrated books on 'water'.
- A collection of plastic bottles and containers of different shapes and sizes.
- A range of different-sized funnels.
- A collection of different-calibrated measures (5 ml spoon to 2 litre measure).
- A collection of containers of different shapes which hold the same amount of liquid.

Time and weather:

- A simple faced working analogue clock fixed at a reasonable height for children to see.
- A collection of well illustrated books about time, seasons and weather.
- Cardboard clock faces, clock stamp and pad, clockface photocopiable masters.
- Resources for timing games.
- Tockers, 1 min, 3 min and 5 min timers; stopwatch.
- Large well designed teaching clock.
- A collection of old dead clocks and watches including digital timepieces; a sundial somewhere in the school grounds.
- A date and weather recording board.
- Basic weather-measuring equipment, thermometer, barometer, weather vane, rain gauge.

Computer software

A range of quality computer software supporting number, shape, handling data and elements of measures is available for different models of computer. Educational software is constantly being developed and many schools are supported by LEAs, who buy licences to distribute copies of software. It is recommended that teachers find out what is available and consult up-to-date catalogues of software suppliers. The names and addresses of the main suppliers of nursery and infant software are listed at the back of the book.

Television programmes

The BBC and ITV programmes for schools broadcast mathematical programmes for young children, for example, the BBC programme 'Numbertime'. The series is also available to buy on video together with accompanying computer software. As with computer software, television companies are always developing new programmes. It is worthwhile teachers consulting the TV press or sending for a free timetable from the BBC and ITV. These list all the educational programmes together with recommended age ranges and the times they are planned to be shown each year. The addresses for these are given at the back of the book.

General resources

Although not exclusively for mathematical use, the resource base in a classroom will require a stock of a variety of paper – plain, different-sized squared, coloured and gummed and a stock of writing, colouring and craft tools for cutting and pasting, painting and printing. Materials for creating attractive mathematical displays will also be needed.

Adult helpers

One of the most valuable resources teachers can have in their classrooms is the support of other adults for some if not all, of the time. Adult helpers not only bring an extra pair of hands but often diverse talents as well. It has been recognised that adult helpers are not just valuable in supporting organisational tasks but can also assist with the planning and direction of activities. Their contribution in this area has been shown to be an invaluable help to both teachers and children. It has meant that more groups of children can have the benefit of quality time with an adult during a teaching session. Where a person is known to have a particular talent, there is an added benefit if the person is encouraged to contribute his or her ideas and expertise to the planning and direction of a session.

The class teacher has a special role to play in managing and supporting other 'staff' in the classroom. Assistants will need to be informed about classroom routines and procedures established by the teacher. If they are expected to supervise a group carrying out an activity planned by the teacher, the teacher should ensure that assistants know what the activity is designed to achieve in terms of learning outcomes. After the session, there should be time to share relevant observations on the activity so that the teacher is aware of children's performance for subsequent planning.

Parent helpers who come into school at regular times begin to establish their own routines and often prefer to assist with a particular type of activity they enjoy. In discussion with the teacher, they may even devise teaching aids or bring items from home which they think may be helpful.

Establishing a 'home base' for adults working in the classroom

Teachers and adult helpers require provision for storage of equipment and resources that are for adult use only. Many teachers in early years classrooms no longer use a traditional teacher's desk, preferring to use locker trays or storage boxes. For regular classroom assistants, it is useful to provide a place to store materials and personal effects related to their classroom duties.

Maintaining an effective resource base in the classroom

Once a teacher has arranged the free-standing furniture and organised effective siting and storage for resources, strategies need to be considered to enable the system to operate smoothly. The children will need to become familiar with the surroundings and be told where things are kept. They should also be encouraged, where possible, to take responsibility for getting things out and putting them away. Labelling drawers, trays, bins, etc., accompanied by small pictures/photos for children who are unable to read, can help children with this. It is useful to label classroom fixtures and furniture for older children because they may need to write the name, for example, in the course of measuring with arbitrary units. A wall chart of related resource names and pictures sited appropriately is equally useful. These strategies are helpful in reducing the number of children requiring words written in a wordbook or dictionary.

Tidying routines

One of the perennial problems in maintaining a mathematical resource base is keeping things in the right place. Establishing a set of 'house' rules and daily 'tidying away' routines will go a long way to help with the problem. In practical activity sessions, clearing-away time is always difficult. Experienced teachers will acknowledge that, even in meticulously planned sessions, one can never predict exactly how long activities will last or how long it will take to clear away, with the result that the clearing-away process is hectic. Adult helpers in the classroom can take the pressure off because they can finish tidying whilst the teacher gathers the children together to finish the session. When teachers are on their own, the task is much more difficult because time has to be balanced between supervising clearing away and attending to the children. Where a classroom has a system of portable storage units for resources that can be carried to and from activities, the tidying process is much easier for children and adults to manage – for example, plastic trays and boxes for small resource items; bins or crates for large items; baskets for crayons; and covered tins for felt-tips and pencils. It is also easier for teachers to put away stray items that have found their way into obscure corners of the classroom. One quickly learns to make friends with the cleaning staff. Having a 'bits' tray or a box in a designated place, where cleaners can put things they find, is invaluable.

Maintenance routines

No matter how well organised, there is always a requirement for different areas of the classroom to be 'sorted out' periodically. Young children often combine resources in the course of activities, particularly in free play. It is not unusual to find cars in with the bricks, for example, or an assortment of shapes in the home corner, where they have been used as pretend food. A useful strategy is to prioritise areas in terms of those which require daily, weekly or half-termly maintenance according to frequency of use. For example, with very young children, the home corner usually requires daily maintenance, possibly twice daily in nursery schools, where different children attend in the morning and afternoon. With older children it is pencils that require daily maintenance to ensure that they are sharpened and ready for use.

Pencil management

In many respects pencil management can be very difficult with young children. In considering pencils as a resource, it is important to remember that, for young children, a pencil represents the only writing tool they use in school. They are fragile tools which blunt and break easily, and therefore a plentiful supply is needed. It is also useful to bear in mind that, the better the quality of pencil, the longer it is likely to last. Regular routines for sharpening pencils are important. However, this is one task that the teacher should take responsibility for – children can waste a lot of time sharpening pencils during lessons and pencils are quickly reduced to stubs. Pencil stubs are difficult for young children to control. As a rough guide, it is best if pencils for 'best work' are no shorter than the length of the child's hand, with shorter pencils used for rough work and drawing purposes. When children are carrying out mathematical recording on pieces of paper, a piece of card or another book should be placed underneath to enable them to write or draw as well as they can. As adults we recognise the need for something to rest paper on when we write or draw. Young children, as formative writers, require this important resource. Yet from the experience of the author, the use of 'pressure pads', when young children are working on paper, is much neglected.

Mathematical displays

Displays are an important part of creating an attractive and stimulating classroom environment. Display is also an excellent way to represent visually evidence of children's current work on an ongoing basis and celebrate children's achievements. It is important, however, that work displayed in classrooms should include something that represents the efforts of every child. This does not mean that every display should include contributions from every child. However, it should be possible to ensure that efforts from each child feature somewhere in the classroom at any one time and, where the work is individual, the child's name is displayed. Nowadays, there are lots of attractive materials and helpful aids for teachers to create displays that can be purchased from educational suppliers. These include precut borders, coloured paper mounts (cut to give approximately 1 cm border around A4-sized paper or card) and easy-to-use paper trimmers. A more recent introduction is a machine which stamps out large upper and/or lower-case letters from coloured card for display titles. Many schools discourage the use of Sellotape or heavy-duty staple tackers on walls, because of the damage they cause, and advise that 'Blutack' should be used. Unfortunately 'Blutack' is not very good for mounting large wall displays. However, if walls are pinboarded, the use of an opened-out Bambi stapler fixes items with a relatively discreet staple. These can be pulled out easily by hand without damage to the board or the work displayed. Professional captions for displays are easy to produce on computers, which can be much more creative if the school possesses a colour printer. The process of assembling displays can be made much easier for the teacher if adult help is at hand. Where group or individual creative work is involved, an adult helper can be deployed to work with one group of children at a time to produce the work required for display whilst the teacher is working with other children. The process of lining boards and mounting work is much easier when there are more than one pair of hands available.

　　Ideas for displays with a mathematical focus can arise, for example, from stories, 2D and 3D shape work, collecting and representing data, mathematical topics on measures, art and number pattern work, creating a shop in the classroom or simply specimens of representative mathematical work carried out in the classroom. A useful set of publications on classroom display for all areas of the curriculum is produced by Belair Publications (the address can be found at the back of the book). A useful strategy for creating displays is to plan them out on paper first. This only needs to be a 'thumbsketch' but it helps the teacher to consider the space available and how to arrange items to create the best overall effect. Selecting paper colours which complement each other for backing and mounting work contributes significantly to the overall effect of the display. The addition of 3D effects, such as drapes, plants, books and related artefacts, can improve the attractiveness and interest value of a display. When planning for display, teachers should consider the use of short-term displays, for example, space for mathematical 3D models which may be displayed for a few days, medium-term displays, such as large wall displays representing different areas of the curriculum, and interactive displays, such as a class shop or a 'pattern factory', which are working displays for children to use.

Whilst display work is very time-consuming, it is perhaps one of the most satisfying elements of resource management in nursery and infant classrooms. It creates a sense of pride and ownership for children and adults in the classroom. It is perhaps the best way the efforts of children can be celebrated alongside adult display skills to parents, other teachers and visitors to the classroom. As with all elements of resource management, display requires regular routines of maintenance. Displays need to be changed on a regular basis to reflect work that is currently happening in the classroom and to sustain a fresh, bright and stimulating atmosphere.

Reviewing resource provision

It is important that teachers review the effectiveness of the resource base from time to time, in consultation with other adults who work with them. For example, there may be problems with the arrangement of furniture, which may not be working as well as had been planned, or a change of 'topic' may require a relocation of resources. Teachers often find that the location of furniture and resources works well with one class but not with another.

A useful strategy for reviewing mathematical resources is to target one area at a time, considering the existing provision in the light of any repairs, replacements or new resources required. This process should be carried out in consultation with other adults who regularly work in the classroom and the school mathematics co-ordinator. In this way the review process can take into account the resource requirements at classroom level within the context of the needs of the whole school.

Summary

Resource management in the classroom requires teachers to take stock of the existing provision before organising the room to suit their needs and those of the children. Once this has been carried out, regular routines of maintenance should be established to ensure that the resource provision effectively supports the work carried out in the classroom at all times. The use of adult help can effectively support organisational routines as well as offering valuable contributions to the planning and direction of activities in the classroom. Good organisation and maintenance of resources contribute significantly to the effectiveness of the day-to-day management of teaching and learning and create an ethos where a classroom looks bright, purposeful and professionally businesslike.

10

Mathematics lesson management

Teaching requires a comprehensive and diverse repertoire of strategies and techniques. In the unique circumstances of each classroom only the teacher can determine exactly when, where and how to deploy them.

(Robin Alexander)

Lesson management is the aspect of teaching which draws upon all management skills related to planning for learning, class organisation, management of resources, teaching, maintaining control, assessment and record-keeping. To orchestrate class lessons incorporating all the above elements effectively and appropriately requires practice to develop mastery. Even very experienced teachers acknowledge that some lessons do not go as well as expected. For many student teachers and newly qualified teachers, the orchestration of lesson management can expend a lot of nervous energy because, in the early stages of learning to teach, lesson management can feel like staging continuous performances of different one-character plays without the benefit of any rehearsals.

Planning mathematical lessons

Short-term plans

Short-term plans establish the organisational details of the daily management of teaching sessions. These may be weekly plans (see Figure 10.1) or daily lesson plans. In some nursery schools, where adult helpers are involved in directing activities, teachers provide them with guidance in the form of activity plans (see Figure 10. 2).

Resource audit

Teachers starting to work in a new classroom will initially have to take stock of the resources available to them in terms of time, resources (including adult help) and space (arrangements of furniture and fittings) (see Chapter 9).

Pre Prep 2 - Weekly Planner

	8.40	9.00 — 10.40	11.20 — 12.30	2.00	3.30
Mon 20	Chapel	**Language/Activities/Reading** — Oral news and weather/helper chart; Picture and writing (News/own choice); Activities * see below + playdough, playmobil, jigsaws. Individual reading	**Number** — Make fruit salad - sharing cutting, examining, tasting	**Swimming** — In ability groups/Oxfords	Story
Tue 21 (Assem / Script)		**Dance/Number/Activities/Reading** — Dance - Let's Move tape - Festivities; Number - Heinemann at own level; Activities * + small world, cogs, fuzzy felt; Individual reading	**Language** — Story - Hodge the Hedgehog Discuss hibernation and animals preparing for winter	**Creative Activities** — Mrs. Dobson	Story
Wed 22	Chapel	**Language/TV/Activities/Reading** — Oral sounds - 'o' and 'ow'; Follow-up sheet on 'o' - handwriting - Oxfords; TV - words and Pictures 9.45 - Reading; Activities * + threading, jigsaws, farm	**Number** — Oral number - context sheet; Own level Heinemann; Number songs and rhymes	**Creative Activities** — Clay hedgehogs (follow-up to story); Leaf rubbings to make owl	Story
Thur 23 (Assem / P.S.E.)		**Library/Number/Activities/Reading** — Library and book sharing; Play - Spin a colour and Up the Pole; Activities * + cleversticks, Duplo, plasticine	**Language** — Play Spin-a-letter; New Way books at own level; Finger rhymes	**Outdoor PE/Music** — 2.15 Puppet show - Three Billy Goats Gruff	Story
Fri 24		**Language/Reading/PE** — Drama - Billy Goats Gruff followed by picture and writing; 9.50 PE apparatus - theme body, shape and balance	**Maths** — Shape activities - Teddy Bear shapes and picture making; Heinemann shape cards	**Topic/Activities** — Puppet making; Singing	Story

* Computer - shape game   I-spy table - letter 'o'   House, Water, Paints, Sand
Craft table - junk modelling   Nature table - fruits, seeds, leaves and magnifying glass
Maths table - shapes   Writing corner - tracing

Figure 10.1 Weekly planning sheet for a nursery class

Planning the content: skill audit

In planning the mathematical content of a session, teachers should take account of children's known achievement to date. Activities will then need to be planned according to children's needs in relation to the Desirable Outcomes or Programmes of Study for the National Curriculum. Activities may be planned to take place in a single session, such as a session investigating 'fruit maths'. Alternatively,

High Input Activity Plan

Activity Leader: **Miss Butler**	Date: 14.03.95
Name of Activity: **Scales and Buttons**	
Number of Children: **Two at a time**	Activity Duration: 1 1/2 hrs.

Areas of the Curriculum Covered:
Science, Maths, Language, Concentration, Discrimination

Equipment required:
Scales, Buttons

Space and Layout:
Fine motor skills, table, three chairs

Discussion points and Language to be focused on:
Heavy, Light, Heavier/Lighter, More/less, Balance.

Introduction:

    1. Place weights on table, invite child to participate.

    2. Ask child to say which of two is heavier or lighter

Practical Work: 3. Put scales on table, verify child's guess.

    4. Discuss which side has heavier/lighter content. Ask child to make side heavier/lighter

Review Time and Clearing Away:

    Children to talk about their work to the other groups

Assessment: Observation, discussion, questioning.
Criteria:
Can identify heavy and light objects by handling.
Use words heavier and lighter in comparing two objects.
Fine motor skills, hand-eye co-ordination, understanding.

Figure 10.2 Nursery activity plan for a classroom assistant

activities can be planned to take place within a series of sessions – for example, a maths topic on linear measurement.

In planning the content of a session, or series of sessions, teachers will also need to consider whether the planned work for mathematics will take place:

• as an activity with a small group of children within a range of different curriculum activities in the classroom based on a common theme or topic (a common strategy at nursery level);
• as an activity with a small group of children within a variety of different curriculum activities where children visit each activity on a 'circus' basis or 'integrated day' principle (a common strategy at reception level);
• as a collection of mathematical activities related to a specific area of mathematics, planned at different levels for children working in small ability groups (a common strategy used for children working at KS1 and 2);
• as a whole-class activity focusing on a mathematical investigation or real-life problem, where different outcomes are encouraged according to ability or a problem is divided into separate components for children to tackle in groups (an occasional strategy used for children working at KS1 and 2); and
• as an activity with a mathematical focus carried out as part of crosscurricular topic work within other curriculum sessions – for example, arising from stories, science, art, technology, PE, music (a common strategy used at nursery level and throughout the primary sector) (see Chapter 12).

Establishment of learning outcomes

Learning outcomes should define the mathematical learning in relation to concepts and skills that are planned to be developed during a particular mathematical lesson or activity. For example, in a nursery lesson for a small group of 3–4-year-olds, designed to develop children's knowledge of number names, recognition of written numbers, the order and value of numbers and tag-counting skills (say and touch), the learning outcomes might be as follows:

• all children to count orally as far as possible;
• all children to tag-count objects as far as possible;
• some children to recognise written numbers in sequence as far as possible;
• some children to match objects to written numbers in sequence as far as possible;
• a few children to recognise written numbers out of sequence as far as possible; and
• a few children to match objects to written numbers out of sequence as far as possible.

(See planning for minimum, optimum and extension outcomes in Chapter 17.)

There are also other types of planned outcomes which represent targets for the teacher to achieve during the lesson. For example, one or more of the following may be included in the planning framework for a lesson:

- targeting a group for assessment;
- targeting a child for special help;
- improving the process of dispersing children to group work after whole-class time; and
- improving the management of clearing-away time.

Pre-lesson preparation

A key factor in effective lesson management is for the teacher to be well prepared beforehand, in terms of the resources required for children's and adults' use throughout the session. The use of specific resources stored in a central place in a school may need to be booked out in advance, some of the furniture in the room may need rearrangement and pupil and teacher materials need to be ready for use. Jotting down requirements in terms of pupil/teacher resources, and the layout of furniture to be used, as a pre-lesson checklist, is a useful strategy for students and newly qualified teachers. Whilst attending to other responsibilities, they may forget a critical resource element until they are just about to start teaching. This can be unsettling for the person concerned and may also cause the session to start off badly.

Planning a session from start to finish

Setting the scene

A good beginning is very important as it establishes the tone and purpose of a session. In sessions which are planned around some form of mathematical focus, the National Numeracy Project consultants have recommended that, prior to the introduction of the session, KS1 teachers should consider including a mental arithmetic 'warm-up' session, lasting approximately 10 minutes.

Warm-up time

Playing a whole-class mental arithmetic game for 10 minutes at the beginning of a session can help to settle the class and focus their attention – for example, continue the count or pattern games played in a circle, and washing-line games with number cards for counting-on/back or ordering numbers, where different children are each given a card and have to peg their card on the line in turn in the order prescribed by the 'rule' of the game. There is also a variety of quickfire calculation games that can be played where the teacher prescribes the 'rule', for example, 'Add 1'. Random numbers can be held up on cards or presented orally to children for children to play the game (Edwards, 1997). Other examples of whole-class mathematical activities include:

- oral counting, finger and number rhymes, songs and mathematical stories;
- everyday class routines including registration, lining up, getting into groups, collecting and counting money, clearing away;
- highlighting special times of the day, events such as children's birthdays, recording the date and changes in the weather, reading times on a class clock; and
- mathematical activities included in music, movement and dance lessons, including timing children getting changed, as well as activities in class assemblies and on educational visits.

A useful text in this area is Anna Lewis (1996), *Discovering Mathematics with 4 to 7-Year-Olds.*

Introduction and exposition activities with a whole class or group

The introduction to a session normally includes a brief explanation to the whole class about what is to happen in the session and, where group work follows, to explain what each group will be doing. It is also the time used by teachers to demonstrate and explain any new mathematical work to the whole class, highlight new key words or language involved and invite children to participate in demonstrations, questioning and discussion. Where recording is required, it is helpful for the teacher to explain what children are expected to do and present a model of what is expected.

It is important that the teacher does not introduce too much at once, focusing on the new knowledge and skills that children are required to learn in order to carry out subsequent practical work. For young children, it is useful to demonstrate specific skills through examples and, where possible, invite children to take part in demonstrations. Ruth Merttens (1997) describes this as 'maths-on-the-rug' time and recommends that a small easel with a flipchart or large piece of paper for the teacher and/or the children to write on can provide a focus for young children's attention in the same way a wall chalkboard creates a focus for older children. Before introducing new work, it is a good idea for the teacher briefly to refresh children's minds about previous work they have carried out in the area. The following shows an example of an introduction to a lesson on shape to a group of nursery children:

> Today we are going to learn some more about shapes. Last week we learnt about some special shapes. Who can remember their names? (circle, square).
>
> Daniel, can you find a circle in my box? Good...show it to the rest of the children.

(Other children in group invited to find a known shape in the box.)

Our new shape today is called a triangle (hold up big triangle). All of you say it with me... Let's count the corners...

Abdul, can you find a triangle in my box? Good. What colour is your triangle? (Other children in group invited to find a triangle in the box.)

Here is a picture of lots of different triangles, let's count the corners on them... How many corners do they all have?

David, come and hold up this big triangle... Vicki, come and hold up this big circle... Samantha, can you tell me the difference between the circle and the triangle?

(Two more children hold up a square and a triangle) John, can you tell me the difference between a square and a triangle?

We are going to do some special things with triangles today. Some of you are going to make some triangle-shaped biscuits with Miss —— and Mrs —— is going to help some of you to decorate plates with triangles. When they are all finished we shall have a triangle tea party.

I also want to see if you can find one thing shaped like a triangle in the room to go in our triangle box. Remember we only want different things. If your shape is already in the box then don't put it in.

Managing whole-class sessions

One of the important keys to success to starting whole-class sessions is to create a settled atmosphere and be able to command everyone's attention. In theatres, this is achieved by putting the lights down. In classrooms, where teachers do not have the benefit of this 'magical effect', it requires careful planning and direction. Whole-class sessions usually occur at the beginning of the day or after break-times. These are points in the day when children are particularly unsettled and it is important to establish clear rules and routines to avoid problems occurring. In nursery schools and many reception classes, the first session of the day is often planned as a free-play session. Children know that, after reporting to the teacher, they are able to disperse to activities. In infant schools, at the beginning of sessions, rules are often set where children are expected to walk in quietly to sit in the carpeted area, sit in their 'places' or line up by the door to be led in by the teacher. With a new class, these rules are not learnt automatically and the children may require some practice. It is better that a teacher anticipates problems and formulates clear procedures which children are able to respond to than having to resort to shouting at children when things go awry.

Once the children are settled, there is the task of commanding the children's attention. In a similar way to an actor, the teacher should use his or her voice, body language and 'business' to captivate his or her audience. Speech should be articulate, expressive and sufficiently loud for children to hear and want to listen. Muffled and droning speech, as well as speech that is too loud, can make children restless. Sharing eye contact with individual children during the session can help to make them feel personally involved. Movement and activity through demonstration can focus interest, particularly if children are invited to participate through questions and practical activity. Children are always eager to be involved and rules need to be established as to how children will be selected to answer questions or participate in an activity – for example, establishing a procedure where children put their hands up without calling out and reinforcing it by regularly reminding children that they will not be 'picked' if they do call out.

Another important strategy is to ensure that the session does not go on too long because children start to lose interest and become restless. Fifteen minutes is a useful guideline. Careful planning can ensure that the 'business' of the session is explicitly covered in a stimulating and businesslike fashion, including time to go over key points, before children are dispersed to work in groups.

Dispersing children to work in groups is often seen as a problem spot in a teaching session. One of the most effective strategies, when a teacher has no adult help, is to decide which groups are going to require the least supervision to get started with their work and send them away to work first, leaving the group that is targeted for teacher input until last. Where another adult is available to work with a group then that group can be one of the first to be dispersed.

Planning practical work for small groups

In planning practical work for small groups of children, it is important for the teacher to decide whether the learning behaviour involved in the activity represents the exploration of new or *epistemic* learning, or an activity which is designed for practice and mastery of previous learning – *ludic activity* (Hutt, 1979) (see Chapter 1). Activities which are designed to stimulate epistemic learning behaviours should be planned as high-input work, where an adult works interactively with the group for most of the time, directing the activity and asking questions and encouraging children to develop ideas. Activities which are designed for practice and mastery can be planned as low-input activities which require little teacher input. However, low-input activities should not be planned just to keep children occupied. According to the Cheshire Unit for Pupil Assessment (1992, G 3), low-input activities are: 'fundamental to the curriculum and in themselves will have required high input teaching at sometime. They need to have been established and skills learnt for them before-hand. A whole school policy in these educational activities gives security for children and maintains continuity and harmony within the school.'

Low-input activities will always be much richer if adult input can be given at some stage during the activity. The involvement of an adult will give status to the activity and create opportunities for discussion and the development of ideas.

Planning the content of practical activities

When planning the content of practical activities, teachers will need to cater for children working at different levels of ability and/or rates of working. Different levels of expected outcome should be taken into consideration and clear plans should be established for children who finish their work quickly. The planning of activities with open-ended outcomes is particularly helpful to enable children of different abilities to work at their own level (see Chapters 11, 12 and 17).

Managing practical mathematics activities with small groups

Managing the organisation of practical work for small groups of young children demands a variety of skills, especially if the teacher is the only adult working in the classroom. In this situation, it is not practical for a teacher to give all the groups the kind of activities which require high teacher direction. If this happens, a teacher is likely to discover that he or she is working in overdrive, rushing round the classroom like a one-armed paper hanger, with little or no time to offer effective direction or support to any group, with the atmosphere in the classroom being less than calm. A strategy commonly used to avoid this scenario is to plan a range of activities requiring a balanced amount of high, medium and low teacher input, which provides opportunities for learning and practice side by side (see Chapter 1). A teacher is then able to spend some quality time with a high-input group, it is hoped without too many interruptions, before circulating round other groups.

Where additional adult help is available during a session, assigning an adult helper to work with a group of children significantly reduces the workload of the teacher. Another group can be given quality time, and the person is on hand to help direct clearing-up proceedings. For example, in a class of four groups, a teacher may plan the session with a high-input activity for teaching a new concept to one group. At the same time the teacher may plan a medium-input activity for the second group to practise a concept, working with published scheme materials, whilst the two other groups carry out low-input tasks, comprising work to be finished off, followed by structured play activities.

It is helpful to organise teaching sessions using a points system, for example, 5 = high input, 3 = medium input, 1 = low input. A teaching session planned for four groups, with only one adult present, should contain activities up to a maximum of ten points to work effectively, i.e. one high-input group, one medium-input group and two low-input groups. A teaching session with two adults present could have a maximum of fifteen points, allowing for two high-input activities and a range of combinations of medium and low-input activities (Edwards, 1995). Figure 10.3 shows a lesson planned using high, medium and low-input activities.

If a teacher feels overwhelmed with demands from children it is often because too many high-input activities have been planned to take place at the same time. On the other hand, it is important to re-emphasise that low-input activities should not be used predominantly as low-level 'time fillers'.

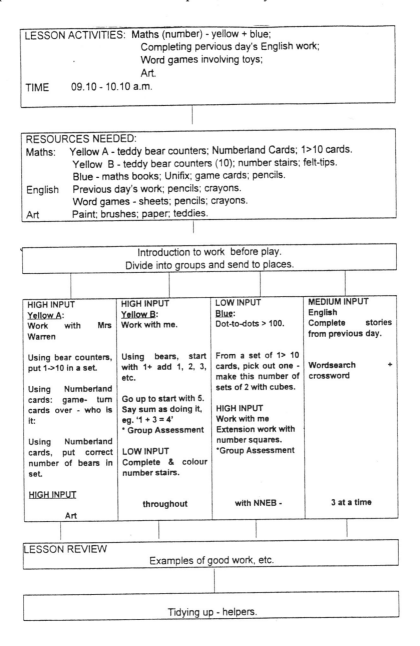

Figure 10.3 Year 1 lesson plan involving high, medium and low-input activities with planned assessment opportunities

'Withitness'

When teachers are actively involved in working with a group, it is important that they position themselves so that they are also able to keep an eye on what is happening in the rest of the class. Jack Kounin (1970) defined this skill as 'withitness', where the teacher constantly scans the classroom during the course of a session. It is particularly important with young children, in relation to safety, to be able to recognise situations where they may be likely to injure themselves or other children. The skill of 'withitness' also enables teachers to diffuse minor problems and disruptions during the course of a session by engaging pupils in eye contact or through the process of *public audit*, where the teacher engages a child through a personal comment (Wragg, 1993) – for example, 'Sarah, have you finished your maths?' Children soon get the message that their teacher has 'eyes in the back of his or her head'. If a problem persists, it is better for the teacher to go to the problem rather than try to impose control from a distance by shouting. In this way the problem can often be dispelled without disrupting the whole class. If this fails, the teacher can dissipate a problem through moving the main instigator to sit close to the teacher for a while. When a child displays persistent aggressive or disruptive behaviour it is better to try to negotiate a contract with the child after the lesson and support the child in sustaining the contract through encouragement and praise when behaviour improves. Public humiliation is the least effective strategy.

Clearing away and review

The transition between practical work in groups, involving clearing away and settling children again as a whole-class group, can also cause problems. The establishment of well planned storage for resources and clear tidying procedures can reduce tension at these times. Planning for practical activities should include time for clearing away in preparation for bringing the session to a conclusion. Planning time for review at the end of a session gives an opportunity for celebrating children's efforts by encouraging children to share work they have done with the whole class. It also gives an opportunity for the teacher to recapitulate on the main teaching points of the session and establish whether children have understood.

Assessing children's performance

During the course of a teaching session teachers will need to monitor children's performance in mathematics, as part of a continuous assessment process, through incorporating assessment opportunities within their planning and informally monitoring children's work by circulating around the class. Sometimes guidelines are offered within whole-school policies for assessment but it is more commonly left to individual teachers to devise and implement their own strategies for assessment at classroom level. There is a range of assessment techniques that teachers can use according to the age of the children and the type of activity to be assessed (see Chapter 15).

Keeping track of children's progress

A manageable system of record-keeping should be devised to record formally and/or informally significant outcomes of individual children's performances within a teaching session. For nursery schools, this may include a list of children who have visited an activity. In infant schools, many teachers are moving towards the use of group records, which are seen as more manageable than maintaining whole-class or individual records (see Chapter 20).

Factors associated with high standards of achievement

According to Ofsted (1994), the following factors related to lesson management are associated with high standards of achievement in primary-age children:

- teachers had satisfactory or good knowledge of the subject they were teaching
- teachers demonstrated good questioning skills to assess pupils' knowledge and challenge their thinking
- teachers made effective use of exposition, instruction and direct teaching
- teachers used a good balance of grouping strategies including whole class, small group or individual work as appropriate
- teachers used ability grouping effectively.

Other factors included (*ibid.*):

- clear objectives for the lesson
- good management of lesson-time
- effective use of other adults in the classroom
- appropriate range of teacher assessment techniques
- well established classroom routines providing minimal disruptions to tasks and teaching
- good classroom organisation of resources and materials
- effective planning of pupils' work.

Evaluating a lesson

The evaluation of a lesson enables the teacher to analyse critically what has happened in a lesson from start to finish and set targets for subsequent action. This should involve an assessment of the children's responses to the lesson and to what extent the planned learning outcomes have been achieved. In addition, the contribution made by the teacher through organisational planning, resource management and teaching should be assessed.

Assessment of learning

This enables teachers to use their professional judgement, through observation and examining evidence of work carried out by children, to establish whether the planned work was explained effectively and pitched at the right level. Indications that this may not be so are shown in:

- children who found the work easy and finished quickly with no help;
- children who were very unsure of what was expected of them and needed a lot of help to get started; and
- children who had difficulty with the work and showed no real indications of understanding even with help.

This kind of critical analysis gives vital information to the teacher to guide subsequent planning. It can also assist teachers in deciding which children are ready to move on, which children require more practice and which children may need work at a lower level (see Chapter 15).

Assessment of planning, organisation and teaching

This enables teachers to assess critically whether:

- the content planning matched the needs of the children;
- the classroom organisation supported the proceedings;
- the resource provision was adequate;
- adult help was effectively deployed to support the proceedings;
- explanations were sufficiently clear for children to understand what they had to do;
- time taken for the introduction, activity work and conclusion was well balanced;
- they were able to give quality time to one or more groups during practical work;
- transitions between whole-class time, practical group work, clearing away, review time and class dismissal went smoothly; and
- they were able to maintain a good level of control of the class throughout the lesson.

(See Chapter 15.)

By identifying elements that were successful, and those that were less successful, teachers are able to target areas for improvement in a subsequent lesson. For student teachers settling into a new class, it may seem that quite a lot goes wrong in the first few days. It is worth considering the strategy of listing problems in order of priority, in discussion with the class teacher, and focusing on one or two elements at a time.

It is important to realise that the perfect lesson is a rare experience.

Experienced teachers acknowledge that even if the planned elements seem to be going well, spontaneous events that occur in a classroom full of young children are likely to disturb the proceedings – for example, when a child is violently sick, a paint pot is dropped or water is spilt, to name just a few scenarios which represent 'gremlins' to the best laid planning and preparation.

Writing lesson plans and evaluations

Lesson plans should be *working* documents written in a way that is easy to read and interpret. Concise notes and bullet points are more practical to refer to than screeds of text. It is useful to attach daily lesson plans and any relevant assessment sheets to a clipboard. This enables the teacher to have the documentation to hand and notes can be jotted down on the proceedings, which can be referred to when writing the evaluation (see Figure 10.4).

Lesson planning and inspection visits

Bill Laar (1996), a registered inspector, offers this advice to teachers in an article in *The Times Educational Supplement*:

> Good planning can be succinctly and effectively set out on a sheet of A4. Even in the midst of apparent catastrophe, inspectors will find in careful planning evidence of the vital components of good teaching… such planning will go a long way to securing the sympathy and positive judgement of an inspector… So much that teachers achieve with pupils by day is created through solitary planning by night. Inspectors and others will understand the full importance and value of that if they are given a chance to share it.

Summary

Orchestrating successful teaching and learning events, to ensure that the general needs of the class, as well as group and individual needs, can be catered for, brings together all the organisational, decision-making and interpersonal skills of teachers. Preparation and the ability to anticipate and deal effectively with problems increase the chances of success. To sustain continuity in teaching and learning, the mathematical content of a lesson should be planned in relation to evidence of what children already know and understand, with assessment and evaluation processes guiding decisions about what should follow. Teachers should also consider ways in which their input can be improved as part of the process of professional development.

Students in training are expected to produce detailed lesson plans as evidence of their ability to consider the many aspects involved in lesson management. They are also expected to write detailed evaluations as evidence of their ability to analyse critically the proceedings and use the information to guide future actions. With respect to experienced teachers, lesson plans and evaluations may not be written down in such detail. However, the processes required are just as thorough and will need to be made as explicit for the purpose of inspection.

Lesson Plan 1

Subject:	Mathematics
Title:	length
Focus:	starting learning language for measurement of length.
Time/Duration:	Thursday 18th January 1996 - 1.20-2.15pm 55 minutes
Number of children:	6

Leaning Outcomes:
1. Understanding language - Tall, short, wide, narrow, thick, thin, length
2. To show understanding visually on sheets provided and orally.
3. To be able to put things in order.

Organization: Children will first listen to the story which will be used as the stimulus for the activity. This will be done in the library because they will be able to concentrate better. Then we will go back into the classroom, we will start by sitting on the carpet so the children can see the blackboard and then move to a separate table.

Preparation: I will need to make sure the library is free and we will need the multi-link and the black board. Check that Mrs. ✱✱✱✱ the class assistant is free to help translate.

Introduction:
1. Read the story in the library with the class assistant translating it into Punjabi.
2. Return to the classroom and introduce the language on the blackboard.
3. Show the children visually what is meant by the words using multi link.

Practical Work:
4. Sitting at the table explain the sheets prepared
5. Sheet on tall and short
6. Activity: Find things taller than their pencil.

Review Time and Clearing away: Ask the children about what they have done.

Assessment: Observation, discussion with the children and questioning.

Criteria:
1. Can listen, focus attention.
2. Understanding of the language tall, short etc.
3. To be able to understand visually and orally.
4. To show understanding of comparisons.
5. To be able to order things.

Figure 10.4 Lesson plan and written evaluation for group work in a reception class

Lesson Evaluation 1

1. Assessment of Learning.

Martin

Martin is ready to go on to ordering in more detail, he understood the story, although he was distracted and kept looking around the library whilst it was being read. He understood the language and showed this by his completion of the activities. He did not need much help.
We gave Martin a little task on ordering and comparisons, he is ready for this.

Maryam

Maryam understood the story, she answered questions about it and on it. She completed the activities well and showed understanding of the language and of comparisons.

Reheem

Reheem showed some understanding of the story, but did not answer any questions. He needed quite a lot of help to complete the work. Needs more work on language.

Chenise

Chenise focused well on the story and showed some understanding of it. She needed a lot of help with the tasks and needs more work on language.

Shamrez

Had little understanding of the story and did not answer any questions. Needs individual help with tasks, because he does not understand the language or the concepts being introduced.

Rosina

Had all her attention on the story-listened to it being read in Punjabi. Needs individual attention and like shamrez much more work on the language involved in measuring.

2. Assessment of Teaching

The story went well, especially because it was also read in Punjabi. This meant that all the children should have been able to understand it. We went to the library so that the children were distracted as little as possible.
I think our lesson idea moved on to quickly for most of the group, except Martin and Maryam. We did not time the lesson right, the story took longer than expected so we had to continue the activity after the break. We did not leave enough time to round up and review the lesson.

3. Course of Action
  Setting Targets:

Martin	Start work on the concept of ordering and reinforce the language.
Maryam	Start work on the concept of ordering and reinforce the language.
Reheem	Much more work on the language involved in measuring.
Chenise	Much more work on the language involved in measuring.
Shamrez	Much more work on the language involved in measuring.
Rosina	Much more work on the language involved in measuring.

Teaching and organizational targets.

The next lesson we will focus on the language and use more concrete examples.

Figure 10.4 Lesson plan and written evaluation for group work in a reception class (continued)

11

Planning mathematical activities
1. Number

Nursery and reception level

Number activities at nursery and reception level are best planned as interactive practical work. In this way number work can be directed through structured play activities, small-group games and taken as a focus for circle or whole-group time. Within this framework, opportunities should be planned for children to learn new number skills, develop mental skills and to use and apply learnt skills in practical contexts to develop mastery.

Counting and number recognition

- Counting, matching and writing numbers (Desirable Outcomes).
- Ordering and sequencing objects and events (Desirable Outcomes).
- Sight counting, conservation of number, counting on/back (working towards level 1).

Planning considerations

Counting

Young children need a wide range of activities that enable them to count groups of people, objects and actions using number names and touch/tag counting, and to know that the last number they say represents the number of the set. This is the *cardinal* aspect of numbers. Familiarity with number names should be extended as counting skills develop. These activities can be incorporated within all aspects of school life. They can be integrated into planned activities for all areas of the curriculum, arise through spontaneous moments within the course of a school day or presented through singing games involving counting, finger and number rhymes, and stories.

Matching and writing numbers

Children need to see numbers and watch them being written. The use of a number frieze and displays around the room, together with a collection of illustrated counting books, can help to familiarise children with written numbers. Children should also be given opportunities to recognise numbers in everyday contexts – house, telephone, bus and car numbers, prices in shops, numbers on clocks and dials, and on computers and calculators, etc.

Flashcards or paper plates with numbers on can be used to play recognition games in group time and for children to match numbers to objects. It is also useful to plan opportunities for children to draw numbers in the air, in sand, with paint or chalk, and model numbers in clay, Plasticine or dough. Tracing over dots is a helpful way to develop children's number-writing skills. There should also be opportunities for children to copy numbers on paper and be encouraged to develop their number-writing skills freehand from memory. In addition, activities should be provided for children to find or draw a specified number of objects. When children have a reasonable grasp of counting and writing numbers, activities can be planned where children write numbers alongside their own pictures of groups of objects.

Ordering objects

Children should be given opportunities to recognise visual relationships between the size and order of objects, through ordering objects by size from smallest to largest and *vice versa* in familiar contexts. In the early stages they are often only able to discriminate visually between the 'big one' and the 'small one' and the notion of 'middle-sized' or 'in-between' is more difficult to understand. The story of *The Three Bears*, for example, can provide an ideal starting point to introduce this principle, where the story can be acted out using teddy bears, chairs and bowls to generate understanding. This can lead on to ordering three different-sized bottles, pencils, etc., increasing the number to four, then five, etc.

Sequencing events

Pattern recognition is a vital element in developing children's mathematical understanding. Through early experiences of repeated patterns and sequences, children are able to generalise 'rules' and mentally predict progression. Children's first experiences of pattern arise from routine events in their daily lives. Early activities can be centred around asking children to talk about familiar routines, such as getting up and getting dressed, and getting ready for bed at night. Simple short story sequences can be read to children with questions such as 'How did the story start?' 'What happened next?' In addition, there are many commercial activities which are designed for children to put pictures in order of sequence. As children's skills of pictorial recording develop, they can make zig-zag books where they can draw their own sequences of events or story sequences.

Sequencing objects

Before children start to order objects into patterns or sequences, they need to practise their skills in threading beads, setting out objects in a line and printing with objects in random configurations. When children demonstrate they are able to match simple given patterns using objects correctly, then activities can be structured for them to copy and continue patterns – for example, matching sequences of objects or actions for simple 1:1 patterns, and continuing the sequence:

- red, blue; red, blue...
- boat, car; boat, car...
- clap, jump; clap, jump...

As children's familiarity with pattern develops, more complex sequences can be introduced, such as 1:2 patterns (red, blue, blue...) and 2:2 patterns (clap, clap, jump, jump) and growing patterns (1:2:3, 1:2:3). If young children are expected to draw or print sequence patterns it is useful to use strips of paper rather than sheets as this helps them to sustain the linear principle of the pattern (see Figure 11.1).

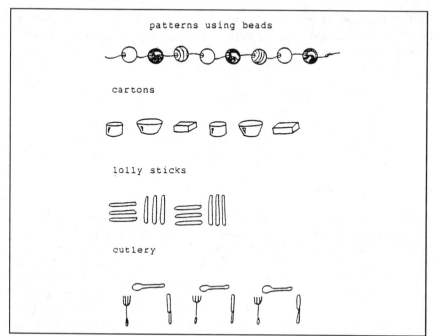

Figure 11.1   Building sequence patterns with objects

Children should also have experiences of recognising pattern on fabric, wallpaper, bricks, paving stones, etc. There are some well illustrated 'first books' which present pictures or photographs of patterns on artificial and natural objects which can be used for discussion.

Sight counting

As children become more skilled at counting, the need for touch counting or pointing to objects diminishes and the skill of sight counting begins to develop (sometimes known as *subitising*). This is when children start to recognise numbers on dice or dominoes, for example, and perform simple counting activities with small numbers of objects in their heads. Dice, dominoes and playing card games can assist in the development of sight counting. However, it is important to ensure that children recognise, for example, that 5 can be configured in different ways and not just as the well-known five-dot presentation on dice, dominoes and playing cards. Experience of finding different ways to arrange counters or cubes is helpful with this process. The BBC television series 'Numbertime', features the numbers 1–10 in different configurations and in different contexts.

Conservation of number

The principle of conservation of number is defined as the ability to recognise that the numerical quantity of a set of objects does not change if the position of the objects is altered. For example, if 4 blocks are built into a tower or spread out in a line the quantity remains the same. Activities should be planned which encourage children to handle groups of objects and count them in different configurations. It is also important that children have experience of counting sets of different, yet related, objects, such as a set of four different cars. This is so they realise that it is not the cars that are important, but the 'fourness' of the cars.

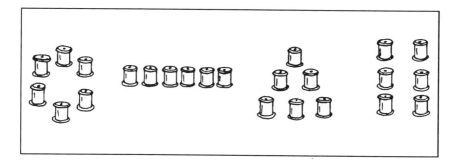

Figure 11.2   Different arrangements of six objects

Counting-on/back

To help develop children's mental skills at counting-on and back, oral games can be planned where children count on/back in ones from a given number. Activities can also be planned where adults play simple track games using dice with small groups of children. The use of a 'washing line', pegs and large numbered cards can offer the basis for many count-on/back games (the teachers' cards in the *Abacus Mathematics Programme* contain many ideas for washing-line, card and dice games at different levels of difficulty – see 'Useful resources' at the back of the book for further details). Playground markings, in the form of a number snake or track, can introduce children to the first principles of counting-on/back using a numberline.

Early steps towards addition and subtraction

- More/less/fewer, pairing, ordering and sequencing; one more/less; counting-on/back (Desirable Outcomes).
- Combining and partitioning sets, number fact patterns (addition and subtraction) (working towards level 1).

Planning considerations

More/less/fewer

Early visual/verbal comparisons arise naturally from everyday life experiences and through play. Directed activities with sand, water, in role play, construction and outdoor play, etc., can provide a wealth of opportunities for children to gain first-hand experiences of visual comparison. Activities planned to promote visual comparison also encourage the development of early estimation skills. Discussion and questioning can promote the appropriate use of comparative numerical and measurement language.

Pairing/matching

Activities should be planned which enable children to match pairs of objects and associated pairs, for example, cups and saucers, and to use the language 'more/less/same' appropriately. When children have developed matching and counting skills, their skills can be extended by comparison questions – for example:

- How many more boats than cars?
- How many fewer cars than boats?

Ordering and sequencing numbers; one more/one less

Number songs and finger rhymes present a useful context for work with increasing and decreasing collections, where the rhyme can be acted out or presented in picture form. When children have started to tag/touch count successfully and can order at least three similar objects by size, they can be introduced to building 'staircases' of blocks, rods or countable objects, or playing one more/less games with dice or numbered cards. The use of washing lines (for example, pegging handkerchiefs on the line or using numbered sheets of paper, putting them on or taking them off one at a time) shows the collection increasing or decreasing. The story of *The Very Hungry Caterpillar*, together with a wall picture of the story, is a useful way to create an attractive visual aid to demonstrate this principle.

Counting-on

In developing skills of counting on using addition, it is important that children learn to count-on from the number of the first set and not start back at the beginning of the count. The encouragement of 'finger counting' is helpful when children are counting-on one and two with small numbers, as this can represent a first stage towards abstraction (Haylock and Cockburn, 1997). As numbers get larger, this becomes more difficult for children to master (see Chapter 3). From counting on one, this can be extended to counting-on two, etc. As children's counting skills develop, they should be encouraged to count-on orally from numbers other than one. Mental work can be developed by using sets of objects as a starting point, for example:

• Take out two cars from the box. If you took one more, how many cars would you have altogether?

moving on to 'Let's pretend' scenarios:

• Let's pretend there are two cars in a car park. If another one drove in, how many cars would be in the car park?

Counting-back/take away

Activities should be planned which give children plenty of practical experience of counting out objects orally, taking one, two, three away, etc., and counting what is left. Again, it is helpful to encourage children to use their fingers to count back/take away one or two from small numbers. As children become more confident they should be given opportunities to count-back orally in ones, twos, etc., from a variety of given numbers. Mental work can start with objects, for example:

• I (teacher) have three sweets. If I give one away, how many will I have left?

leading on to 'mental scenarios' such as:

• Let's pretend there are three birds sitting on a branch. If one flies away, how many are left?

Combining sets

Through the experience of combining two sets of objects into a single quantity to find out 'how many altogether?', children are able to recognise the relationship between the 'real-life' mathematical statements of addition – for example: 'Two apples and three oranges. How many altogether?' and the corresponding 'number sentence' 3 + 2 = 5. Finger counting is also useful where, in this example, a child may use two hands, holding up three fingers on the first hand and two on the second and then adding them together. Where possible, it is important that teachers encourage children to count-on – 'four, five' from the three fingers rather than counting all the fingers in ones.

Partitioning sets

Partitioning sets involves splitting a set to form component sets. For example, in partitioning a set of four, it can be split to form a set of three and one; two and two; or four and zero. Through partitioning activities, including use of fingers, children develop an understanding of the fact that numbers can be made in different ways. Children should also begin to recognise, for example, that one and three, and three and one, have the same total (the *commutative law*) (see Figure 11.3).

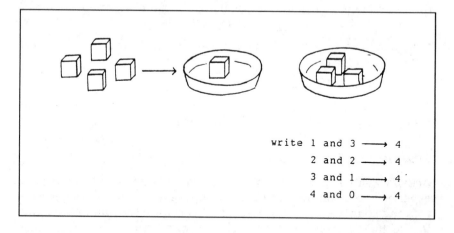

```
write  1 and 3 ──→ 4
       2 and 2 ──→ 4
       3 and 1 ──→ 4
       4 and 0 ──→ 4
```

Figure 11.3 Partitioning 4 using margarine tubs

Number fact patterns

First 'story' activities can arise from investigations with different arrangements of small numbers of objects, for example, 'Ways to dress Teddy' with red, blue and yellow T-shirts and shorts. To develop children's understanding of pattern in relation to early addition and

subtraction, the patterns derived from 'Number Stories' are important
stepping stones towards developing familiarity with number bonds,
doubling numbers, etc., as an aid to mental calculation (for example, the
'Story of Five': see Figure 11.4).

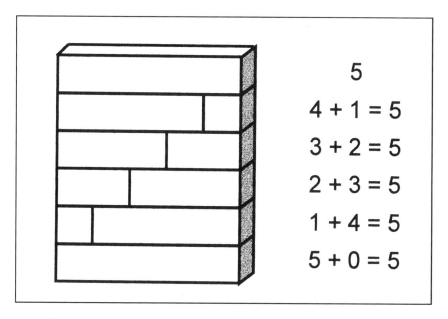

Figure 11.4. 'Story of 5' represented with Cuisenaire rods

Mental arithmetic

Evidence of mental arithmetic skills is shown when young children can
perform simple addition/subtraction by recognising the number of a
small group of objects by sight *(subitising)* and being able to add one
more or take one away in their heads. This can then be increased to two
more/two less, etc. In this way children are able to become familiar with
the 'rule' of the pattern and become more confident to perform the
calculations mentally. Work with a numberline can support children's
work with counting patterns, as the patterns can be quickly spotted and
generalised (see Figure 11.5).

Mental arithmetic can also be facilitated by familiarity with number
facts, particularly when children can understand that, for example,
reversing 2 + 7 to 7 + 2 and looking for familiar doubles 2 + 2, 3 + 3, or
near doubles 3 + 4, can make calculations easier. Work with calculators
can encourage young children to explore what happens when numbers
are input into the calculator, experimenting with number patterns and
sequences to fill the display and experimenting with the operation
buttons.

Figure 11.5   Counting in tens activity

Recording

The first records of children's work with addition and subtraction will be through evidence of their ability to carry out activities practically with objects and verbalise their experiences. Written/pictorial recording emerges when children are able to draw marks or pictures on paper to represent their experiences and talk about them. Whilst it is desirable to encourage children's recording skills, it is important that doing and talking are seen as the main ingredients in developing young children's understanding of number. First recording may include combinations of marks, pictures and/or numbers. Any form of standard recording for addition and subtraction should only be introduced when children are able to:

- (orally) count-on/back confidently;
- show some evidence of sight counting and counting-on/back mentally;
- demonstrate evidence of an understanding of the processes of addition and subtraction through practical work;
- use informal recording methods to represent numerical ideas; and
- write numbers confidently and reasonably accurately from memory.

However, even when children can perform and record addition and subtraction calculations using standard methods, their own informal methods may be more appropriate in certain contexts and should not be discouraged because it demonstrates that the child is attempting to make sense of the mathematics.

Number: KS1, levels 1–3

The planning of number activities at KS1 should be no different in principle from those at nursery and reception level. Adult-directed practical activities should form the basis for work where new learning is involved, with opportunities for developing mental arithmetic skills, using and applying number skills in problem-solving and investigational contexts to develop mastery, and containing activities planned for practising number and recording skills. In planning number activities at KS1, it is important that children are given opportunities to explore and develop familiarity with the workings of the number system, from early counting to place value and to use and apply the four arithmetical rules in practical contexts where they are encouraged to develop mental arithmetic skills. The main processes of thinking and reasoning required for children (and adults) to perform arithmetical tasks happen inside their heads. Paper and computer screens are the means by which thinking and reasoning processes can be recorded. Hopkins *et al.* (1996) assert that, where the majority of activities provided for young children are 'sums' on paper with 'cubes', '. . . they may be able to read numbers, count the cubes, add or subtract them, then count again and write the answer. They may also have got the idea of putting two lots together, for add, and taking some away for subtract, but they are not calculating'.

The processes performed in these types of activities are principally mechanical and do not draw sufficiently upon children's thinking and reasoning skills. The focus for planning number activities should, therefore, centre around the development of mental rather than mechanical skills.

Counting to place value

Extending children's counting skills beyond 10 to 100, on to 1000 and beyond, can be carried out with oral counting, work with numberlines, number rectangles and squares. As well as counting-on/back in ones, children should be encouraged to count-on/back in twos, tens, fives, etc., and to have experiences of counting-on from numbers other than 1 in different contexts – for example, counting-on with 5ps, 10ps, 20ps, 50ps; 5 minute, 10 minute, 15 minute, 30 minute and 60-minute intervals. Building numberline and number square count-on/back patterns also forms the basis for multiplication and division. Work with very large numbers can be introduced through work with a calculator. Work with negative numbers can also be introduced through the use of calculators and numberlines from +10 to −10, and children can be made aware of their application through recording cold weather temperatures.

The introduction of principles of place value, defined as recognising that the position of a numerical digit in a number or sequence of numbers determines its value, should be introduced when children have familiarity with counting and ordering numbers to at least 20. First work is understood more easily if activities are planned for children to build the pattern of tens and units with numbers 10–19 with Cuisenaire rods or Dienes apparatus (see Chapter 3, Figure 3.1). Pattern work can then continue 20–29, 30–39, etc., until children have 'found the rule'. Once children have established the rule, practice games can be planned, for example, with a set of shuffled 1–100 numbered cards, where children select a card and say or record the number in tens and units. The same processes can be applied to hundreds and thousands. Work with spike abaci or home-made HTU baseboards can help children to understand the function of zero in the number system.

Four rules work: developing mental calculation skills using number patterns

Pattern is a very important element in enabling children to understand the relationships between numbers and how numbers can be manipulated in calculations using addition, subtraction, multiplication and division. When children are encouraged to build number patterns, they are focusing on what is the same in the pattern, for example, 'add

2'. Through this process, they are able to identify the 'rule'. Initially this may be 'always the number next door but one'. As understanding develops, this will include, 'always an even number when the starting number is even, always an odd number when the starting number is odd'. Also, the pattern of add two contains a repeated last-digit pattern of 2, 4, 6 , 8, 0, 2, 4, 6, 8, 0, which is rhythmic when numbers are counted orally (rhythmic patterns are also obvious when numbers are counted orally in fives and tens). At a later stage, children will be able to connect the same rules to patterns of 'add 20', add 200, etc. According to Haylock and Cockburn (1997), it is this sense of pattern in number that is the foundation for success and confidence in handling calculations, whether written or mental, or a combination of the two.

The 'story' of ten

One of the most important number relationships to be understood is addition and subtraction stories of ten. Since the number system is base ten, knowledge and instant recall of these number facts represent a key skill in manipulating numbers throughout the system. Children can build these facts in pattern form by using Cuisenaire rods or by colouring squared paper (see Figure 11.6). This form of spatial representation of the pattern, showing one of the pairs of numbers increasing by one as the other decreases by one each time, can help children's initial understanding far more than if facts are presented as random 'sums'. The pattern work can be further developed to facts about 20, 30, etc., until children become familiar with the 'rule'.

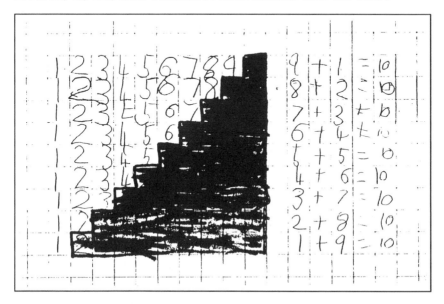

Figure 11.6   'Story of 10'

Addition and subtraction through ten

One of the calculating skills children find difficult is addition and subtraction through 10, 20, 30, etc., with numbers 6–9 (see Chapter 3). Building addition and subtraction patterns with these numbers using Cuisenaire rods can help children to develop instant recall and begin to recognise doubles or near doubles as an aid to calculation. Through extending these activities at a later stage with Dienes base-ten blocks and a ThHTU baseboard, children will be able to see how the pattern relationships continue through the number system, for example:

6 + 7	60 + 70	600 + 700
7 + 7	70 + 70	700 + 700
8 + 7	80 + 70	800 + 700, etc.

Use of number squares and rectangles

Hundred squares present a very special spatial arrangement of numbers 1–100 which enable children to see the relationships between numbers beyond 10. For example, the number 56 is between 55 and 57 in the 'fifties' line; it is also below 46 and above 66 in the numbers ending in 6 line, with a difference of ten between each number.

Through the use of a number square, children are able to build a variety of addition, subtraction and multiplication patterns. Starting from any number, children can build horizontal, vertical and diagonal patterns using addition and subtraction. This can be developed to more complex patterns (see Figure 11.7).

Work with numbers through 100 can be developed by extending the number square into a 1–200 rectangle. Similarly, if a hundred square is beyond the counting range of children, the square can be reduced to a 1–30 or 1–50 rectangle. Number squares can also be used which contain, for example, the numbers 200–299, which enable children to begin to recognise that patterns can be repeated anywhere in the number system.

Work with number squares is a valuable way of developing children's mental facility with addition and subtraction of one and two-digit numbers. The visual, spatial presentation of the numbers enables children to discover rules of addition and subtraction patterns quickly, to recognise the inverse relationship between addition and subtraction and make connections between related calculations, for example 34 + 3 and 74 + 3. However, it is equally important for teachers to ensure that children are given plenty of opportunities to apply their calculation skills in the context of real-life situations, for example, through counting money and giving change.

Multiplication patterns

Multiplication can be introduced through repeated addition patterns

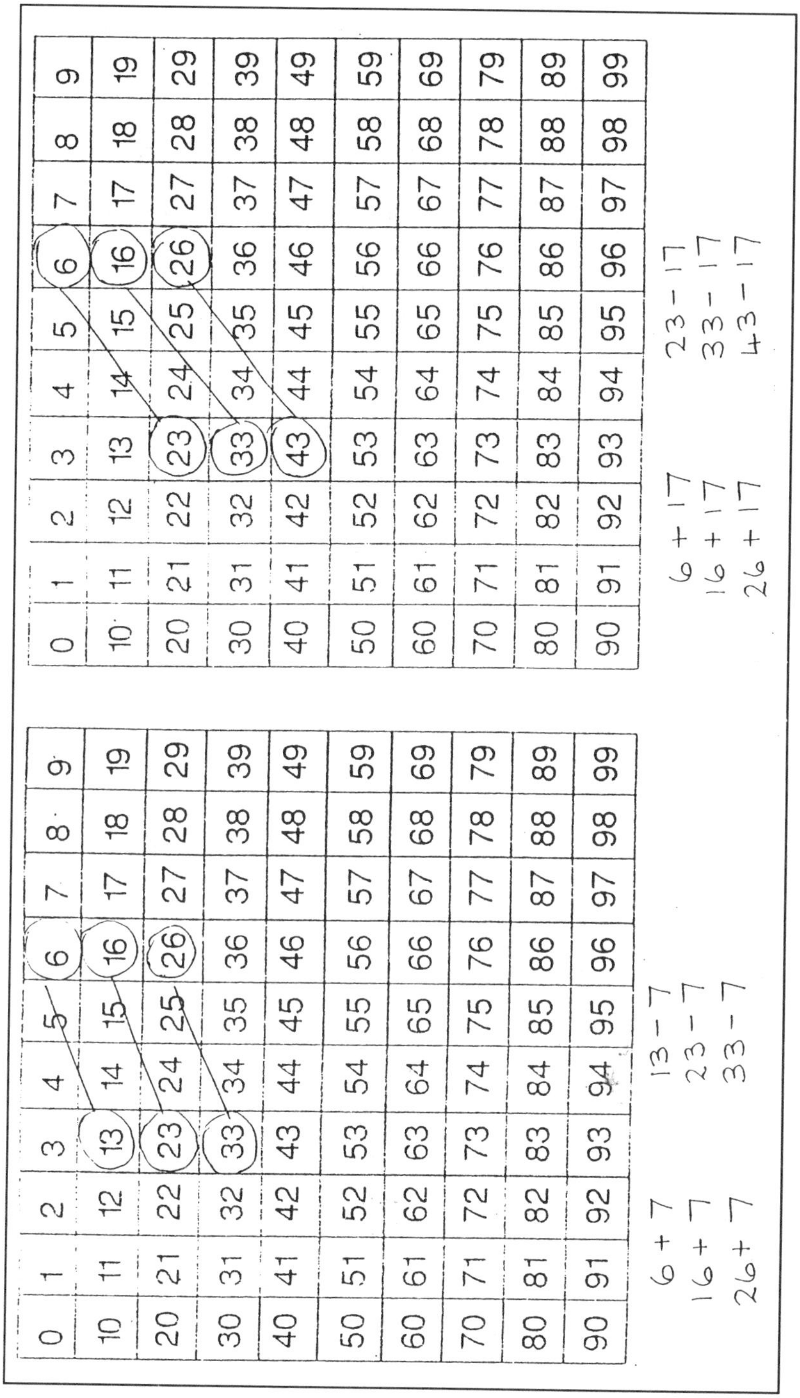

Figure 11.7 Related addition and subtraction patterns on a number square

using a numberline and 'colouring-in' patterns on a number square. Children should also be given opportunities to operate multiplication in real-life contexts, for example, in multiple buying where one item costs 3p. How much will five items cost? Other activities can include problem-solving with objects – for example, one car has 4 wheels. How many wheels for 8 cars? These problems can be more effectively solved if children are shown how to record a table of the 'pattern' – for example:

Cars	Wheels
1	4
2	8
3	12
etc.	

If children can explain the rule, this represents a first step between finding patterns and establishing early algebraic generalisations. The above example represents a model of the 'rule' $n = 4x$ or 'any number multiplied by four'. This type of activity can be carried out with shapes, models children have built, plates of cakes, bags of marbles, in fact almost anything that can be represented in multiple form. A useful resource is *The Pattern Factory* published by Jonathan Press (address supplied at the back of the book).

Learning tables

Multiplication tables enable children to develop instant recall of multiplication facts. Knowing the two, ten and five times tables should be regarded as a minimum for KS1. However, it is important that learning tables is not just a mechanical exercise but includes recognising the relationships between the tables and using the range of patterns in the tables to solve problems in everyday contexts.

Division: grouping and sharing

There are two processes that can be used for developing children's understanding of division and this can confuse children in the early stages. (See Figure 11.8.) To avoid confusion, it is better if the process of *grouping* is used to introduce division because it leads children to consider remainders from the outset (see Figure 11.9).

Sharing should be used in relation to 'equal shares' and for later work, in developing an understanding of fractions of numbers (see Figure 11.10). Both methods of division can be understood more effectively if children are presented with opportunities to create different arrays of objects or pictures, or use Cuisenaire rods, to demonstrate the principle. For example:

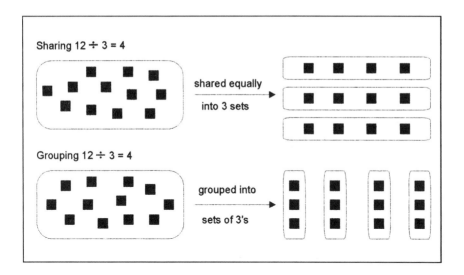

Figure 11.8   Sharing and grouping

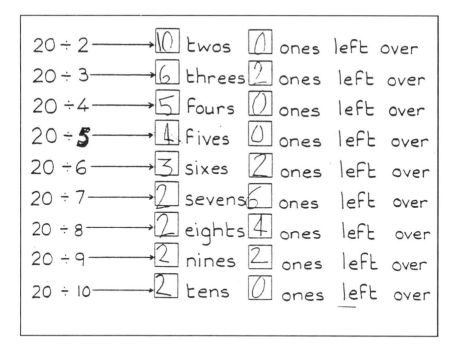

Figure 11.9   Building division patterns with remainder

Grouping

Grouping objects can be introduced using a variety of arrays and can include the principle of remainder; e.g. 13 ÷ 2.

Sharing 12

OOOOOOOOOOOO   OOOOOO   OOOO
                OOOOOO   OOOO
                         OOOO

In this way children are also able to make connections between multiplication and division processes and recognise the inverse relationship between the processes, i.e.:

12 × 1	6 × 2	4 × 3
1 × 12	2 × 6	3 × 4
12 ÷ 1	12 ÷ 2	12 ÷ 3
12 ÷ 12	12 ÷ 6	12 ÷ 4

Fractions

Early work with fractions is usually carried out through practical work with cutting apples, cakes, sandwiches, etc., into halves and quarters. This is then developed through spatial representations of dividing regular shapes into equal parts, through folding and cutting paper shapes and later through children drawing round shapes on paper or drawing shapes on squared paper and dividing them into halves, quarters, etc. These experiences with fractions lead on to later work with fractional relationships between numbers, where the *whole* number array can be divided into equal parts and children can begin to understand the relationships between equivalent fractions and possibly begin to work with addition of fractions (see Figure 11.10).

Applying number skills to real-life problems

For children to use their number skills to solve real-life problems they need to know what calculations are needed. With young children, the first stages are to make a model of the problem using objects. For example, in sharing cakes, having real cakes or pretend cakes will help them to model the problem. At a later stage, children can be encouraged to draw a picture of the problem to work out the solution. A further stage is for children to represent the problem with rods or cubes. The last stage is for children to represent the problem with a 'sum'. Older children who have a good understanding of the mathematics will feel more confident in representing the problem as a 'sum'. However, in cases where children are less confident with the formal representation, they may still be able to solve the problem successfully by inventing their own strategies, which might include a combination of pictures, marks and/or numbers (see Chapter 2).

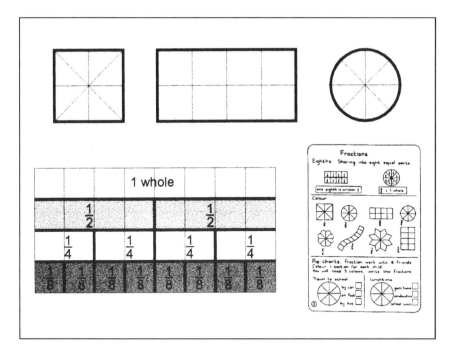

Figure 11.10   Work with fractions of shapes

Work with calculators

Pocket calculators are used routinely by adults worldwide in the course of their daily lives. It also needs to be emphasised that calculators are not a new phenomenon, but simply replacements for the tally stick, abacus, 'ready reckoners', log tables, mechanical adding machines and electronic comptometers of the past, all of which became dinosaurs with the development of the silicon chip and micro-technology. A further development in micro-technology is seen in bar-code readers, which eliminate the need to press any buttons!

In the same way that adults use calculators, it is important that children should know how they can be used to support accurate calculations when they find themselves working with large or complex numbers. However, the best aid to mathematical reasoning is the ability to process information mentally. A calculator should be used to enhance this skill and not used as a substitute. Over-reliance on a calculator can result in children performing 'mechanical' arithmetic without any thinking or reasoning involved, in much the same way as the process of doing pages of sums with cubes mentioned earlier.

Appropriate applications of a calculator

Exploring interesting patterns   For example, putting 9s into the calculator and adding 1 each time: 9 + 1, 99 + 1, 999 + 1, etc.

Generalising   For example, the result when a series of numbers, including zero are multiplied – 2 × 7 × 5 × 0 × 3 × 1 × 9 = ?

Manipulating large numbers   Giving young children confidence and experience of working with numbers beyond the traditional one or two-digit, and later, three-digit calculations.

Working with realistic numbers   Activities for young children, involving mathematical problems, are usually presented in unreal number quantities – for example shopping items costing 2p, 5p 10p, etc., instead of more realistic amounts of 49p, 1.99p; room measurements are given as 6 m by 4 m instead of 6.2 m by 4.5 m. By using a calculator, children can be invited to solve real problems rather than watered-down simulations.

Prediction   For example, 'I can thread 17 beads in 1 minute. I predict that I can thread 51 beads in 3 minutes'. This type of problem can present a useful focus for discussion because, although the prediction is calculated accurately, the result invariably does not match the prediction.

Negative numbers   Often a starting point for discussion about negative numbers comes when a child is experimenting with subtraction on a calculator through repeated subtraction of 1 or where the second number input is bigger than the first, for example 3 − 4. This can be explained with the help of a −10 to + 10 numberline and reference to real-life applications such as cold weather temperatures and using a lift in a building which has a basement below ground-floor level.

Number investigations   One of the first and well-known investigations is 'square sums' that was developed as part of the CAN (Calculator-Aware Number) Project in the 1980s (Shuard *et al.*, 1991). Children draw a square, choose a number to put inside and then try to find four numbers to put on the corners that, together, will total the number inside (see Figure 11.11).

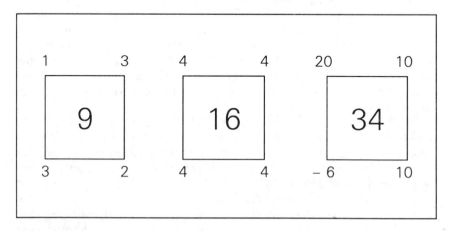

Figure 11.11   'Square Sums' using addition and subtraction

Useful ideas for activities using calculators can be found within the BEAM materials (address given at the back of the book).

Factors influencing standards of achievement in number

Finally it is important to emphasise factors highlighted by Ofsted (1993a) as influencing standards of achievement in number. Where practice was seen as good, there was evidence of:

- well planned work which established clear lines of progression based upon sound assessment of the pupils' abilities;
- teaching which enabled the children to talk confidently about number, to ask and respond to relevant questions, and to receive clear explanations about number operations and relationships;
- mental work including the learning of tables and number facts and involving, where appropriate, the application of number to real-life problems;
- purposeful investigation which strengthened the pupils' understanding of number patterns and relationships, often through work in other subjects such as science and technology;
- consistent and constructive marking of work, including a clear analysis of errors and what needed to be done about them [see Chapter 15];
- well organised classrooms in which the teacher and pupils made effective use of a range of printed and practical materials and achieved a good mix of mental, oral, practical and written number activities.

Summary

Within the context of 'bread and butter' number work, consideration has been given to the current emphasis on shifting from ideas of mechanical 'pencil and paper' arithmetic, to the use of much more dynamic and purposeful activities that enable children to develop their powers of mental reasoning. Strategies have been offered which enable children to develop their mental facility with number, through exploring patterns and applying rules in open-ended mathematical investigations. Strategies have also been offered to assist children with solving real-life problems through encouraging them to use methods they are comfortable with, and recording their solutions with objects or on paper, using pictures or numbers. A rationale for the use of calculators has been presented including appropriate contexts for their application to mathematical work in school. Finally, threads are drawn by highlighting factors reported by Ofsted (1993a) as promoting good standards of achievement in number.

12

Planning mathematical activities
2. Different contexts

Contexts for mathematical learning

Opportunities for mathematical learning arise from every aspect of school life (see Figure 12.1).

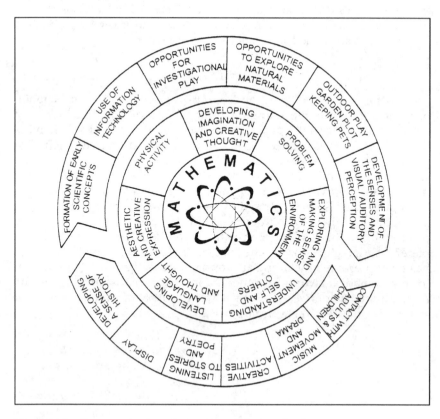

Figure 12.1   Contexts for learning mathematics in school

150

Planning crosscurricular work

The young child is exposed to a myriad of learning experiences, some of which are brief and transitory and others of which are developed and sustained over a period of time. Crosscurricular work can create a focus for young children to make sense of the world around them by enabling them to make connections between their learning experiences. According to Julie Fisher (1996), it enables children to cross the boundaries between traditional subjects and, through activities and experiences, children are able to see how different 'subject' skills can be brought together and applied in real-life situations.

The skill of the teacher lies in planning crosscurricular work which is relevant, interesting and appropriate to the needs of the children. One of the difficulties that may arise from long and medium-term planning is that, because the content of crosscurricular work is planned in advance, the moment of relevance may have passed or timing may become inappropriate. A classic example is represented by a personal experience of a Monday morning in January when there had been heavy snow the night before. The Year 1 and Year 2 children were taken out to build a snow dragon, which became the centre of interest for the day through story writing, measuring the dragon and making a large snow dragon for the wall. In the next room the Year 3 class were busy with their topic on 'Tropical Rainforests'. It is, therefore, important that content should be planned with a certain amount of flexibility, where plans can be adjusted or changed according to circumstances. In the case of the 'Snow Dragon', the planned topics of 'Journeys' suddenly included another dimension. We were able to include children who have travelled to school by sledge that week on 'Our journeys to school graph', and talk about how people travelled over snow (not included in the topic plan!).

Starting points

Sarah Tann (1988) considers that one of the most effective ways to plan crosscurricular work is to consider the following strategies. Starting from:

- a concept, for example, growth, pattern, time;
- an interest, for example, a class visit, a special event, a story, toys; and
- a problem, for example, litter in the playground, making a maths game, creating a class shop.

Topic-related crosscurricular work can be planned to be carried out over a few weeks, a few days or occur as a spontaneous happening. It is particularly important that the work is not wholly teacher engineered, that there is opportunity for children to have some input in the direction the work may take. Bright suggestions from children can add impetus and stimulate interest and excitement in the work (for the teacher as well as the children!).

Mathematical opportunities arising from crosscurricular work

In incorporating mathematical elements into crosscurricular work, 'natural' connections can be established through, for example:

- *Science* Exploration of materials and properties of shapes, measurement, collecting and interpreting data, recording changes in the weather.
- *English* Stories, poems and rhymes with a mathematical focus, making books; writing stories and acting out 'mathematical' plays, for example, *Three Billy Goats Gruff*.
- *Information technology* Software for data handling, recognition and exploration of shape, playing number games; exploration of space and distance (using programmable toys such as Roamer, Pip and Pixie).
- *History* Sequencing events, language related to the passage of time, for example, long ago, old, new, last year; biographical life lines, time lines and time cycles (seasons); making a birthday graph; stories set in a historical setting; story of the history of 'time'.
- *Geography* Numbers, patterns, 2D and 3D shapes in the environment; following directions through the language of movement and position, for example, up, down, left, right, in front, behind, etc. Making maps, plans and models of real or imaginary places. Stories about journeys and different countries, or in relation to children's holiday experiences. Routes from home to school or charting 'Teddy's walk'; collecting and interpreting data, for example, different types of houses; using programmable toys; maths trails and shape hunts.
- *Music* Number and colour songs, repeated clapping and percussion patterns, sound sequences, timing – fast/slow, pitch – high/low.
- *Art, craft and design* Colour, patterns, 2D and 3D shapes, symmetry, tessellation translation and rotation; spirals, spaces and lines; measurement; making a maths game.
- *Design and technology* Making a puppet theatre, creating a class shop, designing a class book, making a working model, etc. all involve elements of using and applying number, shape, space and measures.
- *PE and dance* Properties of shapes through handling balls, quoits, beanbags, etc. Awareness of space through position and movement. Patterns and sequences of movements. Language of measures – high, low, fast, slow, etc. Counting games, such as throwing and catching, bouncing balls, skipping. Groupings, working in pairs, threes, fours, etc.
- *RE* Seasonal celebrations, family and birthday celebrations. Cooking special food, making decorations, stars, paper-chain patterns, Islamic patterns, work on families, collecting and interpreting data. Counting stories, for example *Noah's Ark*.

In all areas, opportunities can be found for counting objects, actions or people.

Mathematical themes

Within the framework of a scheme of work for mathematics, many teachers choose to highlight a particular area or theme for a sequence of units of work. With young children a focus can be taken for a 'Maths Day' or a 'Maths Morning' which can be planned around a particular theme. Within these themes, children are able to explore different aspects of related mathematical ideas, which may be drawn from different attainment targets and different levels at KS1. This is seen to be a very useful strategy to establish a focus for children to use and apply their mathematical skills through a variety of connected experiences. In a report on the teaching and learning of number in primary schools, it was found that 'The pupils whose understanding of number was most secure were those taught in classes where they encountered a variety of experiences which helped them to appreciate mathematical relationships' (Ofsted, 1993a). Possible themes are given in Figure 12.2.

Colour	Size	Patterns	Shape	Estimating
Shopping	Phone numbers	Hands and feet	Lego maths	Maths with sweets
Time	Teddy maths	School maths	Christmas maths	Pairs
Party maths	Pasta maths	Grouping	All about 'five'	Boxes

Figure 12.2   Mathematical themes

Mathematical events

It is useful from time to time to create a spotlight on mathematics by organising a special event. Planning a maths assembly can create a lively focus for whole-class participation, which can be made more special if parents are invited to share in the experience. Competitions such as the following can be organised:

- design a number poster;
- guess the number of cubes in a tin;
- who can find the most ways to make 99? (using a calculator);
- who can do the most 'add 10' sums in a minute? (throwing a cube on to a number square, adding 10 to the number it lands on);
- who can fit the most objects into a matchbox?
- who can thread the most beads in a minute?
- who can do the greatest number of ball bounces?
- who can get dressed the quickest after PE?

Maths trails

A school environment lends itself to creating maths trails, which can be simple collecting trails that can be carried out in the classroom – for example, 'Collect a set' tasks such as 'objects that roll' or '5 things longer than a pencil'. These can be extended to children exploring the school, to count doors; how many different circles they can find, etc. Staff can work together to plan an organised maths trail where children are asked to find things in different areas of the school. Figure 12.3 represents an activity from a maths trail planned in a nursery school.

1 ~ Shapes

Where it is :   Front entrance door.

Look at the large circle on the door; the door as a rectangle; and the rectangles within the door.

Suggested questions:

- "What shapes can you see?"
- "What colours can you see in the circle?"
- "Can you touch some writing?"
- "What colour is the door?"
- "Can you see any smaller shapes inside the door shape?"
- "What shape is that?"
- "How many rectangles are in this door?"
- "Look around, can you spot any other rectangles?" e.g. bricks in the wall.

Mathematical language to be encouraged:

shapes   colours   counting   pattern

Figure 12.3 Sample of an activity from a nursery maths trail

Opportunities for children to work together

Planning activities for children to work together on an activity provides opportunities for peer discussion, collective problem-solving and opportunities for them to learn from each other.

Co-operative play

Very young children are more likely to be involved in parallel play, where they are sharing materials but not actually working together. The first forms of co-operative activity often arise from 'role-play' games – for example, in house play, where roles are often decided by the children before the 'play' begins, and also in activities such as construction, where different 'roles' are established through negotiation (or adult arbitration!). Opportunities for mathematical moments can arise from the following co-operative play scenarios:

- *Real-life role play* Railway set, garage, shop, café, farm, post office, house, zoo, airport, dressing up, puppet theatre, etc.
- *Construction* Junk construction, bricks, pattern blocks, Duplo/Lego, small and large commercial construction kits.
- *Exploring materials* Sand and water; modelling with clay, dough or Plasticine; natural objects (seeds, cones, conkers, shells, etc.).
- *Games* Skittles, dominoes, board, card and dice games, computer games.
- *Outdoor activities* Large equipment – climbing frames, barrels, tyres, nets, slide, earthmounds. Wheeled toys – push-carts, pedal cars, tricycles, scooters. Small equipment – balls, hoops, beanbags, skipping ropes, quoits, etc. Gardening equipment – wheelbarrows, spades, buckets, rakes. Playground markings – number snakes and squares, hopscotch courts, target rings, etc.

It is important to emphasise that simply providing young children with such activities does not guarantee that they have gained any mathematical experiences. When teachers actively involve themselves during play sessions they are able to stimulate *epistemic* learning behaviours through asking questions, encouraging the development of ideas and promoting the use of correct mathematical language. This does not mean that a teacher has to direct activities all the time. It merely emphasises that sensitive intervention at some point during the play can create a focus for a mathematical moment to take place.

Collaborative work

With older children, activities can be planned for collaborative work where joint effort is required to carry out a task. For infant children, this is more successful if activities are planned for children to work in pairs. When children work together they have less need for continuous support from the teacher. In *Curriculum Matters 3: Mathematics 5–16* (DES, 1985), it is emphasised that 'Co-operative activities contribute to the mathematical development of pupils through the thinking, discussion and mutual refinement of the ideas which normally take place'.

The following activities lend themselves well to this kind of work:

- measuring tasks – length/height of objects or body parts with arbitrary or standard units including estimation activities (see Figure 12.4);
- weighing tasks – estimating, balancing and counting objects;
- capacity tasks – estimating, pouring and counting activities;
- timing games – including estimation activities;
- collecting data and making graphs;
- number and shape investigations and problem-solving activities;
- board and dice games including money games;
- computer-number and shape games; and
- work with programmable toys.

For larger groups of children to work together co-operatively requires the group to be no more than four to six children and an adult working with the group to direct a common task, where all children are expected to participate. If managed well, group work presents a good opportunity for assessment (see Chapter 13).

Shape, space and measures

Many of the activities relating to shape, space and measures can be seen to arise naturally from the different practical contexts discussed in this chapter. It is perhaps important to re-emphasise that there is no substitute for exploring real materials and shapes and measuring and comparing real objects. Pictures on paper cannot provide the visual or spatial experiences required for children to understand fully the properties of shapes, or the understanding gained from discussions related to sorting shapes, building with 3D shapes and modelling with junk, making pictures or patterns with 2D shapes, folding or cutting 2D shapes or cutting open 3D cartons.

Similarly with measures, children need to have experiences of making comparisons between real objects and real quantities of water or sand. They need to be actively involved in measuring, balancing, pouring and timing games using arbitrary and standard units, if skills of estimation and accuracy in measuring are to be developed.

Helping children to tell the time is perhaps the only activity where pencil and paper practice actually supports learning, because we wish to draw children's attention to time patterns where, for example, they are presented with the 'rule' for o'clock – 'the big hand is always on the twelve'. Through making different 'times' on cardboard clocks and recording these times using clock faces on paper, children can demonstrate that they can apply the rule. To use real clocks is not practical and to use real time would take for ever!

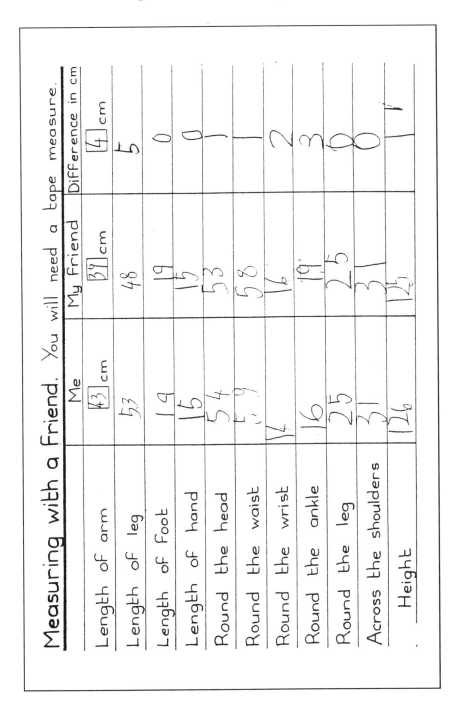

Figure 12.4 Example of a collaborative activity – 'Measuring with a Friend'

Handling Data

Activities for collecting, recording and interpreting data arise naturally from crosscurricular work and practical maths activities. Early work with handling data starts at nursery level with children sorting, classifying, counting and comparing objects, which can lead on to them collecting simple data and creating graphing pictures. Examples of different types of graphing pictures are presented in Figure 12.5.

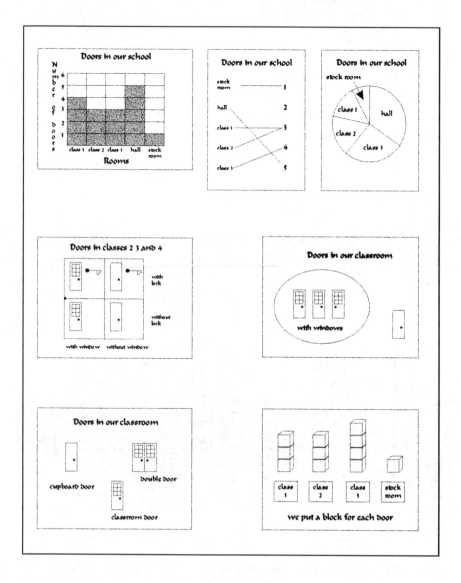

Figure 12.5 Examples of graphing pictures

It is important that graphs are not just representational pictures but used as a focus for making comparisons and discussing numerical relationships (see Figure 12.6). Data collection can also be used to inform decision-making. For example:

A class of children planned to invite their mums for tea. A questionnaire was sent home asking mums to fill in whether they wanted jam or cheese sandwiches and whether they wanted tea or coffee to drink. From the results of the questionnaire, recorded as a tally chart, the children were able to establish how many jam and cheese sandwiches to make and how many cups of coffee and tea were needed.

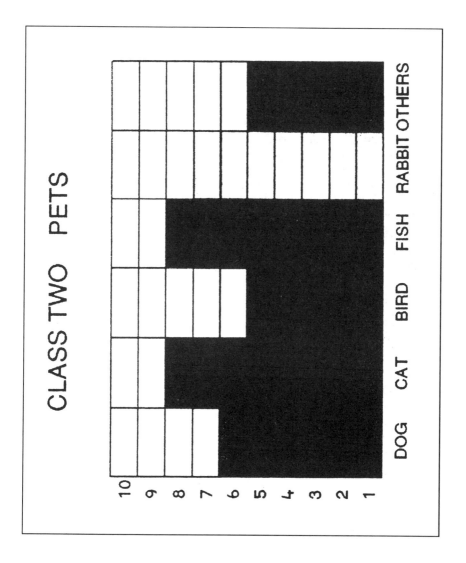

Figure 12.6   Representing and interpreting data using a computer

There are many good computer programs for early work on representing data with a graph. A particularly good series is *Counting Pictures, Counter* and *Counter Plus*. The series starts with simple picture graphs, tally charts and block graphs and moves on to more developed work with block graphs and it introduces pie charts. The third programme in the series develops block graphs and pie charts further and introduces line graphs, plotted points and scatter diagrams (suppliers' addresses are given at the back of the book).

In addition to graph work, children working at level 2 can be introduced to the first principles of working with co-ordinates, through activities involving marking positions on a grid or finding 'addresses'.

Use of open-ended tasks

Where children are expected to demonstrate evidence of their understanding, whether with objects, through pictures or with written mathematical statements, the planning of open-ended tasks gives children opportunities to demonstrate their potential, as well as making the work more challenging. Children are also given more ownership of the work because open-ended tasks place the responsibility for making the decisions involved in processing the task with the child. For the teacher, open-ended tasks can be used effectively to differentiate for ability because they are open to negotiated outcomes (see Chapter 17). The following list represents just a few ideas from many that can be devised to create a range of open-ended activities for young children:

- different ways to line up 3 red cars and 2 blue cars;
- find different shapes that can be made with 4 triangles and 4 squares;
- collect a set of different circles;
- how far can you count?
- find different ways to make 10;
- playing the 'Add 10' game with a number square;
- find different pairs of numbers with a difference of 5;
- find different ways to spend £1.00 (using a set of cards with priced articles);
- 'square sums' with a calculator;
- investigating magic squares;
- find different ways to represent $\frac{1}{4}$ of 16 on squared paper;
- find different ways to arrange 5 squares on squared paper (polyominoes);
- investigating tangrams;
- investigating symmetry with capital and lower-case letters of the alphabet;
- find different ways to balance a reading book;
- find different ways to measure a table;
- find different ways to fill a jug; and
- record pairs of times showing a difference of 10 minutes.

A further benefit to the teacher is that the design of recording activities requires just a title in most cases. Any specific instructions on ways of recording can be given through an example under the title if required or, with older children, this can be discussed and presented on a flipchart for a group, or chalkboard for the whole class to see. In most cases, it means that teachers do not have to spend hours designing worksheets and photocopying them, as this type of work lends itself to being carried out in exercise books of plain or squared paper, unless required for display. If teachers plan for young children to work on paper, it is important that any lettering used for the title and/or for examples of recording should be the best model they can produce for children to follow. The advent of computers and the facility to use different fonts has made it much easier for teachers to create well presented text and labels for displays. It is worth re-emphasising that when children are expected to write or draw on paper, they should be given a pressure-pad to rest on to enable them to carry out the work as effectively as possible.

Use of closed tasks

There are important times when closed tasks are necessary, for example, as an extension to teaching a certain skill, where a level of mastery is required before children are able to use the skill in more open-ended investigational situations (see Figures 11.5 and 11.10). Teachers may wish to devise a series of closed tasks as an assessment test at the end of a series of lessons on a particular area of mathematics to establish what children have learnt. There may also be times when a short series of closed tasks relating to a particular skill is presented to children as a revision exercise. The kinds of recording tasks that do not support the development of decision-making in learning or offer scope for young children to demonstrate their potential are:

- repetitive pages of colouring objects or shapes;
- drawing rings around specific pictures denoting the heaviest/lightest, etc.;
- filling in words or numbers in boxes within prescribed statements; and
- repetitive pages of closed 'sums'.

Whilst the list appears very short, many published scheme workbooks and textbooks for children comprise activities which can be categorised as one, or a combination of, the four elements mentioned above.

Sources of curriculum support materials

One reason for the popularity of published schemes is that activities are ready made and teachers do not have the problem of continuously thinking up ideas for activities. Thankfully, this has been greatly helped in recent years by the production of good-quality publications which present a wealth of ideas and photocopiable masters for teachers to use or adapt for their own use in classrooms. These can be found in bookshops, publishing catalogues, through visits to educational exhibitions, such as the annual education show at the NEC in Birmingham, by attending mathematical conferences or by subscribing to professional journals, such as *Child Education*. Publishers are always responding to recent developments. For example, there are now many publications on the market which feature nursery mathematics and the development of mental arithmetic skills in young children. It is important for teachers to be selective in their choice of published materials. They are not cheap and may turn out to be of little use. Most educational publishers have an inspection service for books where teachers can 'try before they buy' on a sale or return basis.

Summary

This chapter has attempted to present a broad picture of the range of mathematical experiences that can generate opportunities for effective learning in nursery and infant classrooms. A variety of different examples have been presented, representing the wide range of mathematical activities that can be planned for within different contexts. Through discussion in this, and the previous chapter, an attempt has been made to convey that mathematical activities for young children should not be confined to mechanical 'pencil and paper' exercises, but represent a variety of interesting and challenging tasks that develop children's mathematical skills in a range of mental and practical contexts. If developed in this way, mathematics can be one of the most interesting and exciting aspects of the curriculum to teach and, most importantly, for children to learn.

SECTION 4
Managing assessment in relation to mathematics

13

Planning for assessment

> Assessment is linked, inextricably to teaching and learning. We have to know what children have learned, where they are finding difficulties, and by implication, what new learning opportunities should be offered, in order to structure teaching and the content of lessons.
>
> (Clemson and Clemson)

The *Non-Statutory Guidance* for administering the National Curriculum states that 'Teacher Assessment is part of everyday classroom activity' (NCC, 1991, para. 6); and that time has to be planned for assessment opportunities to be incorporated as an integral part of teaching in all primary schools. The guidance from SCAA (1995a) recommended that the equivalent of one hour per day should be spent on the teaching and learning of mathematics. During that time, some form of planned assessment should take place.

Fitness for purpose

It is important for teachers to decide which assessment opportunities should be planned into their timetable on the basis of 'fitness for purpose'. It is important for teachers to decide which elements require priority in terms of planning regular assessment opportunities and which ones are only required on an intermittent basis. Ruth Sutton (1991) suggests that:

> it helps to consider the statements of attainment in terms of the *frequency* with which they are encountered as children progress through the key stage. By the

163

end of the key stage, all attainment targets will have been checked, but some of them are encountered regularly, while others may only crop up once or twice.

This can be seen in relation to Statement 5 in the Desirable Outcomes for mathematics – 'recognise and use numbers to 10'. Children are involved in recognising and using numbers in many different contexts during the course of their time in school. The teacher does not have to make an assessment each time this occurs, but select appropriate opportunities to make an informed judgement.

Teachers have a range of assessment techniques at their disposal: observation, questioning, testing or self-assessment. In deciding which strategy to use, teachers need to be clear about whom and what they are assessing. When assessing younger children, strategies may be different from those used with older children.

Validity

Attention needs to be paid to factors that might create bias or inconsistency, thus rendering the process invalid in empirical terms. For example, in assessing mathematical competence, a child who finds reading difficult may not be able to read a mathematical question. However, if the question was presented orally, the child might be able to perform the task competently. According to Ruth Sutton (1991), 'the assessment has to focus on what you want to find out about'. In the case of the example given, the focus should be on mathematical competence and not reading ability.

Reliability

In carrying out assessments teachers should ensure that the process is as reliable as possible through giving attention to variables that can affect the outcome of the assessment. The main variables that are likely to affect the process of assessment are:

- Inconsistency in interpretation of the criteria, where the meaning of criteria statements can be interpreted differently by different people carrying out the assessment. For example, the statement 'beginning to develop mathematical understanding through practical activities and talking about them' is open to interpretation and the use of such criteria needs to be discussed by all staff involved in assessment in order that consistent interpretations can be made.
- The amount of involvement of the person carrying out the assessment can affect the outcome. With young children carrying out practical tasks it is natural for teachers to try to give them the best chance of success, maybe by simplifying the oral phrasing of a task when a child indicates that he or she has not understood what he or she is expected to do. However, care has to be taken that prompting and guiding does not take the form of showing children what to do or doing it for them!

It is therefore important that teachers establish collective guidelines on ways to administer assessment tasks.

- Teachers also need to be careful that preconceptions of children do not colour the way in which their performance is judged – for example, having different expectations of neatly dressed children compared with scruffy children, or having preconceived expectations of a child on the basis of an elder sibling's reputation (good or bad).
- The environmental situation in which an assessment takes place can significantly affect the outcome. Teachers need to consider the application of consistency where possible. Fitting assessments into spare moments takes no account of the backdrop of distraction from classroom noise or interruptions; an assessment carried out on a Monday morning is likely to generate a different outcome from one carried out on a Friday afternoon when children may be tired.

Standardisation of procedures

A key element of assessment is the establishment of consensus about standardisation of procedures through shared experiences of all staff involved in the process. This should be carried out prior to any planned assessment taking place and a set of procedures for carrying out assessments should be established that represent 'the best fit between purpose, validity, reliability and manageability' (Sutton, 1991). The process of standardisation should be seen as the professional tool which attempts to safeguard children from inaccurate and unfair judgements made through invalid and unreliable assessment procedures. However, it is by no means an easy process to establish consensus in terms of standardisation. Teachers often hold strong personal views which can create tension and disagreement and principles may have to be implemented on a trial and review basis phased in over time. Ruth Sutton (1991) advises that 'standardisation is greatly helped by a prevailing atmosphere of professional confidence, mutual respect and a wish to find consensus, in the best interests of the children'.

Managing assessment opportunities in the classroom

Time management

Consideration of time management and ways in which classes are organised is needed so that teachers are able to plan and implement assessment opportunities within their teaching programmes.

Use of adult helpers

One strategy which can assist in planning for assessment opportunities is to use time when other adults are available in the classroom. As Headington (1997) states, 'assistants can support teachers by supervising groups of children carrying out mathematical tasks, or supervise a group of children carrying out art work whilst the teacher works with a group doing mathematical work'. To enable this principle of worksharing to be as effective as possible it is important to ensure that assistants are well briefed beforehand and that the outcomes of a session are discussed afterwards. Assistants can also be involved in assessment by recording notes about children's performance during teaching sessions (Headington, 1997).

Classroom organisation

Alexander *et al.* (1992) state that 'classroom management and organisation are particularly crucial to the quality of assessment'. A classroom organisation where children are encouraged 'to be autonomous, to work collaboratively and to work on open-ended tasks' (CUPA, 1992, G1) can reduce demands on the teacher. Resources should be organised to encourage independent learning, where children have easy access to mathematical apparatus which is well stored and clearly labelled. Additionally, children should be familiar with procedures when they are 'stuck' and to know how to work collaboratively – so they can help each other, (*ibid.*, G2).

David and Wendy Clemson (1994) suggest a set of strategies for children to use in lesson time when they cannot get on, which can also be made into a visual aid in the classroom for children who are not yet readers (see Figure 13.1).

Figure 13.1 Strategies for children who are 'stuck'
Source: Clemson and Clemson, 1994, p. 136

Planning group assessment

It is not feasible to assess more than a few children at a time with any real measure of accuracy and it is useful if children are clustered by ability for the purpose of assessment. In this way a teacher is able to obtain a more accurate impression of an individual child's performance in relation to the 'norm' of the group. Teachers are also able to set tasks appropriate to the generalised ability of the group. Individual children's performance can then be assessed against a manageable set of clear criteria which define the knowledge to be learnt and the skills to be acquired. For example, for a balancing activity with Year 1 children, the criteria might be:

- uses a balance correctly;
- chooses suitable material for the task;
- uses appropriate language when balancing;
- can balance and count objects correctly; and
- can record results in pictorial and/or written form.

Shorrocks *et al.* (1993) recognise that observation of the behaviour of one child when operating in a group can be difficult because a child may be reluctant to contribute to a group's efforts and decision-making. In these instances, intervention from the teacher may be necessary to encourage the child to exhibit behaviour according to the evidence required.

Planning the recording of assessment

Planning how assessments are to be recorded is a critical part of the process. In the early days of the National Curriculum many teachers found themselves bogged down with completing paperwork relating to assessment, to the point where they felt that their teaching was suffering as a result. In the Dearing Report (1994) the situation was reviewed and significant modifications were made to reduce the workload for teachers. In the process of development, schools have become much more circumspect in establishing procedures for recording assessments, managing to reduce the bureaucracy by adopting a whole-school system that is easily managed by all staff involved. Strategies for managing the recording of assessment are discussed in detail in Chapter 20.

Moderation

One of the most difficult principles of implementing an effective system of formative assessment for mathematics in schools is maintaining consistency of judgement. It is recognised that judgement on children's performance can vary significantly in relation to differences in teachers' values – for example, some teachers may value neatness of presentation very highly, where others may value methods of working as more important. Shorrocks *et al.* (1993) state that the terminology used to define criteria for assessment in terms of 'performance verbs', such as *understand, explain, predict, demonstrate, use, know,* is imprecise. It can, therefore, be difficult to establish a standardised interpretation in relation to children's performance. For example, *understands* can mean different things to different people. It can also be interpreted differently according to a child's stage of development.

Agreement trials/standardisation

It is recognised that it is important for teachers working together to share their perceptions about making judgements on children's performance. They should establish, as far as possible, a common understanding about expectations to be set and standards of achievement that are likely to be achieved at the different stages of children's development throughout the school. Many schools hold regular *agreement trialling* meetings to discuss and monitor levels of consistency (CUPA, 1992, E1). This may include examining specimens of children's work and reviewing methods of teaching. It may also include discussion on refining assessment procedures for the purposes of improving standardisation. In one infant school, the staff compiled 'moderation files' for mathematics and English. The files contained annotated specimens of children's work and photographs from the different years at KS1 to represent exemplars of standards of work in all the Attainment Targets at the different levels. In addition, schools are now implementing *peer observation* sessions as a further mechanism to improve levels of consistency throughout the school. Where teachers work in a team situation, perceptions of children's performance can be formally and informally shared on a daily basis and common targets established.

A policy for assessment

The perceived need to standardise procedures for assessment has resulted in schools recognising the importance of creating a whole-school policy for assessment, where procedures are formally set out for all teachers to follow throughout a school. In the City of Birmingham *Mathematics Guidelines* (1992, p. 47) it is stated that 'mathematics in school needs to have a coherent approach to assessment that is compatible with the school's overall policy for assessment'. In this way, a code of practice, generated through shared discussion of the staff, is established in order that 'results are used appropriately to inform future teaching, to ensure continuity and progression and promote higher standards' (Ofsted, 1995).

Implementing review procedures

Any system adopted as a whole-school policy should be subject to regular review as part of the school development plan. Procedures for assessment will require refinement and updating in response to changes that occur at a national and local level. The most important principle of reviewing procedures is to ensure that the assessment system operated by the school is regularly updated in terms of being the best fit for the school and the staff who use it.

The role of the assessment co-ordinator

In small schools this may be undertaken by the headteacher but in larger schools a member of staff is likely to be named as the assessment co-ordinator. According to David and Wendy Clemson (1991), the duties will include:

- providing colleagues with national and local requirements;
- ensuring that school systems are both understood and adhered to across the school;
- providing regular opportunities for evaluation and ensuring that action is taken on the agreed outcomes of evaluation meetings;
- trouble shooting;
- giving colleagues appropriate briefings prior to parents' and governors' meetings; and
- developing moderation and cross-moderation opportunities.

In addition to this, an assessment co-ordinator should be responsible for initiating staff development through in-service training and supporting new members of staff in implementing the systems for assessment adopted by the school. The assessment co-ordinator may also wish to discuss subject-related issues with subject co-ordinators. For example, assessment issues related to mathematics would be shared with the mathematics co-ordinator. Crosscurricular issues related to assessment, for example, gender or cultural considerations, will need to be discussed with the whole staff.

Summary

A programme of consistent assessment procedures should be formally documented as a whole-school policy and implemented, in a standardised form, throughout the school. The principles should be established on a 'fitness for purpose' basis through:

- the appointment of a person responsible for co-ordinating assessment procedures throughout the school;
- attention to validity, reliability and standardisation of assessment procedures;
- consideration of classroom management and organisation strategies to support the planning of assessment opportunities;
- use of a manageable system for recording assessment;
- the implementation of moderation procedures to ensure consistency in the judgement of standards of children's work; and

- the implementation of regular review procedures to ensure that the system is regularly updated.

The process of planning for assessment is not simply about considering ways to assess how children will respond to a given curriculum. It involves decisions about curriculum planning and implementation. It has to take into account the role of the teacher in the assessment process and the ways in which classrooms are organised and managed to support assessment opportunities. Assessment should be planned so that it becomes an integral part of teaching and learning. It should be valued by teachers as the professional tool which enables the monitoring of children's progress and achievements to take place within the context of a fair, consistent and easily managed system.

14

Baseline assessment

Children's mathematical knowledge and experiences represent a personal collection, built up from their time before attending school, continued through their young life at home and in school, and into their lives as adults. Thus it is not unusual, when children first enter school, for individual experiences to range from a child possessing very limited mathematical language, knowledge and skills, to a child who demonstrates a good understanding of mathematical concepts. It is important, therefore, when a child first enters compulsory schooling, for the teacher to try to find out what mathematical knowledge and skills a child has learnt, at home and/or in a nursery setting.

Historical background

In early years settings, teachers have always used the first few weeks of a new school year as a 'settling in period', where emphasis has been placed on getting to know children individually and finding out what they can do. As early as the 1930s Susan Isaacs, in partnership with colleagues at London University and Wiltshire LEA, pioneered the use of the 'infant admission card' (Wolfendale, 1993). During the 1970s many LEAs developed early diagnostic screening procedures which were designed to be administered by teachers when children entered school or during the first term of schooling. These were predominantly used for identifying significant weaknesses in children's experiences rather than as tools for identifying strengths. In recent years, with the advent of the National Curriculum, and priority accorded to raising children's levels of achievements in literacy and numeracy, teachers of reception-age children recognised that identification of children's prior knowledge in these areas enabled them to establish 'starting points' for planning more effectively, according to individual children's needs and abilities.

Entry screening at 3

Most nursery schools that offer provision for 3-year-olds operate some form of baseline screening on entry. This is to identify any obvious physical, auditory or visual discrimination problems that may require support and to gain a picture of children's learning experiences prior to entry. These are used as guidelines for planning purposes and to monitor individual children's progress. Entry screening often takes the form of interviews with children's parents, combined with a simple series of orally explained practical tasks administered to individual children on entry – for example, finding out the child's dominant hand, whether he or she can build a tower of blocks, thread beads or name pictures of shapes, how far he or she can count and write numbers, etc.

DfEE: statutory instruments for baseline assessment

Baseline assessment is compulsory for all children starting school in reception classes from September 1998 as a statutory requirement. Draft proposals for a *National Framework for Baseline Assessment* (SCAA, 1996b) set out the following guidelines.

Purposes of baseline assessment

Baseline assessment schemes should provide formative and diagnostic information to the teacher. To achieve this the assessment should:

- identify the child's strengths and learning needs;
- enable the teacher to plan appropriate teaching and learning activities to meet the child's needs;
- identify the child's individual learning needs including special educational needs;
- provide information that will inform discussion with parents about their child's learning and progress.

(SCAA, 1996b)

What should be assessed?

It is recommended that baseline assessment schemes should be related to the six areas of learning set out in the Desirable Outcomes, with an emphasis on literacy and numeracy. However, there needs to be scope within a scheme to assess children who may achieve more than the stated Desirable Outcomes, and for children who are not yet at that stage.

Mode of assessment

The documentation recommended that baseline assessment procedures should be 'rooted in normal classroom practice and rely on observations made of the children working on familiar types of activities' (SCAA, 1996b). However, the use of standard tasks designed to assess specific aspects of children's learning was seen as valuable, providing that the tasks related to normal classroom activities and were unobtrusive to the children (*ibid.*).

Manageability

Baseline assessment schemes should be as manageable as possible in the classroom. They should involve the minimum amount of paperwork and be able to draw on the support of NNEB and classroom assistants to help with the process wherever possible.

Key principles of baseline assessment

These are set out under two categories. The first category identifies the *essential principles* required of all baseline assessment schemes. The second category identifies *additional principles* which a national framework would encourage as features of good practice.

Essential principles

- ensure equal entitlement for all children to be assessed, including those children for whom English is an additional language;
- be sufficiently detailed to identify individual children's learning needs, including special educational needs, in order to support effective and appropriate planning for teaching and learning;
- enable children's later progress to be monitored effectively;
- involve parents/carers in partnership with the school;
- take place in the first half term of the child's entry to the reception class (or year one if the child enters school at that point);
- focus as a minimum on early literacy and numeracy;
- be unobtrusive for children;
- be manageable for teachers;
- provide outcomes which will contribute to value-added measurement.

(SCAA, 1996b)

Additional principles

- contribute to the child's attainment record over the key stage;
- build on assessments and records from pre-school providers;
- include accounts of
  personal and social development
  physical development
  creative development
  knowledge and understanding of the world;
- be an integral part of the school's assessment policy.

(*Ibid.*)

At the time of writing, baseline assessment scales had been published by SCAA (1997f) for optional use in schools and awaiting scheme providers to submit their schemes for accreditation. This was in preparation for a national pilot of baseline assessment between September and December 1997.

Optional scales for mathematics

The optional scales for mathematics published by SCAA (1997f) comprised:

Mathematics A: Number

1. Sorts sets of objects by given criterion and explains sorting
2. Counts objects accurately
3. Shows awareness of using addition
4. Solves numerical problems with addition

Mathematics B: Using mathematical language

1. Can describe size
2. Can describe position
3. Recognises numbers to 10 and writes 1–10
4. Can explain an addition sum.

The scales are accompanied by explicit instructions for administering the test together with a class and individual record sheet. The four items in each section were selected to fulfil the following criteria:

First item	achieved by the majority of reception children (above 80 per cent) in the reception age range
Second item	achieved by between 40 and 80 per cent of children
Third item	representing the *Desirable Outcomes* standard, achieved by between 20 and 60 per cent of children
Fourth item	representing in most cases Level 1 of the National Curriculum, achieved by less than 20 per cent of children.

(Ibid.)

Interim baseline assessment checks

Many teachers devise and use baseline assessment checks for mathematics in Year 1 and Year 2 classes at the beginning of a new school year, on receiving a new class. Teachers recognise that the processes of continuous assessment are unable to take account of the effects of summer holidays, when learning outside school often takes place or, in some cases, children forget what they have learnt. By using a screening procedure at the beginning of the school year, teachers are able to plan more effectively according to children's needs. It is also seen as a useful tool when a new child joins a class mid-year or after a child has been absent for a long time. Some teachers devise 'quick checks' to precede new work in mathematics. These are designed to test whether previously taught knowledge and skills have been fully understood and to enable a better match of work to children's needs at that point in time. Interim checks devised by teachers can take the form of a short series of questions, orally administered practical tasks or a simple written test, depending upon the age and experience of the children.

It is important, however, that careful consideration is given to the design and implementation of 'home grown' assessment material:

CRITERIA FOR WRITTEN BASELINE ASSESSMENT

1. Able to count number of items to 4.
2. Able to recognise the number 5.
3. Able to count number of items to 6.
4. Able to distinguish between odd and even numbers.
5. Able to solve problems of addition using mathematical language.
6. Able to read and order numbers 1-7.
7. Able to reorder numbers from smallest to largest.
8. Able to complete a sequence counting in 2's to 10.
9. Able to complete simple addition to 5/understand mathematical symbols (+/=).
10. Able to complete simple addition to 10/understand mathematical symbols (+/=).
11. Able to name and match number to word.
12. Able to find unknown numbers equalling 4/applying their knowledge.

CRITERIA FOR MENTAL BASELINE

1. Able to count orally in 1's to 100.
2. Able to count orally in 2's to 50/100.
3. Able to count orally in 3's to 30.
4. Able to solve addition problem understanding mathematical language to 5.
5. Able to solve addition problem understanding mathematical language to 5.
6. Able to solve addition problem understanding mathematical language to 5.
7. Able to solve addition problem understanding mathematical language to 10.
8. Able to solve subtraction problem understanding mathematical language to 5.
9. Able to solve subtraction problem understanding mathematical language to 5.
10. Able to solve subtraction problem understanding mathematical language to 10.
11. Number recognition/formation - No.6.
12. Number recognition/formation - No.12.
13. Able to find unknown numbers that equal 7 using mathematical knowledge.
14. Able to solve subtraction problem understanding mathematical language to 10.
15. Able to solve subtraction problem understanding mathematical language to 10.

Figure 14.1 Interim baseline assessment check for Year 1 children

MENTAL ASSESSMENT - QUESTION SHEET

1) Count as far as you can in 1's.

2) Count as far as you can in 2's.

3) Count as far as you can in 3's.

4) 2 add 1.

5) 4 add 1.

6) 2 plus 3.

7) What is the total of 3 add 3.

8) 2 take away 1.

9) 3 subtract 2.

10) What is the difference between 6 and 8.

11) Write in figures the number 6.

12) Write in figures the number 12.

13) Write two numbers make 7.

14) 9 is more than 5 - how many more.

15) What is 10 less 6.

Figure 14.1   Interim baseline assessment check for Year 1 children (continued)

BASELINE PROFILE: MATHS - NUMBER

WRITTEN TEST - DATE: 11/02/97

NAME	1	2	3	4	5	6	7	8	9	10	11	12	COMMENTS	COURSE OF ACTION
ANEELA	✓	✓	✓	✓	✓	✓	✓	✓	✓	✓	✓	✓	Excellent addition showing understanding of the mathematical language. Able to find ways to make 4 using her knowledge of addition. Excellent grasp of add and even numbers	Aneela is ready to move on to addition of higher numbers up to 20/30. Ready for subtraction using key language and can investigate the relationship between addition and subtraction.
BRETT	✓	✓	✓	✓	✓	✓	✓	✗	✓	◁	✓	✗	Completed sequences in 1's good but not in 2's. Good knowledge of odd/even numbers. Addition to 5 good but addition to 10 problematic. Knowledge of language of addition was good. Unable to find ways to make 4	Brett will benefit from practising to count in 2's. He needs more practice in addition to 10 and number bonds/pairs to 5/10. He is not yet ready for subtraction, however once he has grasped addition to 10 he will be.
HAMZA	✓	✓	✓	✓	✓	✓	✓	✗	✓	✓	✓	✗	Addition and understanding of language was excellent. Completing sequence in 2's proved difficult as well as applying his knowledge of addition to find ways to make 4	Practice counting in 2's, move on to addition to 20/30 and reinforce number pairs/bonds. Ready for subtraction and key language and the relationship between addition and subtraction.
HENNA	✓	✗	✓	✗	✓	✓	✗	✗	✓	✗	✗	✗	Weak knowledge of odd/even numbers. Addition to 5 excellent, however addition to 10 was problematic. Understanding of language of addition was good. Sequence in 2's not correct. Could not find ways to make 4	Reinforce odd/even numbers. Practice counting in 2's. Practice addition to 10 and number pairs/bonds to 10. She is not yet ready for subtraction, however once she has grasped addition to 10 she will be.
LEANNE	✓	✓	✓	◁	◁	◁	✗	✗	◁	◁	✗	✗	Not able to identify the number 5, however her addition was promising getting some right both to 5 and 10. Good attempt at odd/even numbers. Did not understand language of addition. Counting in 2's was a problem. Couldn't find ways to make 4.	Practice number recognition - she may have misunderstood the question as she carries out some addition well. Reinforce language of addition. Leanne would benefit from practice of number pairs/bonds to 10.
SHUKRIYAH	✓	✓	✓	◁	◁	✓	✓	✓	✓	◁	✓	✓	Good attempt at odd/even numbers. Addition to 5 is excellent. Addition to 10 is promising but several mistakes. Could not complete the sequence in 2's	Practice odd/even numbers and addition to 10. She will benefit from practice on number bonds to 10 and can also begin to investigate the relationship between addition and subtraction.
SOMIA	✓	✓	✓	◁	✓	✓	✓	◁		✗			Attempt at odd/even numbers. Addition to 5 was good, however addition to 10 was problematic. She does not understand the language of addition. Sequence in 2's is not correct. Could not find ways to make 4	Reinforce odd/even numbers and language of addition. Practice counting in 2's, addition to 10 and number pairs/bonds to 10. She is not yet ready for subtraction, however once she has grasped addition to 10 she will be.

✓ - Topic mastered.   ◁ - Needs practice.   ✗ - Needs re-teaching

Figure 14.1 Interim baseline assessment check for Year 1 children (continued)

BASELINE ASSESSMENT PROFILE

MENTAL TEST - DATE: 11/02/97

NAME	1	2	3	4	5	6	7	8	9	10	11	12	13	14	15	COMMENTS	COURSE OF ACTION
ANEELA	✓	✓	X	✓	✓	✓	✓	✓	✓	✓	✓	✓	✓	✓	✓	Counting in 1's and 2,s excellent. Good attempt at 3's. Addition and subtraction excellent. Good knowledge of mathematical language.	Move on to counting in 3's and 5's. Addition and subtraction of higher numbers and focus on the relationship between them.
BRETT	△	X	X	✓	X	X	X	X	X	X	✓	✓	X	X	X	Problems counting in 2's and 3's. Counted in 1's to 49. Addition was problematic and Brett could not understand the mathematical language or carry out subtraction.	Practice counting 50-100, then in 2's. Needs to work on addition using mathematical language and also number bonds/pairs to 10. Then move on to subtraction and key language.
HAMZA	△	△	X	✓	✓	✓	✓	✓	✓	✓	✓	✓	X	X	X	Problems counting in 2's and 3's. Counted in 1's to 52. Addition was excellent with good knowledge of language. Carried out addition for subtraction problems.	Practice counting 50-100, then in 2's. Work on number bonds/pairs to 10 to aid mental recall. Addition of higher numbers and move on to subtraction and associated vocabulary.
HENNA	△	X	X	X	✓	X	X	X	X	X	✓	△	X	X	X	Problems counting in 2's and 3's. Counted in 1's to 49. Does not fully understand language of +/-. Does not understand subtraction. Reverses her 2's.	Practice counting 50-100, then in 2's. Reinforce addition to 5/10 (number pairs/bonds) and key language. Once achieved Henna can move on to subtraction to 5/10.
LEANNE	X	X	X	✓	✓	✓	X	X	X	X	✓	✓	X	X	X	Counted in 1's to 19. Could not count in 2's/3's. Good attempt at addition but did not understand some language. Did not understand subtraction.	Practice counting in 1's. Reinforce addition to 5/10 and language. Leanne can also work on number pairs/bonds. Then move on to subtraction and associated language.
SHUKRIYAH	✓	△	X	✓	✓	✓	X	X	X	X	✓	✓	✓	X	X	Counting in 1's excellent, 2's needs some practice. Language of addition gave Shukriyah some problems but a good try. She did not understand subtraction.	Move on to counting in 2's then 3's. Addition to 20 - reinforce the language. Practice number bonds/pairs to 10. Then begin work on subtraction and associated vocabulary.
SOMIA	X	X	X	X	X	✓	X	X	X	X	✓	✓	✓	X	X	Counted in 1's to 36. Could not count in 2's/3's. Addition and subtraction was a problem - little understanding of mathematical language.	Practice counting in 1's. Reinforce addition to 10 and language. Then work on subtraction to 10 and language. Practice number bonds/pairs to 10.

✓ - Topic mastered.   △ - Needs practice.   X - Needs re-teaching.

Figure 14.1   Interim baseline assessment check for Year 1 children (continued)

- Are the design and methods of implementation suitable for the age group concerned? For example, orally explained practical tasks, administered on a one-to-one basis would be appropriate for nursery-age children.
- Does the content enable you to find out what you want to know at that point in time? For example, if the first few weeks are planned to cover number, information on children's knowledge of shape is not pertinent.
- Is the 'test' easy to manage and able to be processed reasonably quickly?
- What factors need to be taken into account to ensure that the principle of fair testing takes place? For example, consistency in implementation procedures with all pupils.
- Have language levels in oral or textual contexts been considered in relation to the children being assessed? For example, language may need to be simplified for EAL children. Also some visual clues, in the way of demonstrations or explicit diagrams, may be needed to support oral and/or written instructions.
- Are the test materials well chosen to eliminate 'noise' confusions? For example, if the expectation of the task is for children to identify colour, ensure that the choice of material only presents differences in colour to the child and not differences in shape or size as well. Also, if child is asked to sort triangles from a mixed set of 2D shapes, for example, and all the triangles are red, squares blue, etc., then the child might be led into thinking that 'triangle' is connected to 'red'; that red shapes are always triangles.
- Are there any extraneous factors to be considered that may affect children's performance at the time of testing? For example, time of day, distractions from other children.
- Are the children familiar with the mathematical resources that are planned to be used? Unfamiliarity with equipment can cause uncertainty in children, or with very young children, its novelty factor may create a distraction from the expected task. For example:

A student teacher wishing to assess children in a nursery class decided to use 'Teddy counters' for the purpose. The children had not seen them before and were so fascinated by the teddies that the student found it very difficult to get the children to carry out the tasks she had planned.

A final point, with particular significance to mathematics, is the question of children's understanding of what is being said to them. According to Shorrocks *et al.* (1993):

It is natural for a teacher to respond to any uncertainty in a child's response by asking the same questions in a different way. In this way, the teacher is giving a child further opportunity to demonstrate that they can respond successfully. On the other hand it can be argued that the teacher is invalidating the outcomes, as the responses can no longer be compared, since different demands have been made of different pupils. There is a fine balancing act necessary, on the one hand to guarantee that a child understands the task and the questions being asked and, on the other, to ensure consistency of assessment and comparability of outcomes.

Validity

It is important to recognise that information from baseline assessment programmes is only valid for a very short period of time. It is a vital tool to gain 'first impressions' of children, from which to establish starting points for teaching. However, teachers should avoid fixing labels to children as a result of their performance. Once a child has settled into a class and begins to make progress, impressions can change. Therefore, as soon as teaching commences, the information remains valid simply as a record of the progress a child has made in mathematics from that date.

Establishing teaching groups

The information from baseline assessment can be a valuable guideline for grouping children for teaching purposes. According to Clemson and Clemson (1994), ability grouping within a class makes use of judgements about children's work in relation to others. They point to the danger of setting up fixed classroom 'systems' which enforce a normative distribution of performance. In the worst instances, this can lead to 'pigeon-holing' and 'labelling' children, particularly low attainers in mathematics, which can result in their problems being exacerbated by low expectations from teachers. This issue was highlighted by Anita Straker (1996) as a key concern to be addressed by the National Numeracy Project. It is, therefore, important that group membership is regularly reviewed in relation to the performance of individual children.

Diagnosis and prescription

It is important that teachers recognise that baseline assessment programmes in use at any stage should be both diagnostic and prescriptive to be effective. The process should be viewed as positive, seeking to identify the elements of mathematics a child can confidently tackle at any point in time and the level at which his or her knowledge and skill acquisition starts to falter. This information will establish the 'confidence threshold'. It is this 'confidence threshold' that enables subsequent teaching plans to be matched to the immediate and relevant needs of the child. It also ensures that continuity and progression can be effectively sustained.

Overuse of testing

Whilst the use of interim assessment can be seen as a sensible measure to check out 'confidence thresholds' regularly, it should be carried out as informally as possible. A few pertinent questions in the form of a quiz, at the beginning of a session with a small group, can often be sufficient to refresh children's memories. It is sensible to be cautious about the use of formal testing. Many teachers will themselves remember being subjected to weekly 'quick fire' mental arithmetic tests with the attendant anxiety they created. As David Winteridge (1989) states, 'over-assessing pupils can have really damaging effects, it can discourage pupils and may colour the view of mathematics held by pupils, parents and teachers'. It is important that the use of formal testing has a clear purpose: to diagnose weaknesses, to inform action or to provide a summary of a child's learning to date (for example, in the use of SATs).

Concerns relating to baseline assessment procedures

Parents' concerns

Whilst parents agree with the principle of baseline assessment, there are concerns about children who may still be 4 when they start school and children who are slow to settle into school, who may not begin to show their potential until much later. Parents fear there may be a possibility of these children being labelled as less intelligent from the outset (Maxwell and Hofkins, 1996).

Concerns of teachers

There is concern about national baseline assessment criteria being too narrowly focused and there being little scope to consider the range of talents and qualities in young children that contribute to their performance in school (Wolfendale, 1993). There is also a worry that parents, in wanting their child to do well, may place pressures on children at home to develop formal literacy and numeracy skills before coming to school and the development of important spatial, perceptual and manipulative skills may get overlooked in the process (Maxwell and Hofkins, 1996).

Children with English as an additional language

There are concerns that compulsory baseline assessment in English and mathematics will only serve to highlight the disadvantages of these children without offering anything constructive to support their development in these areas (Maxwell and Hofkins, 1996).

Use of information from baseline assessment

There are concerns that some teachers will not use the results of baseline assessment measures appropriately but maintain their own view of where reception children need to start regardless of evidence of differences in levels of competence and experience (Wolfendale, 1993).

Summary

This chapter has discussed the development of baseline assessment initiatives and the application of baseline assessment procedures in relation to the establishment of 'confidence thresholds' in mathematics. The principles of the national framework for baseline assessment, for all children on entry to reception classes, have been presented but it has not been possible to discuss the details of the procedures because, at the time of writing, they had not been formally published. However, it can be seen that the introduction of compulsory baseline assessment represents a key strategy in the drive to raise standards of achievement in literacy and numeracy. There is also mention of providing outcomes which will contribute to value-added measurement. In the longer term, it is hoped this will bring about a fairer comparison of schools than the raw test scores from SATs in published league tables.

For most teachers of young children, the process of baseline assessment is nothing new and parents generally welcome the idea. There are, however, some reservations on the establishment of a national system of baseline assessment. There is concern that a reductionist approach will be used for the purpose of ease of management in classrooms, which is unlikely to give a full picture of the children to be assessed. There is also concern about the interpretation of results which might lead to premature judgements about children's ability, particularly 4-year-olds in school and children with English as an additional language. However, as the next chapter discusses, baseline assessment is one of many strategies that teachers use in the course of their work. If used well, it can enable teachers to ensure that continuity in children's learning and progression is sustained through times of transition from nursery, or home, to full-time education in school. It can also be used at the beginning of each year, as children change from class to class during their time in school.

15

Continuous assessment

A very important part of the job of a teacher is to guide the child towards tasks where he will be able objectively to do well, but not too easily, not without putting forth some effort, not without difficulties to be mastered, errors to be overcome, creative solutions to be found. This means assessing his skills with sensitivity and accuracy, understanding the levels of his confidence and energy, and responding to his errors in helpful ways.

(Donaldson, 1978)

Continuous assessment enables the teacher to build on what children already know and understand, and directs sustained development in children's mathematical learning. As children change classes and teachers during their primary school career, it is important that continuity of learning and progression are effectively sustained. The process of continuous assessment is the tool by which teachers are able to keep track of children's progress over time. The skills of vigilance and diagnosis, combined with knowledge of the subject and ways in which children learn mathematics, are paramount in terms of the effectiveness of the procedures.

Vigilance

The effective assessment of children's mathematical performance depends on teachers being constantly alert to what is happening during the time children are carrying out mathematical work. It relies on a teacher's ability to observe how children work at practical and written tasks, judging when to interact appropriately, with probing and prompting questions. It is equally important for teachers to listen carefully to children's responses, to intervene where appropriate with clear explanations and/or demonstrations by way of help to support understanding.

Observational assessment

Observational skills are a natural human resource, they are central to our understanding of the world around us and the people we encounter during our lives. As Derek Rowntree (1977) expresses it:

How do we come to know other persons (or they us)?... In the course of our everyday interactions with them we form impressions, tentative at first perhaps, which subsequent experiences of them either increasingly confirms, complicates or else negates. Our everyday assessments of other people come mostly through observation of, reflection on, events and episodes that arise in the course of living, working and playing together.

The skill of observational assessment in the primary classroom, as Colin Conner (1991) states, 'is more than just looking'. It relies on the use of a trained eye to recognise whether children's performance demonstrates *evidence* of understanding of the mathematical knowledge and/or skills being practised at the time. It is also important that the observer recognises that observation can provide vital diagnostic and prescriptive clues from the ways in which children tackle mathematical tasks. An identified problem can be dealt with on the spot, or set as a target for a subsequent teaching session. Written notes on observations are often recorded by teachers at the time in jotter pads. Relevant information is later transferred to formal records in the form of diagnostic and prescriptive statements (see Chapter 20).

Diagnosis

Effective diagnosis is more than identifying that a child has 'a problem'. It is about defining the problem by identifying the root cause. To do this teachers have to carry out a certain amount of detective work, through observing children at work, examining evidence of recorded work and asking probing questions.

In many instances, a teacher is able to recognise that a child is experiencing problems with a particular concept or skill during the course of a teaching session and, within a few minutes, is able to rectify the situation. With more complex problems, the teacher will need to isolate the main cause of breakdown in a child's understanding. For example, a child struggling with addition of tens and units using vertical notation on first observation may appear to have a problem with the mechanics of the process. On further investigation it is discovered that the child has no real understanding of place value and therefore cannot understand what he or she is doing.

Prescription

The establishment of a diagnosis for a medical problem without prescribing a course of treatment does very little to improve the health of the patient. Similarly, in an educational context, identifying the cause of a problem a child is experiencing with mathematics without planning a course of action does very little to help the child.

There are very few teachers who cannot identify when a child has a problem with learning mathematics. However, when defining a problem displayed by a child, teachers are often side-tracked into focusing on the affective aspects of a child's problem rather than pinpointing the weaknesses in cognitive understanding. For example, records include notes such as 'lacks concentration; lacks confidence; unable to work without supervision', which says very little about the difficulties a child may be having in understanding an aspect of mathematics. A more useful statement of diagnosis would be, for example, 'Counts orally to ten but has difficulty with counting objects and recognising written numbers beyond 5 (Action: flashcard game, tracing numbers, matching objects to numbers 6–10)'.

In the above statement it can be seen that notice has also been taken of what the child *can* do (counts orally to ten). The identification of aspects of a task that a child can perform will help the teacher establish a starting point for prescribing a course of action.

Diagnostic assessment in mathematics should be used to identify strengths as well as weaknesses. It is just as important to recognise when a child is performing well and could benefit from some more challenging work. If no action is taken, the child may start to become bored, frustrated or become disruptive, and this may create a harder problem to solve!

Questioning

Teachers ask children questions about their work with the purpose of finding out what they have done and why, as well as to guide children to overcome their difficulties. It is suggested that teachers' questions can be classified into two broad categories, 'probes' and 'prompts' (Mason, 1995).

Probes

A probe involves questioning children about how they reached a solution to a problem, or how they are working on a task, in order to determine current understanding. Probes include questions like 'Tell me how you did that?' 'Why is that the largest?'

Prompts

A prompt involves asking children to consider aspects of the tasks with the aim of helping them to reach an informed solution or to use a more appropriate method. Prompts include questions like 'What happens when you add two to a number?' 'If you change the numbers round (e.g. 2 + 7), do you get the same answer?'

An important aspect of supporting children's learning with prompts is for teachers to ensure that they are guiding children in their mathematical understanding rather than simply telling them what they should be doing. Whilst explanation and demonstration are excellent prompting tools in mathematics, it is important for a teacher to recognise whether a visual prompt has actually supported learning or simply produced a superficial 'copycat' response. This may result in the child being unable to relate necessary understanding to later developmental work in that area.

Explaining and demonstrating

Clear exposition of skills and cognitive strategies to be acquired was strongly advocated in the Cockcroft Report (1982, para. 243). For children to be able to carry out mathematical tasks effectively, it is important that a teacher clearly explains and demonstrates the methods of working at the beginning of the lesson and poses questions to ensure that pupils fully understand the expectations required. Experienced teachers recognise, with a whole-class or group exposition, that it is important to watch out for signs that indicate a child may be unsure or has not really understood what has been communicated. In these cases, teachers need to organise time to offer further explanation and/or demonstration after setting the other children to work. Backhouse *et al.*, (1992) suggest the following ways in which exposition can be used to good effect:

- when starting a new subject with a class, before their different speeds of working have separated them in their achievement;
- when collecting ideas together after an investigation or some practical work;
- to set up challenges for learners to get them to think;
- to stimulate a discussion, an investigation or practical work.

Reviewing work

An important aspect of assessment is planning time to review mathematical work carried out, to recapitulate on the teaching principles of the lesson through the use of probing questions, and to celebrate achievement. This is generally carried out in the final minutes of a lesson and is often accompanied by a mental arithmetic game to keep skills sharp. The National Numeracy Project (1997) recommends that recapitulation on the previous lesson's teaching principles should also *precede* the next lesson. This can help to generate alertness in children, keep skills sharp and also help children to be better prepared for the teaching to follow.

Setting targets

Review may also take the form of an informal verbal exchange between the teacher and a child where work is discussed and targets agreed. In this way the process of review creates vital links between assessment and planning, whilst at the same time facilitating dialogue which is solely focused upon a child's work (CUPA, 1992, F2).

Involving children in self-assessment

There is much to be gained, by both teachers and children, in involving children in the assessment of their own work. Keith Mason (1995) states that children can be guided to reflect on their learning and so become more aware of their strengths and weaknesses. The 'use of child self assessment methods in the classroom can provide insights into children's skills, knowledge and understanding which can supplement teacher's own assessments' (*ibid.*).

Marking recorded work

The most common way for teachers to monitor children's mathematical learning is to 'mark' work that has been completed. With young children, this is mostly carried out in the presence of the child. As children get older and the amount of recorded work increases, teachers frequently use time outside the teaching session to mark 'sets' of work produced by a class. This form of monitoring, focusing on the product rather than the process of completing the work, is more evaluative than diagnostic. As stated by Pollard and Tann (1993), 'there is no opportunity to talk with the children and find out more about how he or she set about the task'. Teachers can involve classroom assistants in marking children's work, which can be an integral part of their responsibility when directing groups of children. It is important that marking should be carried out in the presence of the child whenever possible.

'Ticks and crosses'

The marking of mathematical work has always been associated with marking every correct answer with a 'tick' and every wrong answer with a 'cross'. This can be very time-consuming for the marker. Also the liberal use of 'ticks and crosses' can be intrusive, especially in red pen! For a child who is struggling, a page of 'crosses' can be very demoralising. What is more important is that there should be evidence on the work that it has been seen and discussed with the teacher. For example, this can be signalled with a 'tick' at the bottom of the work and a 'smiley face' for younger children, or a relevant written comment for older children. Taking the opportunity to talk to a child about the work whilst it is in progress is more valuable that marking the finished product.

Correcting errors

Children make different kinds of errors when carrying out mathematical work. These can be performance errors, arising from misinterpreting what they have been expected to do; method or process errors, arising from confusion or lack of understanding of the mathematics involved in the task; or errors that are simply careless mistakes.

Performance errors

Teachers need to keep a particular watch on children when they settle to start a task. It is at this stage that these problems present themselves because children may be unsure about what they are expected to do. Teachers can intervene effectively and carefully re-explain the expectations of the task. In some cases this may mean a child needs to start again. Whilst not endorsing excessive profligate use of paper, the opportunity to make a fresh start on a new page or worksheet can work wonders in re-establishing a feeling of motivation in a child. A page that is viewed as 'spoilt', by a child, will often produce a half-hearted response from therein. As adults we frequently experience 'false starts' and have the option to throw it in the bin and start again. It is easy to forget that children need that option too.

Process errors

Misunderstanding related to the process or method of a task should be spotted, discussed and re-explained before a child has journeyed very far. This will enable a child to proceed with confidence from that point. In this way the child will not be faced with being told to repeat the whole task again.

Careless errors

The occasional careless arithmetic error can be discussed and amended on the spot with the use of an extra box beside the 'sum' – for example:

$$3 + 5 = 9 \ \square$$

Errors of number reversals within the work can be discussed and amended on the spot, with the aid of an eraser. However it is important for teachers to signify that a correction has been made on the child's work. This will ensure that children receive clear messages that accuracy is important and parents do not get the idea that their child is a budding Einstein! For example, the symbol **C** can be written beside the correction – $25 + 7 = 32$ (C).

Targeting children for extra help

In the case where there is a clear problem with understanding and the work contains several method or process errors, this is a clear signal to the teacher that some extra help is required. It may not be possible for the teacher to devote sufficient time to a child in the same session and work may have to be deferred and targeted for a subsequent session. In these cases it is sufficient to signify that the work needs re-teaching and some symbol to denote this is required – for example, the symbol **R** placed somewhere visible on the page to prompt learning support action at that point.

Evidence of a persistent problem

If a child is still having difficulty after re-teaching, the teacher must question whether the work is too difficult for the child at this stage. Further practice may be required at a lower stage to re-establish confidence so that the child may regain a 'handle' on the understanding required. However, it is important to recognise that repetitive drill and practice of a concept the child does not really understand is inadvisable. It will only serve to dishearten the child to the point where confidence and interest are lost. Children need experiences of success and satisfaction in order to sustain momentum and interest in what they are doing. Many children can be greatly helped by the setting of achievable short-term goals on their route to longer-term success (Cheshire Curriculum Policy Statement 5.6, 1989, p. 13). The strategy of providing a variety of tasks giving an opportunity to the child to experience success is more advisable. For example, mathematical games, open-ended number investigations that children can confidently carry out at their own level and computer activities are very useful in these instances.

Evidence of easy success

Teachers enjoy having children in their class who are highly motivated and get on with their work. Amongst these are the children who consistently appear to get everything right and finish their work before other children. It is important for teachers to take this as a sign that perhaps the work is too easy. It is worth administering an interim baseline assessment to try to establish how far advanced the child is in relation to the rest of the class. This will give some guidelines as to the level at which the child should be working. If the school uses a published scheme, it is no problem to place the child on a higher-level book to offer the child work at his or her conceptual level. However, continuous work in a scheme workbook or from a textbook is not very stimulating and lacks the challenge that can be provided through interactive problem-solving with the teacher and other children. Open-ended mathematical investigations can offer bright children the opportunity to solve problems at a higher level, using their advanced knowledge and skills. Older bright children can be given ownership of work by, for example, devising a maths trail around the school with the support of an adult. If encouraged, bright children will also contribute significantly to the mathematical experiences carried out in the classroom. For example:

> In a Year 2 class a group of children were told to work in pairs to find out the area of objects in the room using transparent centimetre-squared grids. Richard noticed that the window between the cloakroom and the classroom had squares on it, being toughened glass. With his partner helping, he counted the squares along the length and then the width of the window and then used a calculator to find the area of the window. It gave him and his partner a huge buzz that they had done this, especially when they were asked to explain to the class how

they had done it. In the next session other children tried Richard's method using transparent grids and calculators.

Pacing progress

Children of all abilities require time to reflect upon tasks and activities in which they have been involved. Moving children on from activity to activity, experience to experience, without giving them time to reflect, to draw threads together or to come to conclusions, does not produce effective learning (CUPA, 1992, F1). Such 'progress chasing', at its worst, can mean that every time a child begins to understand a new concept he or she is moved on to the next, in a way that can be defined as 'concept surfing' (like the habit of 'channel surfing' using the remote control for a television). This point is emphasised in the Plowden Report (1967, para. 530): 'It takes much longer than teachers have previously realised for children to master new concepts, or new levels of complex concepts. When understanding has been achieved, consolidation should follow.'

The strategy of review, mentioned earlier, needs to be combined with regular programmes of revision. Revision sessions are more effective if they are planned to precede the introduction of new work in that area. In this way the children are more able to make better connections between concepts and skills already covered and the new knowledge to be learnt.

Reviewing progress

Regular review of children's progress, in relation to short-term curriculum planning for mathematics, is an important feature of maintaining an effective match between children's learning needs and the planning of mathematical work in the classroom. Many teachers carry out a whole-class review on a weekly basis, where the teacher critically evaluates the proceeds of the week, the effectiveness of the mathematical teaching that has been carried out and the quality of the responses from children in the class. The teacher then uses this information as the basis for planning the following week's work. From this information he or she will decide which children can be introduced to new work, which children will require more practice and which children require targeting for help. It would also be an appropriate time to review the membership of teaching groups.

Reviewing group membership

Although many children may perhaps remain in the same ability groupings, there may be one or two children who appear to be more suited to working with another group. For example, it would be sensible to change the group of a child when that child is seen to be progressing very quickly and confidently, moving him or her to work with a group of more able children. This will give them the opportunity to try out new work and present them with an element of challenge. The fact that their efforts have been acknowledged by the teacher will contribute a 'feel-good factor'.

Conversely, when a child is showing signs of struggling and displaying anxiety, that child can be moved to work with children progressing at a slower rate. In this way, assessment enables the teacher to respond to the varying pace of children's learning within a flexible context.

Evaluation

As part of the continuous assessment process, the evaluation of mathematics sessions enables teachers to take a broader look at what is happening in their classrooms. In addition to assessing children's performance in the classroom, teachers need to assess their own performance and examine how well this supports children's learning.

Lesson evaluations

By analysing a whole teaching session from beginning to end, teachers are able to judge the effectiveness of their planning. They can evaluate the effectiveness of the organisational arrangements that were planned to support the orchestration of the lesson – for example, methods of grouping children and the deployment of resources. They are able to review, for example:

- the structure of the lesson (time spent on the introduction, practical work, review and clearing away);
- appropriateness of methods of grouping children;
- appropriateness of teaching materials used in the session; and
- whether resource provision supported effective learning.

Evaluating the response of the children

In addition the teacher can review the outcome of the lesson as a whole in terms of the response of the children. For example:

- attentiveness during whole-class work;
- quality of practical work produced;
- contribution to discussion;
- ability to talk about what they had done;
- ability to work independently;
- ability to select and use resources appropriately;
- ability to work co-operatively; and
- the general atmosphere in the classroom, whether children were motivated and on task, or noisy and easily distracted.

(See also Chapter 10.)

Long-term benefits of continuous assessment

Continuous assessment over time offers benefits in terms of long-term planning considerations – for example, teachers can begin to recognise that some concepts and skills may require more teaching than others. Patterns start to emerge relating to concepts which represent common difficulties for children and which can be highlighted for special attention in future planning. Also, through long-term continuous evaluation, teachers begin to recognise particular teaching approaches that have generated consistent success and incorporate them in future planning. It is with these elements that experienced teachers have a significant advantage over newly qualified or student teachers. A student teacher, without the benefit of experience, will need some guidance and support in these areas during the times they are undertaking work in school. Support also needs to be continued whilst they are in their first year of teaching. It is realistic to recognise that the knowledge and skills derived from experience only begin to emerge after a teacher has been continuously teaching the same age group for more than one year.

Even with experienced teachers, if they change age groups, the first year will involve a lot of trial and refining of strategies. Planning for the second year will be more focused, drawing upon the insights gained during the first year. They will have first-hand experience of the range and scope of mathematical work children of that age are likely to achieve during one school year. This knowledge will enable the teacher to develop more effective long and medium-term plans.

Summary

Continuous assessment informs teachers about children's rate of progress and levels of achievement in mathematics over time. Through diagnosis and target setting, continuous assessment enables teachers to make short-term curriculum planning decisions tailored to the mathematical needs of the children. Vigilance will ensure that early diagnosis of children experiencing difficulties takes place and that appropriate action is taken. Regular review of children's work can help teachers make decisions about pacing progression and help them to decide when revision of previous work is appropriate. Regular evaluation of mathematics lessons can help teachers refine teaching approaches and classroom organisation to support learning more effectively. Continuous assessment over time can give teachers a feel for long-term planning considerations which will help to increase their overall effectiveness.

16

National assessment in mathematics

Statutory programme of national assessment

Standard Assessment Tasks

The introduction of the National Curriculum for mathematics in primary schools (DES, 1988) was designed to be accompanied by a programme of national testing comprising a statutory programme of *summative* Standard Assessment Tasks (SATs). The statutory instruments for National Curriculum assessment arrangements were introduced in 1990 by the DES. KS1 SATs were piloted in 1991 in a representative sample of Year 2 classes in state primary schools throughout England and Wales. SATs are now administered by all state primary schools in England and Wales at the end of each KS. The test for KS1 is scheduled to take place in the school year that children reach the age of 7 (in exceptional circumstances the assessment may be administered at a younger or older age). At the junior stage, it is scheduled to take place in the school year that children reach the age of 11 (KS2).

Teacher assessment

Additionally, schools are expected to establish a system of teacher assessment to support the 'determination of level of attainment by assessments' (DES, 1990). The statutory instruments setting out the National Curriculum assessment arrangements for mathematics, (*ibid.*, para. 6: 2) define the procedures for combining teacher assessment and standard assessment. These have been updated in line with the revised requirements (DFE, 1995a) and are summarised as follows:

• Where the results of teacher assessment are the same as the SAT assessment, this will represent the level of attainment for a child to be recorded by the school.
• Where the SAT assessment does not assess an attainment target, for example, AT 1, 'Using and applying mathematics', the level of attainment for a child, to be recorded by the school, is determined by teacher assessment.

• Where the results of teacher assessment and the SAT are different, the level of attainment for a child, to be recorded by the school, is determined by the SAT assessment.

It can be seen from the above summary that, within the procedures for the summative assessment arrangements for the National Curriculum, teacher assessment is accorded a lower status than standard assessment. However, teacher assessment is accorded a very high status in the context of formative assessment. Decisions related to planning and implementing effective mathematical programmes are dependent upon information gained from teachers' monitoring of children's individual progress over time.

SATs for mathematics: primary concerns

SATs were formulated for use in primary schools by the DES (1988) as a national measure to assess standards of achievement, to identify weak or failing schools and to raise standards of achievement over time. However, the design of the mathematics tests for KS1 and 2 contains predominantly closed tasks within fixed parameters, offering children restricted scope to demonstrate their potential in terms of depth of knowledge and mathematical understanding. The level of attainment accorded to a child is derived from the raw score (the number of questions answered correctly). As a measure to assess standards of achievement, there is concern that raw score data from closed-task tests represents a crude instrument with which to make accurate judgements about individual children's levels of achievement.

As a method to identify failing schools, the use of raw scores from SATs is seen as lacking in reliability. Significant affective factors, such as social-class effects, on children's levels of achievement are not taken into consideration.

ENCA 1 project (1992)

A formal evaluation of the 1991 KS1 National Curriculum assessments – the ENCA 1 project (Shorrocks *et al.*, 1993) – was carried out by members of the research team at the School of Education, University of Leeds. Evaluation of the research produced some interesting results, summarised as follows:

• *Birth date* Children in the sample, who were recorded as having summer birthdays (i.e. the younger children in the cohort) consistently performed less well in mathematics than older children in the year group. This applied to both the teachers' own assessments and to the scores on the SATs.
• *First language* Children in the sample, who were recorded as having English as an additional language, performed less well in mathematics than children who were recorded as having English as their first

language (with the exception of Welsh-speaking bilingual children, who proved to be a special case by performing better than their non-Welsh speaking counterparts).

- *Social background* Children in the sample were divided into four groupings, high status, intermediate status (high and low) and low status, by home address and post code, as a measure of social background through neighbourhood status. Children from high-status neighbourhoods performed significantly better in mathematics than those lower down the social scale. There was evidence of a clear relationship between declining pattern of attainment and declining neighbourhood status.
- *Nursery education* Children in the sample, who were identified as having attended some form of nursery education establishment, generally performed better in mathematics than children who had not attended a nursery education establishment.
- *Gender* There was no *overall* difference in the performances of boys and girls with respect to levels of achievement in mathematics, although girls outperformed boys in the mathematical areas of number concepts and number patterns and relationships.

The results of the ENCA project 1 evaluation served to draw attention to concerns raised by teachers and educationalists about SATs. If raw data from SATs alone is used to identify weak or failing schools, then the process would be seriously flawed. Account needs to be taken of differences in background and the different levels of experience of children prior to entry to school. These need to be recognised as important independent variables that can have a significant bearing on how well a child is able to perform in SATs at 7 years of age, despite the excellence of the provision a school can offer. For example, research has consistently pointed to the fact that the type of catchment area and socioeconomic background of children can significantly affect levels of achievement. Teachers express concern that these factors are not taken into account in raw scores from SATs tests.

Value-added factors

It was also recognised that raw scores in mathematics tests do not give any indications of the measure of success of a school. This is with respect to the 'value-added' factors a school can provide, through excellent teaching and learning support. For example, a school serving an area known for social and economic problems may be excellent in terms of value-added progress children have made during their time in school. However, the school could be viewed in a poor light against a neighbouring school achieving higher SATs results.

The notion of hidden value-added factors has now been recognised as a serious issue to be addressed, if individual schools are to be judged fairly in terms of the quality of educational provision they offer.

Monitoring the quality of provision at national level

The school inspection system, managed by Ofsted, ensures that all state primary schools are regularly inspected with respect to assessing the quality of provision, and that reports are published for governors and parents of the school. The issue of value-added factors is also being addressed by the use of baseline assessment programmes in reception classes. With the advent of state nursery provision for all 4-year-olds (DfEE, 1997a), efforts are being made to raise the quality of nursery provision according to a set of prescribed common standards, identified within the Desirable Outcomes for children's learning. This can be seen as an attempt to reduce some of the inequalities of experience prior to children entering full-time schooling at 5.

Desirable Outcomes for children's learning

The Desirable Outcomes underpin the framework for inspection of the national provision for 4-year-olds in nursery establishments as a means of ensuring 'that nursery education is of good quality and provides a sound preparation for the National Curriculum, giving particular attention to the development of early literacy and numeracy' (SCAA, 1996a).

In compiling the Desirable Outcomes, SCAA was asked to take account of the best practice across the full range of under-5s provision in the private, voluntary and maintained sectors.

Desirable Outcomes for mathematics

The goals established for mathematics cover the key aspects of early mathematical understanding and provide the foundation for numeracy. They are stated thus:

> The educational programme is likely to ensure that children by the age of five:
> - use mathematical language to describe shape, position, size or quantity (e.g. circle, cube, behind, bigger than, more).
> - recognise and recreate mathematical patterns.
> - sort, compare and put objects in order, sequence and count, using everyday objects.
> - are familiar with counting games, number rhymes, songs and stories.
> - recognise and use numbers to 10.
> - through practical activities, begin to solve problems, record numbers and show an awareness of number operations such as addition and subtraction and language, such as add one more, take one away, how many altogether, how many are left?
>
> (Ofsted, 1997)

SCAA (1996a), defined the goals for nursery education provision under key areas of early learning: personal and social development; language and literacy; mathematics; knowledge and understanding of the world; physical development; and creative development. However, there is recognition of the good practice that exists in education for the under-5s, where many activities embrace skills drawn from different areas of learning and resources serve different purposes. As stated in *The Curriculum for the Under-Fives*: 'because of the inter-related nature of activities, many resource items are multi-purpose, the approach to using them being significant in influencing the quality of the learning experiences' (Curriculum Council for Wales, 1991, p. 9).

All nursery settings in LEAs with early learning development plans are eligible for funding for 4-year-olds on roll. They are inspected on a regular basis to ensure that there is evidence that 'quality of provision is likely to promote the *Desirable Outcomes* in each of the six areas of children's learning by the age of five years' (Ofsted, 1996). It can be seen that this initiative is laying the foundations for establishing a national level of expectations on standards for children entering reception classes. The Desirable Outcomes are also designed to ensure that children who are failing at this stage are identified early and can be offered specific programmes of help, outlined in the *SEN Code of Practice* (1989).

KS1 SATs for mathematics

The assessment arrangements for KS1 SATs have undergone modification and amendment every year since their inception in 1991. Because of continuous changes in the procedures, it is impossible to present a definitive description. It has, therefore, only been possible to present the arrangements for 1997, being the most recent model available at the time of writing. For later amendments, *teachers will need to consult current published documentation.*

The assessment arrangements for 1997 were based on *The Education Order: Assessment Arrangements for the Core Subjects, Key Stage 1, England* (DfEE, 1995), and *The Education Order: Assessment Arrangements for the Core Subjects, Key Stage 1, England, Amendment* (DfEE, 1996).

Children to be assessed

The arrangements apply to all children in their final year of KS1 – the 'final year' of KS1 meaning that in the next school year those children will be moving on to KS2 programmes of study. Most children will be in Year 2 classes and become 7 years of age by the end of the school year. In order to accommodate the exceptional SEN and gifted child, 'where a child is older or younger than 7, that child should only be assessed if he or she is moving on to the Key Stage 2 programmes of study' (SCAA, 1997a). It is not intended that a child should be assessed more than once at the end of the key stage.

Teacher assessment

The results from teacher assessment are reported alongside the task/test results. Both have equal status and provide complementary information about children's attainment. The tasks and tests provide a standard 'snapshot' of attainment at the end of the key stage, while teacher assessment, carried out as part of the teaching and learning in the classroom, can cover the range and scope of the programmes of study, and can take account of evidence of achievement in a range of contexts, including that gained through discussion and observation.

(SCAA, 1997a)

It can be seen that whilst task/test results still take priority in deciding children's levels of attainment, teacher assessment is recognised as an essential part of the process and accorded equal status with the testing process. To emphasise this, there are recommendations that 'schools should promote the quality of teacher assessment through a range of strategies, whilst avoiding unnecessary workload for teachers' (*ibid.*).

Teachers are required to summarise their teacher assessment, at the end of KS1, for each child and make entries on a pupil record sheet proforma for mathematics and another proforma for English. For each child they are required to enter:

- a level for **each of the attainment targets** for Mathematics at Key Stage 1 (AT1 – Using and Applying Mathematics, AT2 – Number, AT3 – Shape, Space and Measures)
- an **overall subject level** in Mathematics.

(*Ibid.*)

It is emphasised that teachers should use their knowledge of a child's work to judge which level description best fits a child's performance across a range of contexts. To support schools in the task of teacher assessment for mathematics, SCAA has produced guidance in the form of the following publications:

- Consistency in Teacher Assessment: Guidance for Schools (1995a).
- Mathematics: Exemplification of Standards: Key Stages 1 and 2, Levels 1 to 5.

(SCAA, 1995b)

Calculation of subject levels

The calculation of an overall level for a subject using teacher assessment is done by averaging the levels for each attainment target. There is no need for schools to do this as the calculations are carried out automatically by computer, when the pupil record sheets are processed centrally. For English, the attainment targets are weighted equally. For mathematics, the attainment targets are weighted differently as follows:

'Using and applying mathematics' (AT1)   1
'Number and algebra' (AT2)   2
'Shape, space and measures' (AT3)   1

Attainment Targets	Level (b)	Weighting (b)	Level x Weighting (c)
Using and Applying Mathematics	1	1	1
Number and Algebra	2	2	4
Shape, Space and Measures	1	1	1
Total		4	6

Figure 16.1   Calculating the subject level
Source: SCAA, 1997a, p. 25

The documentation presents the example given in Figure 16.1 for mathematics. To calculate the subject level for this child, take the total of column (c) then divide this by the total of column (b) $6 \div 4 = 1.5$. The answer is then rounded up to the nearest whole number. This child has attained level 2. For the purposes of calculation, if a child is assessed as being half-way between level 1 and 2, then the number recorded should be rounded up to the next whole number. Where a child is working towards level 1 in an attainment target, a zero should be recorded.

Recording and retaining evidence

The documentation states that 'schools are required to keep records on every child, including information on academic achievements, other skills and abilities and progress made in school' (SCAA, 1997a). Schools are expected to update their records at least annually but there are no specified requirements as to how, or in what form, records should be kept. These decisions are seen as falling within the professional domain of schools (see Chapter 20).

Timing

The process of teacher assessment need not be completed until after the tests and tasks have been marked; schools may complete it earlier if they wish. The level-1 task for mathematics can be completed at any time during the assessment period, which is from the beginning of January up to four weeks before the end of the summer term. The level 2–3 test should be administered at sometime during the month of May. A fixed deadline for everything to be completed is set each year at about two weeks before the end of the summer term. This is so that 'schools can submit their results for national data collection and enable an early publication of national results, in response to requests from LEAs and schools' (SCAA, 1997a).

The level-1 mathematics task

Since 1995, the assessment arrangements for KS1 have included a task for mathematics at level 1 which is designed to be used with children judged to be working towards or within level 1 in mathematics as a whole. The tasks vary from year to year but, in principle, they represent orally administered practical tasks, where specified outcomes are planned for and the results are recorded by the teacher administering the task. The 'task' is divided into parts, each part designed to test specific mathematical concepts and skills, with a substantial emphasis on number concepts. For example, the 1997 task comprised:

> **Part A**: an activity designed to assess children's ability to describe shapes, to recognise which do not have a given property, for example 'no curved sides' and to classify shapes on a sorting diagram using a set of shapes provided for the task.
>
> **Part B**: an activity designed to assess children's ability to read numerals up to 10; use the relationships 'fewer than' and 'more than'; find pairs of numbers for a given total up to 10; find a trio of numbers which total 10; subtract numbers up to ten using a set of numeral cards 1–10, a set of 'jacket' cards in four colours, displaying 1–5 buttons and large white 'jacket' cards each displaying 10 buttons. (Children also allowed to use familiar number apparatus available in the classroom if required.)
>
> **Part C**: (Optional) An activity designed to assess children's ability to write and compare numbers mentally, and to add and subtract numbers up to 24 (designed to help teachers make decisions whether a child should be entered for the Level 2–3 test).

> (SCAA, 1997b).

The class teacher is responsible for the administration of the assessment process. However, the task may be carried out under the direction of the teacher by any other competent and informed assistant in the classroom. Parents of children within the class should not be involved in the process. Teachers should use their discretion about how best to group the children and ensure that the testing conditions are conducive to all children being able to show the best they can do. In carrying out the task teachers should make sure all the children understand what they are expected to do. Teachers are allowed to adapt wording where necessary to present the instructions in words and expressions that are familiar to the children. Efforts should be recognised and praise offered, as appropriate. Some specific guidance is given to accommodate the needs of children with English as an additional language, hearing impairments, visual impairments, physical disabilities and emotional and behavioural difficulties (*ibid.*). The content and procedures vary each year. Full details of the administration of the task are given in the *Mathematics Handbook* which is published by SCAA annually.

The level 2–3 mathematics test

The level 2–3 mathematics test is a pencil and paper test, designed to be used with all children judged to be working within level 2 or above in mathematics as a whole and provides grades A–C at level 2 (A = highest grade) and an 'at level 3' grade. Children who narrowly miss achieving level 2 through the test are to be awarded level 1. If a child does not achieve sufficient marks on the test to be awarded level 1, then the school should carry out the level-1 task with the child (SCAA, 1997a).

Structure of the test

The test is presented in a booklet and structured into two parts. The first part, comprising five questions, is administered orally by the teacher, with children writing their answers in spaces provided in the test booklet. These questions are designed to test children's understanding of the language of mathematics as set out in the programme of study for KS1. The questions range in difficulty across level 2 of the National Curriculum. They are not timed and children are allowed to write any working out in their booklet. The documentation presents the following examples of the type and range of difficulty of the oral questions:

1. Write the number sixty-seven.
2. What number is three more than seven?
3. Tick the shape which is a hexagon.
4. There are twelve pencils in a packet. Five pencils are taken out. How many pencils left in the packet?
5. Write the number three-hundred-and-sixty-four.

(SCAA, 1997a)

The second part of the test is designed to be read and completed by the child. It is structured so that the easiest questions appear first, progressing in difficulty through the test to the most difficult questions at the end. In this way children can work through the questions until they reach questions which are too difficult for them (SCAA, 1997d). As children work through the test, teachers are allowed to give children any help necessary with reading the questions but no help with the mathematics (SCAA, 1997c).

Use of number apparatus

For the first time since the advent of SATs, teachers were given clear rules about the use of number apparatus in the mathematics test in 1997. The documentation states that 'structured apparatus, consisting of tens and units, can be provided for each child or group working at the same table' (SCAA, 1997a). Children are also encouraged to use any space in the test booklet to include their workings. An example of this is shown from results produced in the report on the 1996 National Curriculum assessments for 7-year-olds (SCAA, 1997d) (see Figure 16.2).

Fig 16.2   Example of a child's workings in the KS1 mathematics test 1996
Source: SCAA, 1996, p. 19

Weighting of marks and marking procedures for the level 2–3 test

Two thirds of the level 2–3 test marks are accorded to number and algebra (AT2), with the remaining third of the marks accorded to shape, space and measures (AT3). Using and applying mathematics (AT1) is not assessed in the level-1 task or the level 2–3 test. The total number of marks a child achieves on the test is used to determine the level of achievement to be recorded on the pupil record sheets. Instructions for marking the test, a marking key and a table for finding the level a child has achieved are in the KS1 *Mathematics Test Teachers' Guides*, provided by SCAA each year to accompany the testing material.

Audit

The statutory responsibility for audit of the standards of administration and marking of both the tasks and the tests is held by the LEA for LEA-maintained schools and SCAA for grant-maintained schools. The process involves the visit of an auditor to the school during the time that assessments are taking place. The responsibility of the auditor is to verify that marking standards are accurate and to ensure that standards of administration of the task and tests for English and mathematics are consistent with other schools. This includes scrutiny of samples of work undertaken as part of the tasks and tests in English and mathematics (SCAA, 1997a).

Age-standardised scores

From 1997, the *Teachers' Guide* for the mathematics level 2–3 test has included a table which enables teachers to convert raw scores to standardised scores, adjusted to take account of the child's age when taking the test. At the time of writing, these conversion tables for mathematics were made available for use on an optional basis only, to provide additional information for reporting to parents about the performance of individual children (SCAA, 1997a).

Adapting the level 2–3 mathematics test for children with special educational needs

The test is designed to be used with all children who are attaining at the appropriate level but additional consideration has been given for children with special educational needs. An enlarged version of the test is available from LEAs and accredited audit agencies. This version consists of tear-off photocopiable masters of each question which are particularly suitable for children with visual impairments. Such children may use their usual magnification aids and the test is also available in grade-2 Braille from the RNIB, free of charge.

For children who have hearing impairments, the questions may be presented to the child in sign language. Children with physical disabilities may have their answers scribed by the teacher or employ the use of a computer. For children with emotional and behaviour difficulties, there is flexibility allowed in that the test may be administered in small parts over a number of sessions, rather than at one sitting. In the case of children who speak English as an additional language, words and phrases in the text of the test may be translated, but no help given with the mathematics being tested (SCAA, 1997c). Full details of these arrangements are presented in the *Teachers' Guide* to the KS1 mathematics test published by SCAA each year to accompany the testing material.

Making assessments at level 4 at KS1

When children achieve very high scores in the level 2–3 test, teachers can decide, taking into account their own assessments, whether assessment at level 4 or above is appropriate. Assessment at level 4 or above in mathematics is carried out by the administration of KS2 tests, assessing levels 3–5 (SCAA, 1997a). The instructions for administering the tests should be followed according to the *Teachers' Guide* for the KS2 mathematics tests published each year by SCAA. If children achieve level 4 or above, the overall subject level should be reported.

Absence, disapplication and modification

There may be children who are unable to complete the KS1 task or test during the allotted assessment period. In these circumstances it is the headteacher's responsibility to decide what should be recorded for the child in terms of level of achievement or, in exceptional circumstances, whether the child will be assessed the following year. It is also the headteacher's responsibility to decide whether disapplication or modification is to be considered. This has to be supported by evidence provided in a child's statement of special educational needs. There may also be the exceptional case of temporary disapplication – for example, a child who has recently arrived from abroad who speaks very little English (SCAA, 1997a). Teachers who have doubts about a child's ability to carry out the task or the test at KS1 should always refer the case to the headteacher. The procedures for dealing with these exceptional cases are presented in full in the documentation published each year by SCAA, which gives explicit details of the assessment arrangements for KS1.

Summary

This chapter has presented the statutory arrangements for assessment at KS1 to be carried out in all state primary schools. The process has been considerably modified and refined since its introduction in 1991. However, there are still tensions that exist in relation to the interpretation of SATs results, in English and mathematics at KS1, as a measure of good or failing schools. This is a particular issue for schools whose population comprises mainly children from low socioeconomic backgrounds. Differences in achievement in children from different social backgrounds are recognised as a highly sensitive area. Any form of measurement can only be taken using broad generalisable categories, such as the neighbourhood a child lives in, as used by the ENCA 1 project research team (Shorrocks et al., 1992). The introduction of compulsory baseline assessment for children in reception classes, on entry to full-time education, is seen as the fairest means by which value-added factors can be taken into account in every school at KS1. However, the underlying concern still remains that the process of testing children at 7 is being used as a measure by which schools are judged, with little educational benefit for the children concerned.

SECTION 5
Managing differentiation, record-keeping and reporting in relation to mathematics

---

17

Managing differentiation

Differentiation – 'The matching of work to the abilities of individual children, so that they are stretched but still achieve success.'

(NCC, 1993)

The management of a differentiated curriculum for mathematics is recognised as one of the most difficult aspects of teaching. Differences in children's mathematical performance in school are affected by a complex range of factors related to natural or inherited tendencies and differences in cultural upbringing, as well as factors related to differences in children's responses to the teaching they receive (see Section 1).

The challenge to teachers is to incorporate strategies for differentiated teaching to cater for the needs of children of different aptitudes and abilities. In this way, teachers can try to ensure that all children are given the best opportunities possible to realise their potential, within the context of mathematical learning in school.

The terms of reference of the National Numeracy Project are centred around raising standards of achievement in mathematics in primary school children. One of the ways the initiative hopes to achieve this is by reframing the way mathematics is taught in schools, to cater more effectively for children with different abilities.

Baseline assessment

The introduction of compulsory baseline assessment, on entry to school, enables teachers to take into account children's different levels of preschool mathematical experience so they can be grouped, according to ability, for planning purposes. It is hoped that this will reduce the problem of more advanced children 'marking time', whilst also enabling teachers to identify and target less experienced children for support.

Teaching methods

Whole-class teaching

One of the problems associated with the teaching of mathematics is the management of teaching to support optimum levels of learning, matched to pupils' different needs and aptitude for the subject. Traditional mathematics teaching has always been associated with whole-class 'chalk and talk' and children carrying out pencil and paper practice of the expounded principles. This strategy has been criticised with respect to teaching primary mathematics. In mixed-ability classes, the use of a 'blanket' approach, where the lesson is pitched at one level, is considered a poor way of ensuring that a lesson has appropriate substance, in terms of challenge, interest and support, for the most able to the least able pupil in the class.

However, the National Numeracy Project (1997) places a lot of emphasis on the use of quality whole-class teaching time as an integral feature of primary mathematics lessons. There is encouragement for teachers to plan whole-class interactive mental arithmetic games, exposition with rehearsal sessions and the use of revision sessions, which address the *general* needs of a class as in, for example, the practice of counting skills. There is also recognition that the *specific* needs of children require interactive teaching carried out with small groups.

Group teaching

Group work has been the principal method of teaching mathematics to young children because, with large classes, it is difficult to hold the attention of all the children for long periods of time. However, one of the problems is that the teacher can only be with one group at a time. Managing to give *quality* time to all groups in one session represents a nigh impossible task. In nursery settings, the use of adult helpers has been recognised as an effective way of increasing the amount of quality time spent with children working in groups. As mentioned in Chapter 10, the use of high, medium and low-input activities in the planning of group work, in nursery and infant schools, can help teachers to target groups for quality teaching time. However, it is important to ensure that all groups receive a fair allocation of teacher time. Ofsted (1995) raised the concern that: 'A weakness of many lessons is that the teacher's time is spent mainly with those who are stuck and insufficiently in direct teaching with all pupils. Too many able pupils or the conscientious quiet ones do not have interactions with their teachers.'

Ability grouping

Once children have started working through the National Curriculum, it is recognised that grouping children by ability is helpful to teachers for planning according to the needs derived from group 'norms'. Work can be planned at different levels, accommodating less able through to brighter children more effectively. Many schools group children by ability from Year 1 onwards. However, the majority of reception teachers operate mixed-ability and friendship grouping, recognising the importance of children's personal and social development at this age, in the same way as nursery schools.

Setting by ability

In larger infant or first schools, with more than one class in each year group, many schools operate a setting arrangement for English and mathematics across Year 2 and/or Year 3 classes. Children are clustered by ability, the number of sets normally depending on the number of classes/teachers in the year group. In some schools additional support is included, for example, where the headteacher takes the most able children within the year group for one session per week or where the special educational needs co-ordinator (SENCO) is timetabled for a session to help children who have been identified with significant learning difficulties in mathematics.

One of the concerns about group work, whether mixed or ability grouping, is when children are grouped together for teaching purposes, they are often working individually and in isolation and not working as a group at all (Edwards and Woodhead, 1996). For group work to be effective, it requires the teacher or adult helper to orchestrate the task, drawing upon all members of the group to participate, in much the same way as an interactive whole-class teaching session.

Individual teaching

In many infant schools, teachers operate programmes of individualised learning for each child in their class, using published mathematics scheme materials where children progress at their own pace through a series of workbooks or cards. The advantages and disadvantages of using published scheme materials are discussed fully in Chapter 6. It is important to re-emphasise that published scheme materials are best used to support, rather than drive, the teaching of mathematics. In relation to managing differentiation, although children work through the materials individually, the structure of progression is the same for all children, making no allowance for individual needs. Since children progress at different rates through the scheme, teaching often has to be continuously repeated on a one-to-one basis, which can be laboriously time-consuming. Through necessity, teachers have to spend more time in supervising the proceedings than being involved in interactive teaching with the children.

The most effective use of individual teaching is carried out within the context of high-input group work. If the children are grouped by ability, the main body of the discussion and questioning can be sharply focused to the 'norm' of the group, and the teacher is also able to direct challenge and pace in individual children. Small-group work can encourage the quieter, shy child to participate in the proceedings. Individual teaching can take place when a teacher reviews a child's completed work on a one-to-one basis and discusses targets with the child. It was reported by Alexander *et al.* (1992) that the best practice is 'where a good balance of whole class, small group and individual work is carried out on a fitness for purpose basis'.

Strategies for planning and managing differentiated work

The matching of work to the abilities of individual children is fraught with difficulty. Every learner has an idiosyncratic disposition towards learning mathematics, which can be coloured or affected by experiences of success or failure at every step along the way. Experience of success can generate confidence, interest and motivation, whereas failure can produce anxiety and disaffection. Performance can be affected not only by a child's aptitude but also by his or her physical state of health, emotional well-being and by what else is going on in his or her life outside school. Whilst teachers endeavour to do their best for the children in their care, they are always limited by the amount of time available. Necessity dictates the requirement for teachers to balance the provision for individual needs against the provision for general needs of pupils. It is, therefore, important that realistic strategies are established to plan and manage differentiated work effectively.

Different tasks for different ability groups

Planning different tasks for groups of different abilities is a commonly used strategy. Teachers take a common concept area, for example, handling money. They cluster children according to levels of achievement in that area and then plan work for each group at the appropriate level. For example:

- Group A: Stories of 5p, record by drawing around coins (new work – high-focus teaching);
- Group B: Stories of 10p, record by drawing around coins;
- Group C: Stories of 20p, record by drawing around coins; and
- Group D: Shopping at the class shop with 20p. Buying different objects with change. Record by writing: I bought a _____ for ____p. I had ____p change.

Use of common stimuli with a whole class to create different tasks for small groups or individual children

Teachers tend to use a common stimuli approach occasionally to create variety. It is useful to have a bank of ideas for mathematical activities that can be applied in various ways, to achieve different outcomes with different levels of ability. For example:

Activities with pattern block animals at different levels at KS1:

- Children to make an animal using 10 pattern blocks, then ask a friend to make its twin.
- Children to make an animal using 10 pattern blocks then make a graph of the blocks they have used and compare their graph with a friend.
- Give each different-shape block a monetary value, asking children how much their animal is worth. Whose is worth the most/least?
- Children to make an animal using 10 pattern blocks and drawing around the shapes to make a picture, then make a graph and give the graph to a friend. Ask the friend to make the animal from the graph without seeing the picture. Compare the picture and the animal made from the graph; look for similarities/differences. Ask, 'is it easier to make the animal by using a picture or a graph?' Why is the graph more difficult?

Other ideas include:

- 'Teddy Bear Maths' where all children bring a teddy bear to school for sorting, classifying and counting (nursery).
- 'Allsorts Mathematics' – investigating the mathematics in a box of liquorice allsorts (nursery – level 2).
- 'Smartie Maths' – same as Allsorts but not recommended for very young children – they can't resist eating them! (level 1–2).
- 'Telephone Number Maths', where children find out how many different 'sums' they can make using two numbers each time, three numbers, etc. Adding all the digits together using a calculator, whose makes the highest number? Multiplying the digits: this creates an interesting result if they include the STD code – can they find what causes it? (level 2–3).

Open-ended tasks

A large proportion of the mathematical work prescribed in published schemes is presented in closed tasks, which set fixed parameters and give no opportunity for children to demonstrate the full range of their capabilities. Closed tasks allow for no differentiation apart from the different rates children work through activities. Additionally, much of the work in published schemes is often passive practice work, where little challenge or opportunity for decision-making is offered. By planning open-ended tasks, the payoff for teaching and learning is extensive:

• they can be used with children of all abilities in a class;
• they can be used for whole-class, group or individual teaching;
• they present able children with stimulation and challenge;
• they do not confront less able children with failure;
• children can experience success at all levels;
• children have ownership of the work produced;
• they can demonstrate different levels of children's capabilities;
• they can involve decision-making at different levels;
• they can be used for collaborative work to promote discussion;
• combined with direct teaching, teachers can pitch expectation, discussion and questions at the right level to match the work to the capabilities of individuals in a class or group; and
• the design of open-ended tasks is less time-consuming for a teacher to prepare than worksheets (the content of teacher-produced worksheets often represents more of the teacher's work than the child's!).

(See Chapter 12 for examples of open-ended tasks.)

Planning work at minimum, optimum and extension levels

Traditionally, activities for mathematics, particularly closed arithmetic tasks, were planned anticipating basic performance outcomes – 'right' or 'wrong', 'finished' or 'unfinished'. More recently, with the increased use of open-ended investigations and problem-solving activities, performance outcomes are seen to be more flexible in relation to variations in the skills children are able to bring to a task.

As mentioned earlier, one of the advantages of using open-ended activities is that they can be used with children of different abilities at the same time. To help plan these activities, in terms of defining possible learning outcomes for different levels of ability, some teachers outline different levels of expectation in terms of minimum, optimum and extension levels of performance:

• *Minimum*   What every child should know and understand by the end of the teaching session.
• *Optimum*   What most of the children will know and understand.
• *Extension*   What some children will know and understand.

For example, in a lesson planned for 4-year-old children to name and identify a circle, a triangle and a square:

• *Minimum*   All children, each given a circle, a triangle or a square of the same colour, can identify the shape by name. When asked to hold up a named shape, are able to do so.
• *Optimum*   Most children, given a set of mixed shapes comprising

circles, triangles and squares of different sizes and colours, will be able to sort and classify them by name into subsets of circles, triangles and squares.

- *Extension* Through questioning, some children are able to describe differences between circles, triangles and squares by counting the edges and corners and recognise that all triangles have three edges and three corners, all squares have four edges and four corners, all circles have no edges and no corners.

Differences in mathematics and language development

It is important to consider that children's reading and writing skills may not be as well developed as their mathematical skills. In planning work for these children, activities may have to be modified to reduce the amount of reading and writing required. For example, instead of writing out mathematical sentences children can be given a table to complete (see Figure 17.1).

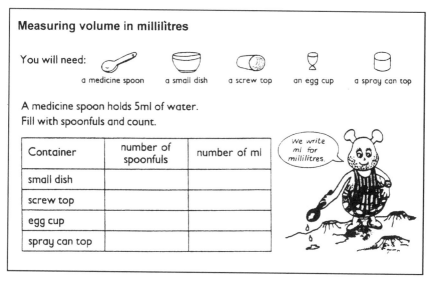

Measuring volume in millilitres

You will need: a medicine spoon, a small dish, a screw top, an egg cup, a spray can top

A medicine spoon holds 5ml of water.
Fill with spoonfuls and count.

Container	number of spoonfuls	number of ml
small dish		
screw top		
egg cup		
spray can top		

We write ml for millilitres.

Figure 17.1 Level-3 measurement activity for children with reading difficulties
Source: Edwards *et al.*, 1998, p. 32

Flexible use of working time

The principle of applying more flexibility to the time young children spend on mathematical work in school is more practical at infant level, where all the children attend full time. In nursery settings, many children attend part time and teachers have to work within the constraints of rigorous schedules to ensure that a balance of key learning experiences is provided. In infant schools there has always been a tradition to timetable sessions for teaching core skills in English and mathematics during the morning session, either before or after the mid-morning break. This is considered to be the 'prime time' of the day, when young children are more receptive to learning. In the afternoons they are more likely to be tired.

Many infant teachers recognise that a conventional timetable, with lessons starting and finishing in line with 'breaks' during the day, does not cater effectively for children's different rates of learning. There is always a problem because some children have not been able to finish their work, whilst others have finished early and are ready for something else. This has resulted in some infant schools adopting the strategy of planning *free-flow mornings*. This is where a particular area of the curriculum is targeted for high-input work for a whole morning and other areas are incorporated as medium and low-focus activities to offer variety and a change of pace.

Free-flow sessions

A free-flow programme ensures that each group will receive high-input teaching at some point during the morning. An example of a free-flow session with a focus on mathematics carried out with a Year 2 class of 32 children grouped by ability is as follows:

High-focus task Repeated addition/multiplication using numberlines for the less able and number-square patterns for the more able.

Medium-focus task Sets of graded English comprehension cards that children were familiar with working through.

Low-focus tasks for mathematics Dice, domino, playing card and number-square addition games, where children were familiar with the rules.

Low-focus tasks for English A computer spelling activity, silent reading, using the listening centre and role play with dressing-up clothes.

Adult support To assist with the organisation, the full-time NNEB was assigned to lead a high-focus mathematics activity. Also, a parent who came to help on this morning was designated to hear children read one at a time, throughout the morning.

Figure 17.2 illustrates the organisation of the lesson.

The use of free-flow sessions establishes the mid-morning break as an interlude and time does not have to be taken up with clearing away. Towards the end of the session, before mid-morning break, the teacher can begin to take stock of children's work so far and decide how children should proceed. Teachers have found this method of organisation helpful in supporting differentiation because time can be allocated more flexibly for children who have not finished their work. Children who complete their target work during the first session and/or the second session can be

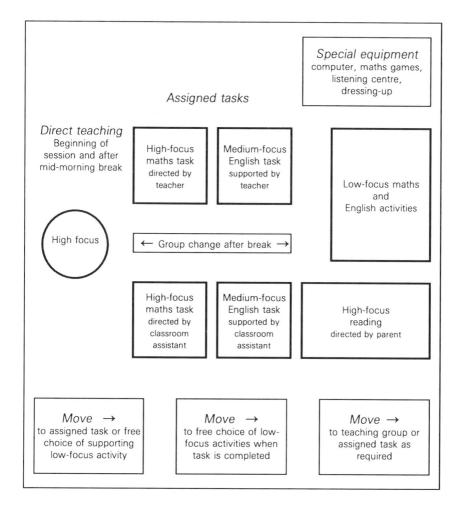

Figure 17.2   Free-flow teaching session

assigned to other purposeful activities for the remaining time.

Teachers who have implemented free-flow sessions successfully have found that the working time is less fragmented, children respond well to the working pattern, there is less unfinished work (children often wanting to do more rather than less work) and the atmosphere in the classroom is busy but relaxed. Also, events in school life, such as a photographer arriving, do not drastically affect the routine.

Extending working time for mathematics

Many schools are involving parents with helping their child at home with mathematics. This has benefit for children of all abilities in extending the time available for mathematics. It also enables teachers to ask parents to give their child some specific help when a problem is noticed with a child's mathematics work in school. The principle of parent partnership with mathematics in the early years of schooling is discussed fully in Chapter 7.

Some schools also run maths clubs at lunchtime or after school. These mainly take the form of 'fun' maths, where children work collaboratively playing mathematical games, carry out interesting investigations and problem-solving activities or work with interactive mathematical games on the computer.

For children identified as having difficulties with mathematics, a few schools have been able to assign a period on the timetable for those children to spend time with the SENCO for extra support. Usually, however, time with the SENCO is more likely to be used for children targeted for support with language and reading (see Chapter 18).

Summary

This chapter has attempted to identify some of the key strategies to manage differentiation in the classroom, with specific reference to mathematics. Whilst the list is not exhaustive, other strategies are mentioned elsewhere in this book that serve to help the teacher with this difficult task. It is important to emphasise that differentiation is inexorably linked to assessment. Without effective assessment procedures in place it is impossible for a teacher to fine tune differentiation, to the extent where there is a close match between individual children's learning needs and curriculum provision. The guiding principles are given below:

Differentiation by:

1) **Task**

- different materials for different groups;
- whole-class work with different outcomes; and
- open-ended investigational work.

2) **Outcome**

- different responses expected from different children; and
- variety and level of recording.

3) **Pace**

- rate of working; and
- rate of development.

4) **Organisation**

- methods of grouping;
- teaching methods;
- time management; and
- use of adult and parent help.

18

Supporting low attainers in mathematics

Problems associated with learning mathematics

Mathematics has a long history of being labelled as difficult to learn.
Because it is perceived as difficult, successful performance in mathematics at school carries with it many positive connotations in our society.
Being 'good' at maths is associated with 'being bright' and signifies
competence and quick understanding. Being 'poor' at maths carries
negative connotations, associated with 'being thick', incompetence and
slow understanding.

Despite associations with difficulty, children are conditioned at home
and in school to recognise from an early age that learning mathematics is
an important and expected part of growing up. Therefore, children who
experience problems with learning mathematics not only develop
feelings of frustration and anxiety but also a growing sense of personal
inadequacy. This can lead children to becoming frightened of
mathematics, showing symptoms of panic when confronted by
mathematics, attempting to avoid learning mathematics because of fear
of the subject or declaring their hatred of the subject in later life.

Factors related to low attainment in mathematics

Mathematical learning experiences at home

The mathematics children learn at home can vary enormously. Factors
that significantly affect the amount of time spent talking and playing
with a child before coming to school are: the family's socioeconomic
circumstances; whether there are older or younger brothers and sisters;
whether it is a large family or a small family; and whether there are close
links with nearby relatives. This can mean that some children will arrive
in nursery schools with evidence of an understanding of mathematics
which represents achievement in most, if not all, the Desirable
Outcomes. At the other end of the spectrum, some children will arrive
in nursery schools with very little prior mathematical experience.

Rate of learning

A child's rate of learning in mathematics, relative to others of the same age, can be an indication of a child's aptitude for the subject. A child working at a significantly slower rate indicates that learning maths may be difficult. However, it is important to recognise that whilst a child's progress may be slower than others of the same age, the child will still need to cover the same developmental stages at a slower rate, perhaps requiring more steps along the way to achieve understanding. Unfortunately, the notion that children can jump steps to 'keep up' and 'catch up' later is not uncommon practice, particularly if a child has been absent from school for a long period of time. An illustration of the 'catch up' principle in action comes from a personal experience of children who had recently transferred from an infant department to the junior department in a primary school:

> A few children who transferred to the junior department were working with numbers to ten, still requiring support from structural apparatus and numberlines. Within the first week the whole class were seen being taught formal vertical notation of addition tens and units. When the teacher was asked about this in relation to these children, the reply was: 'They are in the juniors now, it's time for them to start this work or they'll never catch up.'

Whilst the teacher's actions were based on concern for these children, whole chunks of important foundation work on understanding the principles of place value were being missed out, providing a recipe for these children to experience difficulty with arithmetic throughout their junior years.

Strengths and weaknesses

The nature of mathematical activities may also affect children's rate of learning because different areas of mathematics expect the application of different skills – for example, activities involving computation require number and arithmetical skills, whereas activities involving shapes require spatial and manipulative skills. It follows that some areas of mathematics may be easier for children to understand than others. Where an area is perceived as 'easy' by a child it can represent an area of strength or a 'stronghold'. If a task presented is related to a child's 'stronghold' in an area of maths, then the child is more likely to approach the task with confidence and his or her rate of learning will be faster than when a task is related to a weakness.

Short-term memory

Poor short-term memory can cause significant problems for children learning mathematics. In extreme cases this can prevent a child from starting to tackle a piece of mathematical work. The child may forget some or all of the teacher's instructions and be left with no clues on how to start. A child may not be able to 'hold' the visual image of a number and transpose the digits in copying the number – for instance, writing 15 as 51. In attempting computation (trying to add 16 to 27, for example), the child can be confused as to which numbers to add first, have difficulty 'holding' the first part of the sum in his or her head whilst attempting to compute the second part and finally being unsure of the right sequence to record the answer 43 and not 34, (Chinn and Ashcroft, 1993). Vertical notation algorithms often cause difficulties for children with poor short-term memory, particularly if they are set out on a chalkboard for children to copy. Very poor short-term memory may indicate dyslexia in a child.

Long-term memory

Learning mathematics also relies to a large extent on the importance of having a good long-term memory. Since mathematics is largely hierarchical in nature, new learning is difficult unless prerequisite ideas are remembered – for example, the digits 0–9 must be remembered if the child is to write them on recall. Children who have poor long-term memory find difficulty with making connections between new learning and important features of previous learning because they have forgotten the earlier work, especially if there has been a significant time lapse in between.

Visual-spatial/auditory perception

The very early stages of learning come primarily through our senses. We learn about our world from what we see and hear and from experiences gained through touching, feeling and handling objects and later, through experiences of more developed hand/eye co-ordination (gross and fine motor skills).

If any of a child's sensory mechanisms are weak from birth then vital elements in early mathematical development may be impaired. In cases of severe sensory disorders with sight, hearing and psychomotor control, these have generally been identified well before children arrive in school. However, in cases of children with moderate or slight disorders, these may not be highlighted until a child enters school, when the child's difficulties become apparent in relation to the performance of children of the same age.

Children, whose mental reception and organisation of sensory experiences has been 'fuzzy' rather than sharply focused from birth, will have a slower rate of development. For example, children with weak visual-spatial organisation will experience difficulty with discriminating forms and matching shapes, from the outset (Abercrombie, 1963). Similarly, when auditory sensations are reduced, a child will have difficulty in relating sounds to experiences, in connecting language to actions and in interpreting verbal instructions (Compton and Bigge, 1976). Importantly, the degree of learning by imitation through watching and listening will have been impaired. Thus a child with a sensory weakness may not have developed the necessary skills sufficiently to cope with learning the range of mathematics normally expected for children of their age.

Translating perception to abstraction

What a child perceives is real: a ball or a set of balls. When a child is working with numbers he or she is working with the unreal or in the 'abstract' mode. A child who has difficulty in learning mathematics often requires a lot more assistance with translating perceptions into abstractions. An important aspect of this work relies on teachers ensuring children establish understanding through making appropriate connections between objects, language, pictures and symbols, as discussed in Chapter 2.

Children with English as their second language

Children's reception and organisation of mathematical experiences in the brain will be more difficult if their verbal thinking processes are in a different language from the language of instruction and communication in school. This is often very apparent when children first come to school, when their previous experiences have been processed entirely in their first language at home. Establishing meaning in a new language will serve to slow children's mathematical development until familiarity with the new language is mastered so that the child is able to bypass the translation process and begin to think in the new language. Equally, a child may be competent at performing aspects of mathematics practically, but the child's experience may not extend to translating ideas into written form in the new language.

Many schools with a large proportion of children whose first language is not English are able to employ the services of a support teacher to work alongside children, assisting them in translation. However, these teachers are often shared between classes and priority is understandably given to deploying their time in sessions involving reading and writing rather than mathematics.

Difficulties with reading

Mathematics has its own language and symbols and this can bring further problems. For example, the + symbol has different 'names' – it can mean 'add', 'plus', 'more' and also 'positive'.

A child needs to be able to read instructions and the wording of mathematical problems accurately. The wording of mathematical problems tends to be precise and so needs accurate reading and interpretation (Kibel, 1992). A child who cannot read key words or misses small words will have difficulty with the work. It is also important that instructions written by the teacher are clear and unambiguous. For example:

Instructions written by the teacher: 'How many cups fill a jug?'
The child came to the teacher carrying a jug with plastic cups inside and said: 'There aren't enough cups!'

Social and emotional factors

It is difficult for teachers to understand fully why children behave the way they do because of the idiosyncratic nature of inherited tendencies and cultural upbringing. Certain aspects of children's personalities may be as a direct result of genetic endowment from their parents. Similarly, children's attitudes and the way they respond in school may be directly related to the style of upbringing they have received at home. The ways in which children behave can have a significant effect on their disposition to learn in school. It is important that teachers are able to recognise certain observable behaviours, exhibited by children in classrooms, that may represent indications that a child has associated problems with learning mathematics.

Lack of social co-operation

These observable behaviours include:

- a child's inability to carry out mathematical tasks without unduly disrupting the activities of others;
- not being able to take turns or share equipment with others;
- behaving aggressively to other children;
- demonstrating a general inability to relate to adults and other children;
- disregarding the feelings of others and being viewed as unfriendly or naughty by other children; and
- cannot be easily reasoned with.

It is important to emphasise that these behaviours are not exclusive to mathematical activities and signify normal immaturity in very young children in any social context. Firm and friendly guidance helps children to learn to become more responsive in the context of social interaction in school both with their peers and adults. Where these behaviours persist into a child's infant career, it is important that teachers develop positive strategies to deal with them, based upon proactive rather than reactive responses. Many schools have established policies for positive behaviour management, where clear strategies are laid out for teachers to follow. A useful text in this area is James and Brownsword (1994).

Inattentiveness

Distraction is a healthy human trait and our minds, eyes and ears are frequently drawn to matters or events other than the task in hand for all sorts of reasons. Nursery-age children are often guided by fascination and interest. If something attracts and excites their attention they are naturally drawn to it and will often leave what they are doing to satisfy their interest and curiosity. In the infant classroom, we should be concerned about children who rarely listen, whose attention frequently wanders and who exhibit uninhibited hyperactive actions. This may relate to the recently acknowledged medical condition, attention deficit disorder, or be a symptom of an allergy to a specific foodstuff, exemplified in the discovery that tartrazine in orange squash caused a hyperactive reaction in many children. If a child consistently exhibits inattentiveness outside 'normal' prevailing behaviours, it would be important to discuss this with the child's parents because they may wish to seek medical advice. Within the context of 'normal' inattentiveness, this could simply be as a result of boredom. Children who find mathematics difficult require challenging and interesting tasks to inspire them. The challenge for the teacher is to provide such tasks.

Lack of personal organisation skills

Everyone accepts that few adults are blessed with the gift of being very methodical and highly organised people. In the case of children who lack personal organisational skills, this is often simply an indication of immaturity or lack of skill training at home. Through the routines of everyday school life children are supported and encouraged to develop a good sense of personal organisation and independence. However, there are a few children where this problem significantly inhibits their progress, particularly in mathematics, and may be related to the perceptual problems mentioned earlier. In the classroom, this represents children who demonstrate a lack of ability to plan or organise mathematical tasks sequentially and are always requiring help or suggestions as to the next step. They are also frequently careless or inexact and find tasks which require methodical processing tiresome or frustrating and their level of perseverance is low.

Passivity

Children who exhibit behaviours related to passivity are ones who rarely show any interest, initiative or self-sufficiency and are always needing teacher/adult support to carry out mathematical activities. At the nursery or reception stage this can be an indication that a child has not been proactive in his or her own mathematical development and has had little stimulation at home. These children often show a marked preference for social play and physical activities in areas which are not structured to develop mathematical thinking. In older children, this problem is recognised when a child generally produces the minimum level of work and when left to his or her own devices, rarely completes assigned tasks. Whilst this may be a sign that the child has a lack of personal organisational skills it is often an indication of disaffection and low achievement. Positive encouragement needs to be given to these children in the form of interesting and achievable tasks.

New situations

Many children experiencing a change of school, or even going up into a new class, find the experience very unsettling for a while and take time to adjust to the different systems in place. However, there are some children who display very low tolerance to change and in extreme cases show symptoms of distress or fatigue when they are presented with new and unfamiliar work.

Identification of low attainment in mathematics

Professional knowledge and experience of the range of mathematics children may be expected to learn and the 'normal' rate of progress of children within a given timespan, can give teachers arbitrary guidance to whether a child is above average, average or below average, in relation to other children of the same age. However, early identification of pupils who demonstrate low levels of achievement in mathematics is important so that learning support can be offered as soon as possible.

Baseline and continuous assessment

The implementation of baseline assessment on a child's entry to school is vital in assisting teachers to establish children's prior learning in mathematics. Baseline assessment techniques also represent valuable diagnostic tools to assist with early identification of special educational needs in relation to mathematics. The process of baseline assessment is discussed in full in Chapter 14.

The implementation of continuous assessment as part of teaching programmes for mathematics can track an individual child's progress and identify any difficulties that a child may experience at any time during the programme and enable the teacher to plan an appropriate course of action.

Strategies for supporting the low-attaining child in mathematics

Partnership

It is important to try to establish good relationships with the child's parent(s) where they support their child by helping him or her at home. With children identified as having problems with mathematics this is often difficult to do. It is not unusual to find that parents have an aversion to mathematics because they found it difficult at school and feel reluctant to become involved. Parents with large families often feel they do not have the time, especially if there is a young baby and younger children to be cared for at home. However, if a good relationship is established, there is benefit for all concerned, particularly for the child. When a child experiences difficulty it is often accompanied with feelings of anxiety and failure. This can be reduced if the child can see that his or her parent(s) and the teacher have a shared interest in supporting and encouraging his or her success in overcoming difficulties. Strategies for implementing parent partnership are discussed in more detail in Chapter 7.

Finely graded steps

It is important that teachers recognise that children's different rates of learning represent an important factor in relation to planning considerations, particularly with respect to the child who is struggling with some, but not all, areas of mathematics. Finely graded steps should be planned for 'problem spots', whilst challenges can be planned for 'strongholds'. This emphasises the principle that children should build experiences of success on to their existing framework of knowledge and experience, rather than endure repeated failure or frustration.

Little and often

Children with poor recall can be helped if the principle of 'little and often' is adopted, where topics are revisited on a frequent basis and new learning is introduced on the back of revision of relevant previous learning each time. Children's memory skills can be exercised and developed through activities which involve chanting numbers, rhymes, tables, and playing mental and memory games such as pelmanism. For children who find difficulty with translating information from one place to another, the use of individual activity sheets can help to 'hold' the information whilst the child carries out the workings on the sheet.

For children with problems with number recall some teachers use types of pictograms, for example, making a '2' into a swan. In this way the picture acts as a mnemonic association to help children remember the shape of the number. Pictograms designed as an aid to assist recall are given in the published maths materials, *Numberland*, (Edwards and Wild, 1990, for nursery and KS1 children) and *Starmaths*, (Edwards, *et al.*, 1988, for low attainers in mathematics at KS2). In *Numberland*, for example, the numbers are drawn as 'number houses' and stories are written about characters who live in the houses (Figure 18.1).

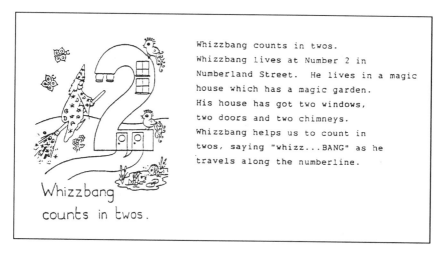

Whizzbang counts in twos.
Whizzbang lives at Number 2 in
Numberland Street. He lives in a magic
house which has a magic garden.
His house has got two windows,
two doors and two chimneys.
Whizzbang helps us to count in
twos, saying "whizz...BANG" as he
travels along the numberline.

Whizzbang
counts in twos.

Figure 18.1 'Whizzbang'
Source: From Edwards and Wild, 1990

Objects, language, pictures and symbols

If children are experiencing difficulties with abstract number concepts it is important they are encouraged to work with objects or pictures, with a teacher or adult to 'scaffold' the learning . For any new work, however, the support of objects and/or pictures and teacher interaction is critical in establishing firm foundations in understanding, as discussed in Chapter 2.

Number patterns and relationships

Planning arithmetic activities around patterns and number relationships can actively help children to feel more confident about working with numbers mentally. Strategies to encourage mental arithmetic skills can help children to reduce their need for apparatus at all stages. Where children find difficulty with arithmetical calculations, teachers can direct children towards strategies which make calculations easier, (see the 'grasshopper methods' in Chapter 2*).*

Visual demonstrations, pictures and labels

A teacher can help by giving visual demonstrations of mathematical activities children are expected to carry out. Where children are expected to follow textual instructions, the use of simple direct language accompanied by picture clues is helpful (see Chapter 17, Figure 17.1).

Similarly, labels for equipment in the classroom can be accompanied

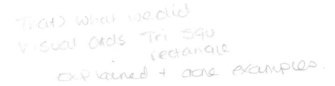

by a picture for ease of recognition and 'key words' can be displayed prominently. If children have difficulty in carrying out written recording in sentences, an equivalent alternative can be devised where children express their results by drawing pictures accompanied by labels and/or numerals.

Setting achievable targets

Setting realistic targets for a child to achieve, followed up with praise, can go a long way to restoring feelings of confidence and interest in mathematics in a child who is showing signs of disaffection. If this is carried out at the beginning of a session, the child is given a clear idea of what is expected and is able to respond accordingly. However it is important not to set expectations too high or too low. The use of open-ended tasks is helpful, where positive outcomes can be achieved at any level. Open-ended tasks do not intimidate children at the outset and can offer a framework for a negotiated level of achievement. It is also important to plan time to review the targets with the child when work is completed and to praise success. This process is a key feature of the HighScope Model, where children are encouraged to plan, do and review their work on a daily basis (Hohmann *et al.*, 1979).

Peer tutoring and collaborative work

Children who experience difficulties with mathematics often value the opportunity to work alongside a brighter child, particularly if the child is a friend. This can increase motivation and they can benefit from sharing discussion and often learn a lot from working with another child, where they are likely to feel less inhibited than working with a teacher.

Changing to a slower track

It is important that children are able to make mental connections between previous knowledge gained and new knowledge to be acquired. A child who is distressed or confused by a new piece of work is indicating that the work is too difficult or that work has not been explained clearly enough and a revision of the teaching should be undertaken. In the case where a child is persistently confused or distressed it is an indication that the child is constantly having difficulty in understanding and needs to progress at a slower rate with sensitive encouragement. If the class is grouped by ability, moving a child to work with another group working at a slightly lower level is helpful. However, if a child is already working with the 'less able' group, the child will need to be targeted for individual learning support when the teacher is working with the group.

Involving outside agencies

It is important that teachers identify any signs that children may be at risk from visual-spatial/auditory perception weaknesses that are not recorded in the school medical record. Whilst they may not have the expertise to make a specific diagnosis, a referral to the school medical service for a 'specialist check-up' can help to diagnose more obscure problems. For example:

> Lesley, aged 5, appeared a very bright and articulate child. Her reading and number skills were well above average for her age. However she had problems with fine and gross motor co-ordination. She did not enjoy PE and appeared to find manipulative activities difficult. This was discussed with her parents and a recommendation for a 'check up' was made. Lesley was diagnosed as having a 'crosslateral orientation' where her left eye was dominant combined with a motor dominance of the right-hand side of her body. It was helpful to everyone, including Lesley, to be able to understand why she had these difficulties.

Children identified with special education needs

It is important that a whole-school policy is established for learning support in mathematics for children who have been identified as having special needs. In the *Special Educational Needs: Code of Practice* (DES, 1989), the code recommends the general adoption of a staged model of special educational needs, where parents are informed at every stage. The recommended procedure for children who need the 'first stage of support' is for children to be given extra help by their teachers within the usual learning situation. Children with greater needs have some form of timetabled support from a nominated member of staff, who may be the special educational needs co-ordinator (SENCO). It is also recommended that schools involve outside help, from LEA learning support teams, to write individual education plans (IEPs), and they may also be involved in the teaching programme for children with greater needs. Many schools establish partnerships where parents are actively involved in helping their child with mathematics at home.

One of the most important considerations in establishing special support programmes for mainstream children is recognising the need for these children to maintain continuity in their daily classwork. Too frequently children with significant learning difficulties are taken outside their classroom for special support at an appointed time during the day. These children either miss out on the classwork completely or leave in the middle of an activity. When they return they have difficulty in regaining the thread of the classwork and have little or no time to complete the work. For low-attaining children, this can seriously exacerbate their problems. Their work patterns will be subject to upheaval and fragmentation. They are likely to develop confused ideas about expectations in relation to their classwork and there will be more awareness that they are 'different' from their peers. Strategies should be established to avoid a child feeling 'different' from the rest of the class. In many schools, learning support staff are timetabled to work alongside children in their classroom or plan short sessions at lunchtimes in order to avoid withdrawing children from the classroom during working time.

Role of the special needs co-ordinator

The role of the special needs co-ordinator should be to support and advise staff on the use of specialised resources, procedures and actions that may be taken, to organise in-service training and inform staff of recent developments. The co-ordinator should also be responsible for formulating a policy statement on the entitlement and provision for children with learning difficulties in mathematics.

Summary

This chapter has presented the key factors that are likely to be associated with low attainment and strategies that teachers can adopt in supporting low-attaining children in mathematics at KS1. One of the most important strategies is early identification through baseline assessment and the establishment of a partnership relationship between the parents, teachers and the child concerned to create a positive support network. Teachers should adopt a flexible approach to planning, recognising that children who find mathematics difficult may require smaller steps along the journey, supported by frequent revision sessions. Care should be taken to plan opportunities for challenge and interest through games, puzzles and open-ended tasks planned at different levels of difficulty. Additionally teachers should recognise children's strengths as well as their weaknesses to help generate confidence and success at every level.

When children are working as a whole class, it is important that expectations are sensitively modified for those children who find mathematics difficult, with consideration given for slower children to finish. Planning considerations should also include opportunities for collaborative work, where a less able child can work alongside a more able child in a form where each child can contribute 'expertise' in different ways It is also important that considerations for inequalities arising from gender, social background and culture are sensitively planned for. It is equally important to value and celebrate less able children's work along with others in the class, highlighting and praising effort and including specimens of their work in displays. Where there are children who are identified as requiring special educational support, care should be taken to reduce fragmentation and discontinuity in their classwork and to avoid situations where a child feels isolated from his or her peers.

To ensure consistency and continuity, a policy statement should be formulated through shared discussion with all staff, which presents a cohesive framework for all staff to implement throughout the school.

19

Supporting the gifted child in mathematics

Problems prior to coming to school

According to Felicity Sieghart (1980), the presence of a gifted child in a family can cause significant tension and stress. Often problems start very early in life with the child as a baby requiring less sleep than average, leaving parents exhausted and unready to face the next day. Because speech develops early in most gifted children and they have an insatiable curiosity for knowledge, their parents are often bombarded with questions. They are likely persistently to demand attention in the form of activity and express frustration when this is not forthcoming. For many parents, rearing a gifted child can be difficult and Felicity Sieghart, who interviewed many mothers of gifted children, was

> amazed to find that most of them do not want to have a very gifted child. Some fear the responsibility it puts upon them; others feel inadequate since they are not so intelligent themselves; and another category, who were perhaps frustrated gifted children in their own childhood, anticipate the difficulties their own offspring might have and are fearful for them...several have asked me in all sincerity if there was anything I or anyone else could do in order to change their child into a more ordinary one.
>
> (*Ibid.*)

There are also reported problems with siblings where a very able child can so overshadow brothers or sisters that they become underachievers at school as they cannot sustain the competition (*ibid.*). Parents and teachers who make overt comparisons between a very able and a less able sibling can be very demoralising for the less able child.

Other problems can arise where a parent may be good at mathematics and has very high expectations of his or her child. A large amount of pressure may be placed upon a child to realise the parent's expectations, with the result that the learning of mathematics ceases to be enjoyable and becomes a source of anxiety.

Problems gifted children face in school

Children who are seen as possessing special abilities in mathematics are often less well supported in schools than children identified as having learning difficulties. One reason may be that teachers themselves are not confident in their own mathematical knowledge and feel anxious about their ability to provide suitable work for the mathematically gifted child. This is often compounded by our national cultural disposition to sympathise with the underdog and to judge outstanding intellectual success critically, with derisory statements such as 'too clever by half'; 'clever clogs', etc. (interestingly, the same does not seem to apply to outstanding sporting or artistic achievements). Also, common to our national culture is the fact that modesty is an acknowledged virtue and 'to blow one's own trumpet' is considered 'bad form'. A highly articulate gifted child is often termed as 'precocious'. Faced with this cultural context, mathematically gifted children can find themselves socially isolated and, where a child bears the label of 'gifted' in school, it can work to their disadvantage. According to Joan Freeman (1979): 'Headteachers in Britain are not, on the whole, in favour of recognising the presence of giftedness as a phenomenon. Teachers in some schools see the term gifted as synonymous with demanding parents and difficult children.'

Lack of recognition of their ability and negative social pressures to conform to the 'norm' can create situations where gifted children feel uncomfortable and unhappy about being different from their peers and seek to resolve this by 'hiding their light under a bushel' – resorting to strategies where they are comfortably underachieving rather than striving for excellence.

There is also a perception that a mathematically gifted child is easy to accommodate within a class of mixed-ability children because he or she learns everything quickly and requires little assistance. However, if a gifted child is not presented with work at a level that is interesting and challenging, boredom and frustration can set in and the child may create distractions in the form of disruptive behaviour. It is therefore important that mathematically gifted children are acknowledged as requiring special attention in school, where their problems and talents are recognised and supported intellectually and socially.

Identification of the mathematically gifted child

Baseline assessment

Although there is no clear blueprint as to what represents a gifted child, the first strategy for a teacher to use, which may give some indication of high aptitude for mathematics in children, is baseline assessment. It is important that children who demonstrate they are performing above the expected 'norm', on entry to school at 5, are presented with work at their own level and not be expected to conform to the normative level of the class. This is a particular problem where published mathematics schemes are in use. It is common practice for teachers to start all the children working on the first book of the scheme on the basis of perceived fairness and equality, when in fact some children are capable of much more challenging work.

The planning of mathematical activities according to children's ability, in the early stages of schooling, can be vital in establishing a positive attitude towards mathematical work in school. Take, for example, the case of David in a reception class where mathematical work was being observed:

> The least able group in the class had been set a task by the teacher to colour a triangle drawn by the teacher on a worksheet and to trace the number 1 underneath, whilst the teacher worked with another group at the other end of the room. David, as a member of the group, had scribbled over the triangle with a crayon and was throwing crayons around the room. When asked why he had scribbled over the triangle he replied *'Don't like mafs – s'boring'*. The conversation led on to me inviting him to count for me. David counted to a hundred without any mistake. I followed this with asking him to carry out several tasks of ascending difficulty. David was able to write numbers to 20; perform addition and subtraction with objects to ten without needing to add objects or take away objects from the number of objects given. At the end of the session I discreetly asked the teacher why David was in the less able group to be told that his group were the poor readers.

David, although a bright child mathematically, had been labelled as less able on account of his reading ability. He was already showing signs of disaffection with mathematics at the reception stage on account of the fact that no work at his level had been offered to him and was declaring 'Don't like mafs – s'boring'. It is, therefore, important that early identification of an aptitude for mathematics, though baseline assessment, is supported by the planning of appropriate mathematical activities at the child's own level to offer stimulus and challenge.

Teachers' checklists

It was found by Trevor Kerry (1981), in a study of East Midland teachers, that teachers, through their experiences of teaching bright primary children, had developed the following checklist of characteristics:

* grasp concepts or experiments readily;
* think out problems for themselves;
* show above-average intellectual ability;
* think and understand quickly;
* ask intelligent questions;
* use their initiative;
* make connections back to previous knowledge;
* draw conclusions;
* assimilate facts quickly; and
* have lively and enquiring minds.

Factors associated with giftedness in mathematics

It is important to emphasise that factors associated with giftedness in mathematics are not exclusive, but represent those factors which research has shown to be common to all children who display an above-average aptitude for academic work in school. In identifying the gifted child, it is important to recognise that their talents often do not lie exclusively in one domain, but that certain special qualities distinguish the gifted child as a bright pupil in the context of other pupils in the class.

Mathematical learning experiences at home

As with low attainers in mathematics, the amount of mathematical experience offered to a child at home is a significant factor in whether the child is likely to be identified as mathematically gifted. Joan Freeman (1979) states that 'children whose home backgrounds have enabled them to exercise their abilities and to achieve more highly are far more likely to be identified as gifted than children from culturally poorer homes'.

Untidy writing

Gifted children of both sexes tend to be messy in their handwriting. According to Trevor Kerry (1983), this feature is usually associated with the gifted child's rapid thinking skills, which are often far in advance of his or her writing skills. However, boys appear to have more difficulty with fine motor control than girls, which is likely to show up in their handwriting, whereas girls' handwriting has a tendency to be neater than boys'. For the teacher it is important to recognise the fact that if a child's presentation of mathematical work is messy it should not override the value of the content. Also, mathematically gifted children may carry out a lot of the mathematical work quickly and accurately in their heads. What is presented on paper may be jottings, representing their mental thinking processes, which do not conform to the conventional notation of mathematical work. More flexible teachers try to make adjustments for this. There are, however, some teachers who expect all children to adhere rigidly to the standard notation and this is likely to place restraint on the intuitive mathematical thinking processes of the more able child.

Learns quickly and easily

Gifted children are highly motivated to learn and have the ability to assimilate and memorise knowledge and skills easily. Their ability to make connections back to previous knowledge enables them to progress quickly, as well as sustaining a developing depth of understanding. In terms of mathematical work, the gifted child often does not need to work through all the hierarchical steps to achieve an understanding of a mathematical process or skill. If they are expected to do so, this can represent time when they are carrying out work below their potential which can dull their motivation through lack of stimulus and incentive. Whilst it is not easy for a teacher continuously to plan challenging work for the brighter children, the use of open-ended tasks and investigations which can be tackled at different levels are a strategy successfully used by teachers to offer stimulus and challenge to gifted children.

The use of published schemes, where the brighter child is expected to work rigidly through every page or card, is also a constraint for the quick-learning child. The designs of published schemes are in the main centred around the average child. Where low attainers require extra support to travel through the scheme, appropriate concessions should be made for brighter children to enable them to progress at their own rate. In order to do this, teachers who make flexible use of published schemes can be selective in planning for brighter children so that they only use what the children need from a scheme.

Self-sufficiency

The gifted child is likely to be highly proactive in terms of self-development. They are capable of sustained periods of focused interest on activities in school, often independently of other children. This can be a source of concern for nursery and infant teachers, where high emphasis is placed on children working together. Tables are placed together, children work in groups and are expected to share equipment. When there is a child who is a determined individualist, who may be irritated by surrounding chatter and the noise of children playing nearby and, for example, does not want to share pattern blocks because they are needed to complete a special pattern, this can create tension in the classroom. The teacher has the difficult task of maintaining the social ethos without unduly cramping the style of the gifted child, whilst at the same time trying to treat all the children fairly. It is, therefore, important that the needs of any gifted child in the class should be considered at the planning stage as certain activities may require extra resourcing. For instance, in the case of pattern-making activities, a variety of apparatus should be made available so that children can select, rather than providing only a single resource.

It is important to recognise that gifted children are happy to be with other children but they have less need of the social support of friends and to this extent they are likely to be more self-sufficient. According to Cutts and Moseley (1957), a bright child can find it difficult to relate to children of the same age, often seeking the company of older children for intellectual companionship. At home, they are more likely to be involved in hobbies which do not involve others – using a computer, reading, building, classifying and researching collections. For example, my nephew at 7 years old had an impressive collection of plastic dinosaurs and was able to talk very articulately about each one. In school, the gifted child is very proactive in making use of the resources available and, where resources are richly provided, the gifted child 'was found to be much better able to make beneficial use of them than less able children. They shot ahead' (Kerry, 1981).

As gifted children grow and develop, they can become alienated from their peers who may see them as 'cocky' or a 'know-all'. For the gifted child this can represent a source of tension and anxiety. Arising from a need to be liked and accepted they may resort to underachieving strategies in order to conform and not appear different from their peers.

Curiosity

It is the gifted child's thirst for knowledge and understanding that often distinguishes them from other children. They display a persistent curiosity from a very young age and ask questions of a deep and probing nature. Because their verbal development is advanced they often use sophisticated vocabulary in phrasing or answering questions and may be labelled as 'precocious' by teachers – for example, a child of 5, known for his consuming interest in fossils, when asked what he wanted to be when he grew up replied, 'a palaeontologist'.

Sense of humour

Although gifted children are noted for their committed application to serious intellectual pursuits, they are acknowledged as having a highly developed sense of humour which is above the usual joke culture of young children. For example:

> A child in a Year 1 class was obsessed with drawing tractors which was well known to the other children. On this occasion he was asked to make an observational drawing of a flower. When I looked at what the child had produced the paper was covered completely in black crayon. On asking what he had drawn, a bright child standing beside me answered for him 'It's a tractor in the dark!'

Strategies for supporting the mathematically gifted child

First, it is important that teachers expect to find bright children in their classrooms. The issue of low expectations of teachers is a concern that has been taken up by the National Numeracy Project (1997). Research has shown that schools serving a deprived community have a tendency to set expectations accordingly. Trevor Kerry (1981), reports a head-teacher's comment: 'You won't find any gifted children here; they're all "Council" children.'

Partnership

It is important to establish good relationships with the children and their parents, so that the teacher and parents work together to support the child. In the case of gifted children, parents are often especially grateful for support and advice from school and this helps to reassure them that the school is acting in the best interests of their child. (Strategies for implementing parent partnership in helping children with mathematics are covered in Chapter 7.)

A child-centred approach

The notion of a 'child-centred approach' is viewed as rather outmoded nowadays, with a shift towards an emphasis on whole-class teaching, particularly with mathematics. However, in order to support the gifted child in learning mathematics it is vital to operate a child-centred approach. Since the gifted child is likely to be a self-sustaining and proactive individualist, it is important to start from the child's personal portfolio of mathematical knowledge and experiences as a basis for planning. The teacher needs to adopt a flexible approach to planning mathematical programmes of work for the gifted child as he or she may not need to follow the same steps or routes as the rest of the class. What is important is that the bright child is offered opportunities for stimulating and challenging work at his or her own level, to sustain his or her interest and satisfy his or her desire to learn. A gifted child, although perhaps requiring 'different' treatment from his or her peers, feels a strong need to be part of the class. Whilst requiring the same level of support, encouragement and praise as any individual child, the gifted child may need extra support to be accepted by his or her peers as a respected, if a little unconventional, member of the group.

Teacher as learner rather than expert

There are many teachers who, like myself, are not mathematicians but see themselves, it is hoped, as good practitioners. In the many cases I have experienced a mathematically gifted child in my class, I have found my expertise has increased by learning with the child and I have been delighted that a child has led me to new fields of mathematical enlightenment. As teachers we often feel we have to be seen as the expert, as the fount of all knowledge to the child, whereas the use of partnership in learning can be much more rewarding for the teacher and the child.

Challenging resources

Since gifted children are highly proactive towards their own development and intensely curious, the provision of challenging mathematical resources in a classroom can stimulate their interest – for example, an exciting mathematical computer game with progressive levels of difficulty, complex 2D and 3D constructional apparatus, complicated jigsaw puzzles, mathematical puzzles or board games, including games of strategy such as 'draughts' and 'chess'.

Building on interests

Gifted children often have special interests in the form of collections that can be capitalised upon. For example, the craze of collecting 'POGS' (circular cardboard discs with different pictures on each 'pog') was used by a primary teacher as a focus for mathematical work called 'Pog maths'. If teachers are a little underconfident about designing mathematical activities of this nature, professional journals, such as *Child Education*, run regular mathematical features. These are tried and tested ideas that have been used in classrooms and represent a useful resource for different and interesting ways to present mathematics in nursery and infant schools.

Topic work

Mathematical activities as part of a class theme or topic can help to add variety and interest to mathematical work in the classroom for all children, particularly gifted children, with their appetite for knowledge and understanding of the world around them. Their interest can serve to spark off interest in others. For example:

> Starting a topic on Weather with a Year 2 class it was discovered that one of the TV weathermen, was a close family friend of a bright child's parents. With support from the parents the children wrote to the weatherman and he sent a large pack of material including satellite pictures for the project. This gave an added impetus to the project especially for the bright child, who pestered his mother to ring 'Uncle Michael' so that he could ask him questions. The child concerned became a star in the class and I don't think I have ever known a class of young children so keen to watch the weather report on the television and bring in newspaper weather reports to school for data collection.

The application of mathematics in a crosscurricular context is dealt with more fully in Chapter 12.

Using the school environment

The school environment can provide a wealth of possibilities for mathematical work and opportunities for problem-solving which can be successfully used to motivate and challenge all children including the brighter child. A nursery school, with help from local students, created a maths trail around their school designed for the children to use. In another school, Year 2 infants were asked to consider the problem of safety in the playground. What caused minor accidents and how could safety be improved? Are there ways in which playtimes could be improved? Some schools compile ideas files, which are regularly updated by the staff and kept in the staffroom for reference.

Variety of diet

Gifted children enjoy the challenge of something new and having a variety of interesting mathematical activities. Including all aspects of mathematics helps to motivate the gifted child. There are many publications which present a wealth of ideas for exciting mathematical activities at nursery and infant level. Key publishers in this area are Scholastic, Belair Publications and Claire Publications (the addresses for these are given at the end of this book).

Maths clubs

In some primary schools there is an opportunity for children to join a maths club which may run at lunchtime or for a short while after school. These usually take the form of 'fun' maths where mathematical games are played, puzzles and investigations are carried out and competitions are organised, such as mathematical treasure hunts around the school. They are normally organised for older children at KS2. However, in some schools activities are planned on different levels and open-ended activities are provided so that infant children can join in, thus giving the bright infant child the opportunity to experience challenging work at his or her own level.

Fast-track or accelerated learning

In recent years, with the concern about standards of numeracy in primary schools, some schools have initiated *fast-track* mathematics programmes as a strategy to raise standards of numeracy in able children. These involve concentrated whole-class sessions with an emphasis on mental arithmetic. The principle is modelled on methods used in Pacific Rim countries (Reynolds and Farrell, 1996). Schools in the UK that have been using the approach have evidence in the form of test results which support its effectiveness with able children. The programmes have also been shown to improve the performance of underachievers in numeracy.

Working with an older class

Where a child is assessed as being significantly more advanced than his or her peers, some schools take the decision in consultation with the child's parents to place the child in a class of older children. This is always very carefully considered and is only agreed when it is judged to be the best course of action in the light of reviewing the child's all-round development and his or her relationships with age-related peers. Although there are exceptional cases where this has been successful, it can be an unsuitable strategy on account of concern for the likely social and emotional problems for a child in relating to a class of older children. Wherever possible, schools prefer to keep a child within his or her own peer group. However, there are exceptional cases where enabling a child to work alongside his or her intellectual peers can be more beneficial. There are some schools who operate a flexible system, where a bright child is timetabled to work alongside his or her intellectual peers in mathematics when the child has been identified as having an exceptional ability and aptitude for the subject. The rest of the time is spent in lessons with his or her own age group.

Summary

The academically gifted child, although having been blessed with exceptional ability, can be seen as having to face a difficult journey through life on account of his or her being seen as different and often difficult to cope with by his or her parents, siblings, teachers and peers. They can be highly demanding and individualistic in their approach to learning and find it difficult to relate to their peers on the same intellectual plane. Mathematically gifted children are seen as a particular concern for non-specialist teachers, who may not feel confident in their own ability in the subject to provide appropriate work at the child's own level. There is a tendency for underconfident teachers to programme gifted children to conform to the 'norm', instead of working alongside the child as a facilitator rather than an expert.

The mathematically gifted child requires special learning support in the same way as the low-attaining child. It is important that the child's aptitude for mathematics is identified early and for the teacher to work in partnership with the parents to support the child's mathematical development. The individual nature of giftedness in children requires teachers to adopt a flexible child-centred approach to planning programmes of work and to understand that their style of learning may be different. Their highly developed appetite for learning requires special provision in terms of challenging learning resources and activities at their own level which stimulate interest and enjoyment. Whilst gifted children are 'different', they also need to feel they belong to a class and require support, encouragement and approval alongside their peers. If the social climate of a class is managed well, the teacher will provide opportunities for all children to have their talents, strengths and efforts recognised from the least able to the brightest children in the class, thus creating a general atmosphere of respect and empathy between all the children.

20

Managing record-keeping

Record-keeping is the last stage in the process of teaching, not the first.
(Shipman)

Monitoring progress and continuity

Records of achievement are vital professional tools for teachers, in the same way that case notes are vital tools for the medical profession. The process of keeping records is fundamentally centred around monitoring continuity and progress in children's learning. It is the formal mechanism that enables teachers to document the formative and summative assessment of individual children. It also represents evidence for audit purposes, in the context of professional account-ability. It demonstrates, at nursery level, that teachers are monitoring children's progress in the six areas of learning defined in the Desirable Outcomes. It provides documentary evidence that KS1 teachers are undertaking the statutory requirements to deliver the National Curriculum and monitor children's progress through the framework of attainment targets and levels.

For a system of record-keeping to be effective it has to fulfil important criteria. As a result of a Schools Council Project (Clift *et al.*, 1981), a group of primary teachers considered the following criteria to be important. To:

- chart pupils' progress and achievement;
- communicate information to other teachers;
- ensure continuity on transfer to other schools;
- guide a replacement or supply teacher;
- serve diagnostic purposes;
- provide information on the success or failure of teaching methods or materials;
- inform interested parties – parents, psychologists, etc.; and
- provide a general picture of the school for headteachers, governors, etc.

In the context of nursery and infant schooling, to establish an effective system of record-keeping, each school has to establish a frame of reference. This should be established through shared perceptions of the staff on what represents a manageable system for record-keeping. This will then need to be formalised into a set of procedures to be adopted throughout the school. According to Conner (1991), 'The most effective systems of record-keeping in schools are those which tend to emerge from the organisation and structure of the teaching'. The process is therefore organic rather than clinically imposed. This is supported by the statement in the inspection review on *The Teaching and Learning of Mathematics* (DES, 1989c):

> The best records included information about the work covered, the equipment used, the evidence of concepts understood, the skills practised and samples of work as well as comments about the child's attitude to mathematics. These records were also used as a basis for planning future work for the class, groups and individuals.

With access to a photocopier, it can appear easier for a school to adopt a formula devised by a publisher or by another school. However, in reality, a formula approach can never fully accommodate the particular requirements of an individual school. The most important part of the process of developing a 'formula' for a particular school can only be carried out through the collective discussion of the staff over time. It needs to be recognised that, even when the staff in a school have formulated a set of principles for record-keeping, these principles will require to be reviewed and updated on a regular basis, through staff meetings or INSET days, as part of a school's development programme.

Fitness for purpose

Record-keeping for mathematics should be viewed as different from English. Whilst there are similarities in the principles, the approaches can be very different. For example, a record of a child's piece of writing indicates a great deal about a child's level of ability and development of writing skills, whether it represents simple marks on a page to a detailed account incorporating the correct spelling, grammar and punctuation marks. A record of a child's mathematical work will often only represent what a teacher or published scheme has asked for, especially if the task is closed. It is for this reason that records of achievement in mathematics rely upon good assessment skills of observation and detective work on the part of the teacher concerned.

Strategies for recording achievement in mathematics

There are different strategies for monitoring children's progress and achievement in mathematics, which all have useful contributions to make, depending on what is being monitored. However, it is important to use a variety of methods on a 'fitness for purpose' basis to confirm and validate judgements. Informal teacher records, which may be jotted down in a notebook, should contribute to the compilation of more formal whole-school record-keeping systems. Some local education authorities have devised sheets or profiles for all schools to use in combination with their own 'in-house' procedures. However, the main body of record-keeping procedures for individual schools will be those that have evolved internally.

The recording of assessment

It is important that record-keeping is recognised as the process through which assessment procedures are formalised and not the actual process of assessment itself. As emphasised by Alexander *et al.* (1992) 'the pre-condition of good records is good assessment'. In the context of monitoring children's mathematical performance in infant and nursery schools, the following strategies are commonly used in conjunction with each other.

Field notes

These are used to record notes from observations on individual children whilst they are performing mathematical tasks. This can be carried out on an informal basis where 'snapshots' of successful achievement or evidence of concern are jotted down during a teaching session and described in relation to the task carried out by the child. However, it is important that 'when writing down observations as opposed to opinions, that it provides an accurate description of a specific event and describes the setting sufficiently to give the event meaning' (*Schools Council Working Paper 75*, 1983). For example, the following notes were compiled by a teacher directing a mental arithmetic number game with a group of less able Year 2 children:

Lindsay, Darren, Claire, Stephen, Mark, Joanne.

Oral games – children take a counter from a box for correct answers in each game, counted up at the end of each game.

Count orally to 20 together and individually.

All children coped O.K.

Count on 1 game.

No problem – everyone quick off the mark – even Lindsay and Claire. Lindsay really enjoyed this.

Count on 2 game.

Mark and Joanne no problems. Stephen and Darren used two fingers but O.K. Claire and Lindsay resorted to guessing. Showed them two finger method. Claire tried but was unsure. Better with a numberline. Lindsay doesn't understand the finger method, hit and miss with a numberline.

Lindsay sussed the scoring. She started to take extra counters out of the box to win – she got irritable when I stopped her – I gave out counters myself.

Abandoned Count on 3 Game – tried count back 1 game.

Mark and Joanne no problems. Stephen sussed the game after the first round. Darren and Claire – numberline – they got quicker but needed numberline. Lindsay seemed to cope O.K. – kept looking at Claire's numberline – difficult to know whether she was able to do it without support – she obviously wants to win!

After the session Lindsay said, 'Mrs Smith can we play that game again tomorrow?'

Will use more games with this group. Must have a go with Mark and Joanne next week with numbers beyond 20.

Individual record sheets

These are used to record information about children's progress over time. The first example shown (Figure 20.1) is a nursery 'picture' record for mathematics where the child colours in a bead to record that he or she has been able to perform a particular skill. The use of picture records is an effective way of involving young children in the process. Most importantly, the sheet conveys very clear information to the teacher about what the child has achieved and what action needs to be taken whenever the sheet is consulted. However, the importance of shared values amongst the staff using the record is essential in the overall management and interpretation of the document.

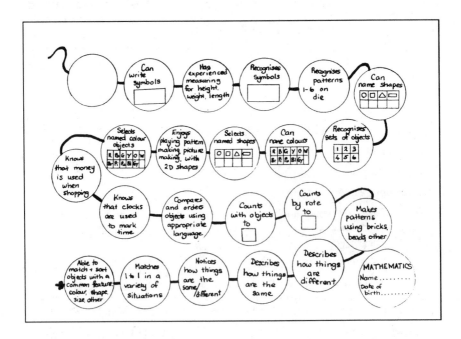

Figure 20.1. A picture record for mathematics

The second example (Figure 20.2) represents an individual record sheet for a child working at KS1. This type of record is useful because it contains information about an individual child's progress in mathematics throughout KS1. It can provide information for the next teacher on a child's progress to date. By charting what the child has covered, it will reduce unnecessary repetition of content so that progress and continuity can be sustained. It can also provide information on a child's strengths and weaknesses in mathematics and documentary evidence of any action taken. In this way a detailed picture of a child's mathematical ability, interests and ways of working is included as part of monitoring a child's mathematical development. Again, a record of this nature requires the staff of the school to establish a collective interpretation of the document.

Recording by checklist

Checklists or ticklists are seen as a quick and effective way to manage the recording of achievement for a whole class on one sheet of paper, presented in a format similar to a register of attendance. The benefit of using a ticklist can be seen when a teacher requires all the members of a class to have experienced a 'turn' at an activity; for example, in using a computer or baking cakes. In this way the teacher can keep track of which children have carried out the activity. A ticklist can also highlight a child's absences when a particular area is covered to indicate that some action needs to be taken when the child returns to school. Ticklists are recognised as very useful at nursery level, where children often move freely from activity to activity. The teacher or helper directing an activity can use the list to keep account of who has visited the activity.

One of the problems with ticklists in relation to assessing children's performance is, what does a tick mean? Does it indicate that a child has demonstrated competence or understanding or that a child has simply experienced something? It is for this reason that many teachers nowadays make use of a key code to indicate different levels of experience and understanding. For example:

/ = experienced

$\angle$ = needs more practice

Δ = understood

$\cong$* = outstanding work

R = requires reteaching

However, it is important when using a key code as a whole-school procedure that each category is consistently and reliably interpreted by all the staff. This requires regular review of the process and the use of *agreement trialling* discussed in Chapter 13.

Annual Attainment Record
MATHEMATICS - Key Stage 1

Name: _____

Date of Birth: _____   Date: _____

Attainment Targets	Programmes of Study	Attainment Levels		
		1	2	3
1	Using/Applying Mathematics			
2	Number/Algebra			
3	Shape, Space and Measures			

Complete as appropriate:

W		
working towards	covered	competent

Examples of particular progress/achievement

_____

General comments including attitude towards the subject

_____

The following action is to be taken

_____

Signed

Class Teacher _____   Head Teacher _____

Figure 20.2   Annual attainment record
Source: From Edwards and Wild, 1990

Group assessment records

These are often used when a teacher is carrying out a high-input teaching session with a small group of children (see Figure 20.3). The teacher takes the opportunity to carry out an assessment of the group at the same time. Children's individual performance is measured against clearly established criteria and a diagnosis and prescription are recorded for each child in the group in relation to the work carried out. In the example in Figure 20.3 the teacher has used a key, which makes on-the-spot recording quick and easy. The value of such record-keeping is that it is easy to manage alongside teaching because everything required for the task is on one sheet of paper. It is easy to create a proforma so that the procedure can be carried out throughout the school and is applicable to any classroom activity carried out by small groups of children. The process generates concise, useful information about individual children for planning purposes. Information is also generated about the performance 'norm' of a group, whether individual children are performing within that frame of reference or whether the membership of the group should be reviewed.

GROUP ASSESSMENT SHEET

TASK: Class 2 E Work with Number Squares and Oral Counting		LEARNING OUTCOMES: CHECKING POINTS	A.T.	LEVEL
	1	Can build a number square	2	2
	2	Can count down from 10 in 1's		
	3	Can count up in 2's		
SUBJECT: Mathematics	4	Can count up to 100 in 10's		
Date: 13 · 5 · 97	5	Demonstrates an understanding of pattern		

NAME	CHECKING POINTS 1	2	3	4	5	COURSE OF ACTION
Luke Brown	▲	▲	∠	∠	△	Completed Square quickly. Could see pattern All numbers formed correctly. Needs practice with counting on past 10. Use number sq. patts
James Edwards	∠	▲	▲	▲	/	Built number square to 42, missed one number out. Didn't see pattern. Very slow worker Good counting skills. Play some timing games
Georgina Smith	/R	▲	/R	/R	/R	Built square to 25. Many number reversals Rest of square filled with jumbled incorrect numbers Needs help with number formation, oral counting. Try dice games
Bryony Jones	▲	▲	△	△	△	Completed whole square correctly. All numbers correctly formed. Very neat work. Counted well orally used rhymes to help her. Some challenging counting games with square
Robbi Ann Williams	/R	△	/R	/R	/R	Managed up to 15. Some formed backwards. Needs help with number formation and oral counting try count on dice/spinner games
Jonathan King	/R	△	/R	/R	/R	Managed up to 14. Filled rest of square with jumbled numbers. Number formation very poor. Needs help with number formation, oral counting. Dice games

Key / = experienced ∠ - needs practice △ = understood ▲ = outstanding work
R = Reteaching required

Figure 20.3 Group assessment sheet

Self-assessment records

It is widely accepted nowadays that children should be encouraged to reflect on their own achievements through the process of review and target-setting. To place this aspect within a more formal context, children are invited to make recorded statements about themselves. This can take the form of a statement scribed by the teacher, an annotated drawing or written sentences. David Hopkins (1985) suggested a very simple recording procedure appropriate for young children – to rate their work by drawing a face to indicate how they felt about it.

Self-assessment records commonly in use are those which ask a child to consider his or her performance in relation to his or her time in school as a whole rather than focusing on a particular subject, but many of the profomas in use could be easily adapted for that purpose if required. Figure 20.4 is an example of a self-assessment form adapted from the Cheshire Unit for Pupil Assessment (1992).

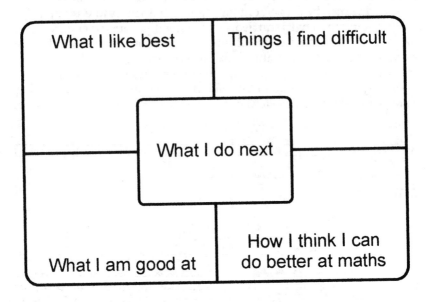

Figure 20.4   Self-assessment sheet

Profiles of mathematical development

A profile of mathematical development usually represents a component of a child's personal file, which includes recorded evidence of a child's achievements in the six areas of learning at nursery level, and in all the National Curriculum subjects at KS1. This will include a portfolio of specimens of the child's work in the form of photographs, annotated drawings, artwork and pieces of written work that represent evidence of the child's progress. The file may also contain other relevant items such as the child's biographical and medical record, a record of baseline assessment, statement of special educational needs, self-assessment records, record of performance in KS1 SATs and copies of annual reports to parents. It can be seen that over a period of time a child's personal file can become very bulky. Storage can be a problem and relevant information can be difficult to access. It is for this reason that schools have found it necessary to find ways to rationalise the process – for example, a single summary sheet is completed for filing purposes (see Figure 20.2). In this way stored evidence is kept to a minimum, with the relevant information presented in a concise and easily interpreted format.

Class journals

Some primary schools have adopted the idea of compiling a class journal. This can take the form of ring files sectioned with the name of each child in the class. The file contains selected specimens of the child's work annotated by the teacher (see Figure 20.5) and a sheet where the teacher records significant landmarks or concerns and discussions with the child's parents in chronological order.

At the end of the school year, the file is passed to the following teacher for the next year's work to be entered. In this way a continuous working record is maintained which can be consulted at any time. In a school where the system was implemented, the headteacher said:

> It is very useful when I have to talk to a parent about a concern with a child. I can refer to the child's journal, see the comments made by each of the teachers and have specimens of work to hand. The only problem is changes of staff, making sure that the new members of staff know how to operate it, otherwise you get gaps in the continuity of the system.

Computer records

The use of computer-generated records of achievement in nursery and primary schools is still mainly something for the future. There are elements of school record-keeping that are often stored on a computer data base for ease of access and updating, for example a child's home address, a contact name and telephone number in case of emergency. Such databases must be formally registered under the terms of the Data Protection Act 1985. In the case of school or teacher-devised records the use of word-processed formats is increasing. However, handwritten statements by teachers on record sheets, specimens of work and reports are still widely recognised as the signatures of professional authenticity. With all written records containing personal details about children it is important that a strict code of 'in-house' confidentiality is observed. This can be a particularly sensitive issue when parents help in classrooms and clear ground-rules must be established.

Evaluation records

Records of lesson evaluations, and weekly and termly evaluations, represent an important component in the continuous process of monitoring the quality of mathematical provision. It also formally represents the process of the teacher as a 'learner' in the context of a learning school. The process of evaluation is both summative and formative. As a summative process, it should serve to review critically what has taken place. As a formative process, it should serve to identify any elements in classroom management that require improvement on a trial or refine basis. The process of evaluation is discussed in more detail in Chapter 15.

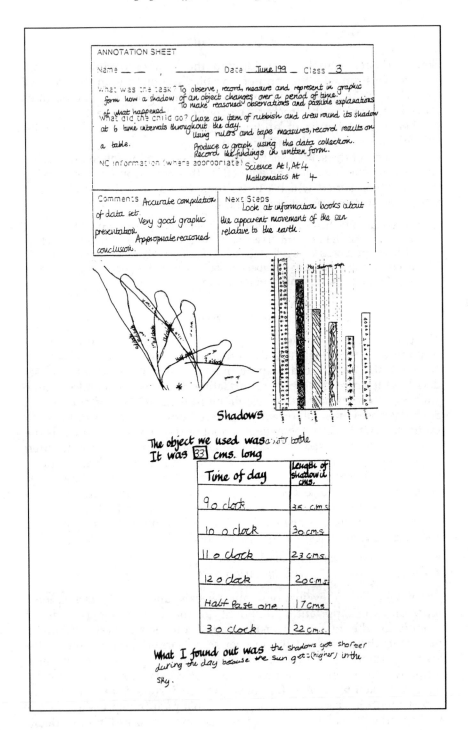

Figure 20.5   Work on measuring shadows by Year 3 child, with annotation sheet

Written reports

The process of reporting and writing reports represents the summative elements of the assessment and record-keeping process. The final chapter of this book is devoted to discussing how these are managed in schools.

Summary

The prerequisite to establishing an effective system of record-keeping for mathematics throughout a school must be an effective whole-school policy on assessment for mathematics. Any system of record-keeping adopted by a school must justify its existence by performing a key role in maintaining continuity and progress in mathematics throughout the school. It is the professional role of the teacher to conform to commonly agreed methods within a school. In addition teachers often develop their own tried and trusted methods which they use on a day-by-day basis in their own classrooms for the purpose of confirming and validating judgements.

The principal role of record-keeping is a formal process by which information, derived from assessment, can be communicated to interested parties. However, in the climate of assessing the competence of teachers, the efficacy of assessment and record-keeping within classrooms, and as part of a whole-school endeavour, has to be seen as representing a professional measure of accountability. In the context of a learning school, it is important that the terms of reference are regularly reviewed and methods refined on a regular basis, to ensure that the system currently in use is seen as 'fit for purpose'. In general terms an effective whole-school record-keeping system should be:

- derived from consensus;
- able to communicate key information on children's progress and achievements to interested parties;
- an active system used to support continuity and progression throughout the school;
- able to involve pupils in some elements;
- easily managed;
- clear and unambiguous to interpret;
- conveniently stored and easily accessible; and
- regularly reviewed.

21

Managing reporting

The final element in the process of managing the teaching of mathematics in the early years is procedures for reporting. In many respects these are the same for all areas of the curriculum. In general terms, the process of reporting represents the collating of evidence pertaining to a particular child or situation and the presentation of a summary of this evidence to date, to inform interested parties. For a system of reporting to be fully effective, it should also be seen as a two-way process of communication, where the process includes opportunities for dialogue and discussion with the parties concerned.

Reports to parents

Written reports

Headteachers have a statutory duty to ensure that a written report is sent, at least once in the course of a school year, to the parents of each pupil for Year R (reception) and above and it must contain the following details set down as the 'statutory minimum' (DfEE, 1997a):

- brief particulars of progress in all subjects and activities studied as part of the curriculum;
- details of the pupil's general progress (e.g. academic, behaviour, special achievements);
- details of arrangements for discussing the report with teachers at the school;
- brief comments for each NC subject studied; (*for year R pupils, only where they have commenced KS1 programme of study*);
- a summary of the pupil's attendance and the percentage of sessions for which the pupil was absent without authority.

For all pupils assessed at the end of KS1

- the pupils' NC levels and a statement that these have been arrived at by statutory assessment;
- a brief commentary setting out what the results show about the pupils' progress in the subject, both individually and in relation to other pupils; *this should give an explanation in cases where there are significant differences between the*

teacher assessment (TA) level and the task/test results;
- a statement where the pupil has been disapplied from any attainment target (AT) under the 1996 Education Act, sections 364/365;
- school and national comparative information, including the proportion of pupils who:
  - are working towards Level 1;
  - were disapplied;
  - were absent from the tasks, tests or TA.

Note: At the end of KS assessment, parents have the right to request written information about their child's level of attainment in each AT of the core subjects on the NC 1–8 scale. Headteachers must provide this information within 15 school days of the request
For all pupils assessed at the end of KS1 the report must include the following details relating to mathematics.

- the pupils' NC assessment levels derived from:
  - the mathematics task/test and TA;
  - finer gradings (A-C) at level 2;
  - KS2 mathematics test (where KS1 pupils attain level 4 or above).

- school comparative information showing the % of pupils (in the current year) at each level of attainment in mathematics by task, test and TA;
- national comparative information showing the % of pupils at each level of attainment in mathematics for the previous year;
- all information must be reported by the end of the summer term of each year.

Discussion with parents

Formal opportunities for parents to discuss their child's progress with the teacher are planned as parents' evenings which normally occur at least once a year in the school calendar. Some schools also operate twilight sessions at the end of the school day on a regular basis – for example, parents of children in a class are informed that their child's teacher will always be available on a certain night of the week after school, for interviews with parents, on an open-door principle. Other schools operate an informal open-door policy at the end of every school day, where teachers are available for consultation when parents pick their children up from school. This is a particularly appropriate procedure for nursery and reception classes, where parents are perhaps more anxious to receive regular feedback on how their child is responding to starting school.

Within formal or informal sessions teachers can take the opportunity to give a verbal report to parents. This should include feedback on a child's strengths, weaknesses and general academic and social progress. In communicating information about a child to parents it is important to deal with concerns in a sensitive way. Parents, particularly those of young children, can be very worried and upset by 'bad news'. It is with areas of concern that the two-way process of reporting becomes very important. Through discussion, perceptions of a child can be shared by the parent and the teacher. A course of action can be discussed so parents can help their child at home. In this way their anxiety will be reduced to some extent because they will feel they are able to do something positive to help their child and, it is hoped, see positive results.

The process of regular two-way reporting also helps to establish feelings of trust and confidence between parents and teachers. It is hoped that this will develop as the child travels through the school to the point where a parent feels comfortable about sharing perceptions and concerns he or she may have about his or her child with teachers.

Reporting to parents should be seen as a positive process, used as an opportunity to emphasise a child's achievements, whilst at the same time weaknesses can be constructively discussed and parents can be encouraged to contribute their support. As a professional process of communication it should also represent integrity and honesty. Whilst there may be elements which may be excluded on the basis that they could represent a breach of professional confidence, be harmful to the pupil or the parents, or involve disclosing information about another pupil, it is important that the guiding principle is that 'parents should be left in no doubt as to how their children are progressing in all areas of school life' (DfEE, 1997a).

Reporting to children

Oral feedback

As part of the reporting process, it is important to keep children informed about how they are doing. For young children there is much to learn about life in school and what is expected of them in the way of behaviour and 'school work'. They are constantly being exposed to new experiences and their only clues to how they should respond come from watching and listening to what is going on around them. It is through indications of approval or censure by their teachers and peers that they are able to refine their view of the world around them and begin to understand what is expected of them.

Teachers of young children, therefore, have a very important role to play in ensuring that their pupils are given positive and constructive feedback on a continuous basis through deserved praise, constructive guidance and encouragement as part of their daily interactions with children. Time should be taken to review and celebrate special effort and achievement at the end of each session, which can serve to present children with models by which they can measure their own performance. However, it is important that review time is not just a platform for brighter children to receive praise but that representative efforts and achievements of all the class are shared and celebrated.

Formal review and target-setting

Within a more formal context, teachers plan opportunities, either termly or annually, to review a child's progress individually. On such occasions, discussion, self-assessment and target-setting can take place. It is important that comfortable relationships are established between the teacher and individual pupils so that review sessions take on more of the form of a 'chat with a critical friend', rather than something a child may feel anxious about. If we consider formal interviews in adult life, and how important it is to make the interviewee feel at ease before launching into probing questions, it may help us understand how a child would feel in the same situation.

Emphasis on achievement

The process of reporting to children should emphasise achievement positively, clearly signalling to children where their strengths lie. Through constructive discussion with individual children, weaknesses can be identified and positive short-term strategies formulated to help children overcome their problems. As experienced teachers know, when there is a glimmer that an individual child is starting to improve, a sprinkle of warm encouragement does wonders for the child's confidence and self-esteem.

Confirming expectations

It has to be remembered that feedback given to children confirms expectations. If no feedback is given, then the child has no guidance on how to measure his or her performance in terms of personal progress or in relation to others in the class. If positive feedback is shelled out liberally and uncritically, children soon catch on to whatever they do that receives praise, and reduce their levels of effort accordingly. If feedback is persistently negative, where a child is constantly criticised for poor work, laziness or bad behaviour, then the child starts to lose heart, gives up trying and begins to confirm the expectation of being lazy and disruptive. For the process of feedback to children to be fully effective it should represent a healthy combination of deserved praise, sensitive encouragement, critical discussion and appropriate censure, apportioned fairly to all members of a class. In this way the process can help towards developing feelings of trust and mutual respect between class teachers and their pupils.

Reporting to other members of staff

Written reports

Summative reports on individual children's progress to date are written to inform the next teacher at the end of each school year so that continuity in progress can be maintained from year to year throughout the school. However, some schools also devise a whole-class report which gives brief details of English and mathematics achievements for each child in the class in the context of ability groups, so that the receiving teacher can quickly scan the report and use the previous teacher's grouping arrangements as a convenient starting point for planning.

Team reviews and target-setting

In nursery settings or in larger infant schools, where teams of teachers work together in a year group, the procedure of a weekly meeting, where time is assigned to review children's work and set targets, has been adopted. This has shown itself to be a useful strategy to identify problems as they arise and enables teachers to target children for specific help in the following week. In this way teachers are alerted more quickly to persistent problems, and support from the SENCO or outside help can be initiated more expediently.

Conferencing

Conferencing occurs when there is significant concern about a particular child. It is common practice for a specific time to be arranged, for interested parties to review the child's case in a more formal setting. This normally involves the headteacher, the SENCO, the class teacher and the child's parents, and may also involve representatives from outside agencies, particularly if the child is being reviewed for the purpose of statementing. In the context of a formal conference the proceedings will need to be recorded. Evidence will need to be submitted in the form of a written report. A child will be assessed in significant areas of school performance to inform any action to be taken.

Informal discussion

The staffroom at breaktimes is often the only place where teachers have the opportunity to share their perceptions of children. Whilst the process is useful to enable teachers to confirm and validate judgements through informal discussion, it is important that the process does not serve to confirm expectations, particularly with children who are frequently grumbled about or praised. Although incidence of this has been rare in my personal experience, there are two examples which come vividly to mind:

Child A
I felt rather apprehensive about receiving child A into my Year 3 class on the back of his staffroom reputation. However, Child A settled in well and after a few weeks I was quite surprised by the amount of mathematical work the child was getting through. He also wanted to do extra work at home. Towards the end of

the year Child A was head and shoulders ahead of his peers and had an insatiable appetite for harder and harder work to the point where it was quite difficult to keep pace with designing increasingly challenging activities. The staff thought that I was being unrealistic when I commented in the staffroom about Child A's work until he joined the next class and the receiving teacher endorsed my opinion. (I found out later that Child A gained a place at Oxford University.)

Child B
Child B had a staffroom reputation for being button bright, highly creative and a delight to teach. On receiving Child B into my class, I had high expectations of what would ensue, but was disappointed that these were never realised. The work Child B consistently produced was very average in relation to his peers and, despite valiant efforts, the reputed 'star' qualities never emerged.

From these two examples it can be seen that care needs to be taken to avoid labels being attached to children, in the case of Child A, a negative stereotype and, for Child B, a 'halo-effect' was created.

Reporting to the headteacher

As part of the headteacher's role to monitor what is happening in his or her school, most headteachers require written forecasts to be submitted at the beginning of each year and/or term. These are generally compiled at formal planning meetings where staff discuss and establish long-term planning considerations for coverage of National Curriculum subjects and topic work. This is to ensure that elements are not duplicated or repeated unnecessarily and that progression and continuity are sustained from class to class. In addition a headteacher may require a written termly summary/review from class teachers – for example, a brief outline of the progress of each class in terms of literacy and numeracy skills.

This is likely to vary from school to school. For example, in a large urban school, the headteacher may require to establish more formal lines of communication in order to keep track of what is going on, whereas in a small village school or a nursery, where the headteacher is involved in day-to-day teaching, communication lines between headteacher and staff may be more informal.

Verbal feedback

There may be times when a class teacher wishes to report an issue to the headteacher. This could be about a child who is causing concern or about an incident in the classroom. The procedures in place will again depend largely on the size of the school. Although headteachers are busy with administration nowadays, they like to be informed of highlights as well as problems. For example, when a class are carrying out some exciting mathematical work, if the headteacher is invited in to see the work, it gives the class a big boost of self-esteem whilst at the same time helping the headteacher to keep a finger on the pulse.

Reporting to receiving schools

Clear guidance is given by the DfEE (1997a) on the procedures for reporting to receiving schools. This applies only to schools where the pupils are of compulsory school age (the term following their fifth birthday):

> Reports must be sent to receiving schools within 15 school days of the child ceasing to be registered at the former school or of the former school receiving a request from the new school. This does not apply if the child was registered at the old school for less than 4 weeks or when it is not reasonably practicable to find out the child's new school.
>
> The reports must contain all statutory assessments in the core subjects, by subject and Attainment Target, indicating the year in which they were made. Both Teacher Assessment and task/test results should be included.
>
> The teacher's latest assessments of the child's progress in each core subject Attainment Target should be sent to the new school. These do not have to be by level but should indicate any significant changes since the last statutory assessment or the pupil arriving at the reporting school and give a fair indication of progress within each core subject Attainment Target.
>
> (DfEE, 1997a)

Whilst the 15-day deadline can be seen to place extra pressure on schools, many teachers see this as a welcome measure, particularly if they are on the receiving end. Often in the past, records from former schools were so late in arriving that they were of little use to the receiving school. In this way there is some attempt made to ensure that continuity and progression are sustained when children change schools.

Reporting to governors and LEAs

The results of KS1 SATs have to be reported formally to the governors and the LEA. This takes the form of written reports, the details of which are made public to parents of the school, but not published nationally except as part of overall national results. The national results for the previous year have to be circulated to all parents with children that have taken SATs in the current year as a measure of comparison. The results of the SATs are taken by LEAs as a measure of good or weak schools. Some weaker schools, identified by poor KS1 SATs results, were targeted for in-service training and support as part of a pilot initiative for the national literacy and numeracy projects.

Summary

This chapter has presented the main processes that schools use in implementing procedures for reporting – first, as a statutory formal measure of accountability to parents, governors, LEAs and receiving schools; and secondly, as formal or informal procedures, operated internally as an important communication network between members of staff and other interested parties. Whilst these procedures are not exclusively related to mathematics, each one will play its part in managing the effective teaching of mathematics in schools.

Reporting represents the final stage in the processes of teaching and learning in school. It serves to present a summarised account of the journey to date and creates a picture of what each child is taking away at that point, in terms of knowledge, skills, aptitudes and interests. It should also represent a two-way process that generates discussion between children, teachers and parents, focused around building the future from examining the evidence of what has gone before.

As a form of communication between teachers it can underpin the structure of whole-school planning for progression and continuity. As a measure of school effectiveness it can help staff assess overall performance, through reviewing the terms of reference, aims and teaching methods and deployment of resources. As schools shift more towards collegiate management and partnership contracts with parents, it is essential that clear lines of communication are established and seen to be open at all times.

Useful names and addresses

Mathematical organisations

AMET (Association of Mathematics Education Teachers), Sylvia Johnson, Sheffield Hallam University, Sheffield.

ATM (Association of Teachers of Mathematics), 7 Shaftesbury Street, Derby DE3 8YB.

Centre for Maths Education, Open Univeristy, Walton Hall, Milton Keynes MK7 6AA.

National Centre for Literacy and Numeracy, London House, 59–65 London Street, Reading RG1 4EW.

NORMAC (Northern Region Mathematics Council), Monsall Road, Manchester M10 8WP.

Mathematical publications

BEAM (Be A Mathematician), Barnsbury Complex, Offord Road, London N1 1QH.

Belair Publications, PO Box 12, Twickenham TW1 1NR.

Jonathan Press/Claire Publications, Tey Brook Craft Centre, Great Tey, Colchester CO6 1JE.

Scholastic Publications, Villiers House, Clarendon Avenue, Leamington Spa, Warwickshire CV32 5PR.

Suppliers of nursery and infant mathematical software

BlackCat Educational Software, The Barn, Cwmcamlais, Brecon, Powys LD3 8TD.

Inclusive Technology, Castle Street, Castleford, Manchester M3 4LZ.

Logotron, 124 Cambridge Science Park, Milton Road, Cambridge CB4 4ZS.

REM, Great Western House, Langport, Somerset TA10 9YU.

Sherston Software, Angel House, Sherston, Malmesbury, Wiltshire SN16 0LH.

Television programmes

BBC Education Information, White City, London W12 7TS.

Channel 4 Schools, PO Box 100, Warwick CV34 6TZ.

Useful resources

Abacus Maths (teachers' cards sets A, B and C) – small-group and whole-class interactive maths activities graded for use in Reception, Year 1 and Year 2 classes.

BEAM: Number Key Stage 1 – a range of active number tasks involving mental and pencil and paper arithmetic.

Developing a Scheme of Work for Primary Mathematics; Teaching Measures; both books contain a wealth of helpful suggestions (*Managing Primary Mathematics* series, Hodder & Stoughton).

Lego Maths – sets of Duplo and pattern tiles supported by a set of laminated cards which present mathematical activities that can be developed from the use of Duplo, for younger children, or traditional Lego for older children.

Longman Primary Maths: Nursery Handbook – a wealth of practical ideas for mathematical activities arising from play contexts.

Mathematics in Nursery Education, (Ann Montague Smith 1997). David Fulton Publishers – contains a wealth of suggestions for planning and teaching mathematics in nursery settings.

Maths on Display, Belair Publications – a well illustrated book to support the creation of mathematical displays in the classroom.

Pattern Animals, Pattern Factory and *Pattern Blocks*, Jonathan Press/Claire Publications – pattern blocks are a versatile resource; the two books support their use in teaching aspects of shape and number work in infant classrooms.

Understanding Mathematics in the Lower Primary Years, Paul Chapman Publishing – a readable book which explains the mathematics at KS1 and gives helpful suggestions for classroom activities.

Bibliography

Abercrombie, M.J.L. (1963) Eye movements, perception and learning, in Reisman, K. and Kauffman, S. (eds.) (1980) *Teaching Mathematics to Children with Special Needs*, Charles E. Merrill, Columbus, OH.

Alexander, R., Rose, J. and Woodhead, C. (1992) *Curriculum Organisation and Classroom Practice in Primary Schools: A Discussion Paper*, HMSO, London.

Anning, A. (1994) Play and the legislated curriculum. Back to basics: an alternative view, in Moyles, J. (ed.) *The Excellence of Play*, Open University Press, Buckingham.

Atkinson, S. (ed.) (1992) *Mathematics with Reason: The Emergent Approach to Primary Maths*, Hodder & Stoughton, London.

Atkinson, S. (1996) *Developing a Scheme of Work for Primary Mathematics*, Hodder & Stoughton, London.

ATM (1987) *Co-ordinating Maths in Primary and Middle Schools*, Association of Teachers of Mathematics, Derby.

Backhouse, J., Haggarty, L., Pirie, S. and Stratton, J. (1992) *Improving the Learning of Mathematics*, Cassell, London.

Barnes, D. (1982) *Practical Curriculum Study*, Routledge & Kegan Paul, London.

Barthorpe, T. (1992) *Differentiation – Eight Ideas for the Classroom*, Desktop Publications, Scunthorpe.

Bath, J.B., Chinn, S.J. and Knox, D.E. (1986) *Test of Cognitive Style in Mathematics – Manual*, Slosson Educational Publications, Inc., East Aurora, NY 14042.

Bechtel, W. and Abrahamsen, A. (1991) *Connectionism and the Mind: An Introduction to Parellel Processing in Networks*, Blackwell, Cambridge, Mass.

Birmingham Curriculum Support Service (1992) *Mathematics in Action: Mathematics Guidelines*, Birmingham City Council Education Department, Birmingham.

Brissenden, T.H.F. (1988) *Talking about Mathematics: Mathematical Discussion in Primary Classrooms*, Blackwell, Oxford.

Bruner, J.S. (1967) *Towards a Theory of Instruction*, Belknap Press, Cambridge, Mass.

Bruner, J.S. (1990) *Acts of Meaning*, Harvard University Press, Cambridge, Mass.

Bush, T. (1995) *Theories of Educational Management*, (2nd edn), Paul Chapman Publishing, London.

Chazan, M., Laing, A.F., and Davies, D. (1994) *Emotional and Behavioural Difficulties in Middle Childhood: Identification, Assessment and Intervention in School*, Falmer Press, London.

Cheshire County Council Education Department (1989) *Cheshire Curriculum Policy Statement 5–16*, Cheshire County Council Educational Services Group, Cheshire.

Cheshire County Council Education Department (1996) *Cheshire Curriculum Policy Statement 5–16*, Cheshire County Council Educational Services Group, Cheshire.

Cheshire Unit for Pupil Assessment (CUPA) (1992) *Primary Records of Achievement*, Cheshire County Council Education Services, Cheshire.

Chinn, S. and Ashcroft, J.R. (1993) *Mathematics for Dyslexics: A Teaching Handbook*, Whurr Publishers, London.

Clemson, D. and Clemson, W. (1991) *The Really Practical Guide to Primary Assessment*, Stanley Thornes, Cheltenham.

Clemson, D. and Clemson, W. (1994) *Teaching Mathematics in the Early Years*, Routledge, London.

Clift, P., Weiner, G. and Wilson, E. (1981) *Record keeping in Primary Schools*, Macmillan, London.

Cockcroft Report (1982) *Mathematics Counts: Report of the Committee of Inquiry into the Teaching of Mathematics in Schools under the Chairmanship of Dr W.H. Cockcroft*, HMSO, London.

Compton, C. and Bigge, J. (1976) Teaching individuals with physical and multiple disabilities, in Reisman, F. and Kauffman, S. (eds.) (1980) *Teaching Mathematics to Children with Special Needs*, Charles E. Merrill, Columbus, Ohio.

Conner, C. (1991) *Assessment and Testing in the Primary School*, Falmer Press, London.

Curriculum Council For Wales (1991) *The Curriculum for the Under-Fives*, HMSO, London.

Cutts, N.E. and Moseley, N. (1957) *Teaching the Bright and Gifted*, Prentice-Hall, Englewood-Cliffs, NJ.

Day, C., Whitaker, P. and Johnston, D. (1990) *Managing Primary schools in the 1990s: A Professional Development Approach* (2nd edn), Paul Chapman Publishing, London.

Dearing, R. (1994) *The National Curriculum and its Assessment – Final Report*, SCAA, London.

Denvir, B. and Brown, M. (1986) Understanding of mathematical concepts in low-attaining 7–9 year olds, *Educational Studies in Mathematics Education*, Vol. 17 pp. 143–64.

DES (1985) *Curriculum Matters 3: Mathematics 5–16*, HMSO, London.

DES (1988) *Mathematics for Ages 5–16 (Proposals for the Secretary of State for Education and Science and the Secretary of State for Wales)*, HMSO, London.

DES (1989a) *Assessment and Statements of Special Educational Needs: Procedures within Education, Health and Social Services*, Circular 22/98, DES, London.

DES (1989b) *Mathematics in the National Curriculum*, HMSO, London.

DES (1989c) *Aspects of Primary Education: The Teaching and Learning of Mathematics*, HMSO, London.

DES (1990) *National Curriculum Assessment Arrangements*, HMSO, London.

DES, Department of Education for Northern Ireland, Welsh Office Education Department (1985) *New Perspectives on the Mathematics Curriculum. An Independent Appraisal of the Outcomes of the APU Mathematics Testing 1978–1982*, Cambridge Institute of Education, Cambridge.

Desforges, C. and Cockburn, A. (1987) *Understanding the Mathematics Teacher: A Study of Practice in First Schools*, Falmer Press, London.

DFE (1995a) *Key Stages 1 and 2 of the National Curriculum*, HMSO, London.

DFE (1995b) *Key Stages 3 and 4 of the National Curriculum*, HMSO, London.

DfEE (1996) *Nursery Education Voucher Scheme: The Guide*, DfEE, London.

DfEE (1997a) *Reports on Pupil's Achievements in Primary Schools in 1996/7,* Circular 1/97, DfEE, London.

DfEE (1997b) *Teaching: High Status, High Standards: Requirements for Courses in Inital Teacher Training,* Circular 10/97, DfEE, London.

Donaldson, M. (1978) *Children's Minds,* Fontana, London.

Dudley Curriculum Support Service (1995) *Mathematics Progression through Key Stages 1 and 2: SEN Co-ordinators Handbook,* Dudley Education Department, Dudley.

Edwards, A. and Knight, P. (1994) *Effective Early Years Education: Teaching Young Children,* Open University Press, Buckingham.

Edwards, S. (1995) Managing differentiation in mathematics at Key Stage One, *Primary Practice,* September, pp. 3–7.

Edwards, S. (1997) Mental arithmetic at Key Stage 1, *Primary Practice,* September, pp. 4–7.

Edwards, S. and Edwards, G. (1992) Building bridges between concrete and abstract conceptualisation of number in young children – a strategy using make-believe signifiers, *Early Childhood Development and Care,* Vol. 82, pp. 27–36.

Edwards, S. and Wild, C. (1990) *Numberland,* Collins Educational, London.

Edwards, S., Wild, C. and Warner, S. (1988) *Starmaths,* Collins Educational, London.

Edwards, S. and Woodhead, N. (1996) Mathematics teaching in primary schools: whole class, group or individual teaching?, *Primary Practice,* September, pp. 4–7.

Ernest, P. (1989) *Mathematics Teaching: The State of the Art,* Falmer Press London.

Fisher, J. (1996) *Starting form the Child?,* Open University Press, Buckingham.

Flegg, G. (1984) *Numbers: Their History and Meaning,* Penguin, Harmondsworth.

Freeman, J. (1979) *Gifted Children: Their Identification and Development in a Social Context,* MTP Press, Lancaster.

Fullan, M. (1982) *The Meaning of Educational Change,* Insitute for Studies in Education, Ontario.

Gagne, R.M. (1970) *The Conditions of Learning* (2nd edn), Holt, Rinehart & Winston, New York.

Gelman, R. and Gallistel, C.R. (1978) *The Child's Understanding of Number,* Harvard University Press, Cambridge, Mass. and London.

Ginsburg, H.P. (1997) *Children's Arithmetic: The Learning Process,* Van Nostrand, New York.

Graham, N. and Blinko, J. (1989) *Zero to Ninety-Nine: Problem Solving on a 100 Square,* Claire Publications, Colchester.

Griffiths, R. (1994) Mathematics and play, in Moyles, J. (ed.) *The Excellence of Play,* Open University Press, Buckingham.

Haylock, D. and Cockburn, A. (1997) *Understanding Mathematics in the Lower Primary Years,* Paul Chapman Publishing, London.

Headington, R. (1997) *Supporting Numeracy: A Handbook for those who Assist in Early Years Settings,* David Fulton, London.

HMI (1992) *Mathematics Key Stages 1, 2 and 3: A Report by HM Inspecorate on the Second Year, 1990–91,* HMSO, London.

Hohmann, M., Banet, B. and Weikart, D.P. (1979) *Young Children in Action: A Manual for Pre-School Educators,* High/Scope Educational Research Foundation, Ypsilanti, Mich.

Hopkins, C., Gifford, G. and Pepperell, S. (1996) *Mathematics in the Primary School: A Sense of Progression,* David Fulton in association with the Roehampton Institute, London.

Hopkins, D. (1985) *A Teacher's Guide to Classroom Research*, Open University Press, Milton Keynes.

Hughes, M. (1981) Can pre-school children add and subtract? *Educational Psychology*, Vol. 1, pp. 207–19.

Hughes, M. (1983) Teaching arithmetic to pre-school children., *Educational Review*, Vol. 35, pp. 163–73.

Hughes, M. (1986) *Children and Number*, Blackwell, Oxford.

Huizinga, J. (1949) *Homo Iudens: A Study of the Play-Element in Culture*, Routledge & Kegan Paul, London.

Hutt, C. (1979) Towards a Taxonomy of Play, in Sutton-Smith, B. (ed.) *Play and Learning*, Garder Press, New York.

Hutt, S.J., Tyler, S., Hutt, C. and Christopherson, H. (1989) *Play, Exploration and Learning: A Natural History of the Pre-School*, Routledge, London.

Isaacs, S. (1929) *The Nursery Years*, Routledge & Kegan Paul, London.

James, F. and Brownsword, K. (1994) *Behaviour Management: A Positive Approach*, Belair Publications, Twickenham.

Johnson, D.C. and Millett, A. (ed.) (1996) *Implementing the Mathematics National Curriculum: Policy, Politics and Practice*, Paul Chapman Publishing, London.

Kerry, T. (1981) *Teaching Bright Pupils*, Macmillan, Basingstoke.

Kerry, T. (ed.) (1983) *Finding and Helping the Able Child*, Croom Helm, London.

Kibel, M. (1992) *Linking language to action*, in Miles, T.R. and Miles, E. (eds.), *Dyslexia and Mathematics*, Routledge, London.

Kounin, J.S. (1970) *Discipline and Group Management in Classrooms*, Rinehart & Winston, New York.

Krutetskii, V.A. (1976) The psychology of mathematical abilities in school children, in Chinn S. and Ashcroft J.R. (1993), *Mathematics for Dyslexics: A Teaching Handbook*, Whurr Publishers Ltd., London.

Laar, B. (1996) An inspector writes: lesson planning, *The Times Educational Supplement*, 12 July, p. 13.

Lévacic, R. (ed.) (1989) *Financial Management in Education*, Open University Press, Milton Keynes.

Lewis, A. (1996) *Discovering Mathematics with 4 to 7-Year-Olds*, Hodder & Stoughton, London.

Liebeck, P. (1984) *How children learn mathematics*, Penguin Books, London.

Mason, K. (1995) *Assess and Progress: A Resource Pack for Teachers of Key Stages 1 and 2: Using and Applying Mathematics*, NFER, Slough.

Maxwell, E. and Hofkins, D. (1996) A mixed reception, *The Times Educational Supplement*, 22 October, p. 13.

McNamara, S., Moreton, G. and Newton, H. (1996) *Differentiation*, Pearson Publishing, Cambridge.

Merrtens, R. (1997) Active ingredients (for teaching numeracy in primary schools) *The Times Educational Supplement*, 26 September, p. 11.

Merrtens, R. and Vass, J. (1990) *Sharing Maths Cultures*, Falmer Press, London.

Moyles, J. (1989) *Just Playing? The Role and Status of Play in Early Childhood Education*, Open University Press, Milton Keynes.

Moyles, J. (ed.) (1994) *The Excellence of Play*, Open University Press, Buckingham.

National Numeracy Project (1997) *Framework for Numeracy Years 1–6*, National Centre for Literacy and Numeracy, Reading.

NCC (1991) *Mathematics, Non-Statutory Guidance*, HMSO, London.

Nias, J., Southworth, G. and Campbell, P. (1992) *Whole-School Curriculum Development in the Primary School*, Falmer Press, London.

Ofsted (1993a) *Mathematics Key Stages 1, 2 and 3. Third Year 1991–1992. A Report from the Office of Her Majesty's Chief Inspector of Schools*, HMSO, London.

Ofsted (1993b) *The Teaching and Learning of Number in Primary Schools: National Curriculum Mathematics Attainment Target 2*, HMSO, London.

Ofsted (1994) *Primary Matters: A Discussion on Teaching and Learning in Primary Schools*, Ofsted, London.

Ofsted (1995) *Mathematics: A Review of Inspection Findings 1993–1994*, HMSO, London.

Ofsted (1996) *Draft Framework for the Assessment of Quality and Standards in Initial Teacher Training*, Ofsted and TTA, London.

Ofsted (1997) *Guidance on the Inspection of Nursery Education Provision in the Private, Voluntary and Independent Sectors*, HMSO, London.

Ogilvie, E. (1973) *Gifted Children in Primary Schools*, Schools Council Research Studies, Macmillan, London.

Pask, G. and Scott, B.C.E. (1975) Learning Strategies and Individual Competence in Whitehead, J. M. (ed.) *Personality and Learning 1*, Hodder & Stoughton, Sevenoaks.

Plowden Report (1967) *Children and their Primary Schools: Report of the Central Advisory Council for Education in England*, HMSO, London.

Pollard, A. and Tann, S. (1993) *Reflective Teaching in the Primary School: A Handbook for the Classroom* (2nd edn), Cassell, London.

Povey, R.M. (ed.) (1980) *Educating the Gifted Child*, Harper & Row, London.

Reisman, K. and Kauffman, S. (1980) *Teaching Mathematics to Children with Special Needs*, Charles E. Merrill, Colombus, Ohio.

Reynolds, D. and Farrell, S. (1996) *Worlds Apart: A Review of International Surveys of Educational Achievement Involving England*, HMSO, London.

Richardson, R. (1996) The Curriculum Co-ordinator: Writing the Curriculum Policy, *Child Education*, Vol. 73, no. 9, pp. 50–1.

Rogoff, B. and Lave, J. (eds.) (1984) *Everyday Cognition: Its Development in Social Context*, Harvard University Press, London.

Rowntree, D. (1977) *Assessing Students. How Shall We Know Them?*, Harper and Row, London.

SCAA (1995a) *Consistency in Teacher Assessment: Guidance for Schools*, SCAA, London.

SCAA (1995b) *Consistency in Teacher Assessment: Exemplification of Standards*, SCAA, London.

SCAA (1996a) *Nursery Education: Desirable Outcomes for Children's Learning on Entering Compulsory Education*, DfEE, London.

SCAA (1996b) *National Framework for Baseline Assessment*, SCAA, London.

SCAA (1997a) *Key Stage 1 Assessment Arrangements*, SCAA London.

SCAA (1997b) *Key Stage 1 Tasks, Level 1, 1997: Mathematics Handbook*, SCAA, London.

SCAA (1997c) *Key Stage 1 Mathematics Test Levels 2 and 3, 1997: Teachers Guide*, SCAA, London.

SCAA (1997d) *Standards at Key Stage 1 English and Mathematics: Report on the 1996 National Curriculum Assessment for 7-year-olds*, SCAA, London.

SCAA (1997e) *Standards at Key Stage 2 English and Mathematics: Report on the 1996 National Curriculum Assessment for 11-year-olds*, SCAA, London.

SCAA (1997f) *Baseline Assessment scales*, SCAA, London.

SCAA (1997g) *Baseline Assessment: Information for Schools*, June 1997, SCAA, London.

Schools Council Working Paper 75, (1983) *Primary Practice,* Methuen Educational, London.

Shorrocks, D., Frobisher, L., Nelson, N., Turner, L. and Waterson, A. (1993) *Implementing National Curriculum Assessment in the Primary School,* Hodder & Stoughton, London.

Shuard, H., Walsh, A., Goodwin, J. and Worcester, V. (1991) *PriME Calculators, Children and Mathematics,* Simon & Schuster, London.

Sieghart, F. (1980) Families under Stress, in Povey, R. (ed.) *Educating the Gifted Child,* Harper & Row, London.

Sinclair, A. and Sinclair, H. (1984) Pre-school children's interpretation of written numbers, *Human Learning,* Vol. 3, pp. 173–84.

Skilbeck, M. (1982) School-based curriculum development: A functionalist/ environmentalist approach to curriculum change, in Barnes, D. (ed.) *Practical Curriculum Study,* Routledge & Kegan Paul, London.

Smith, P.K. (1994) Play and the uses of play in Moyles, J. (ed.) *The Excellence of Play,* Open University Press, Buckingham.

Stenmark, J.K. (1991) *Mathematics Assessment.* National Council of Teachers of Mathematics, Virginia.

Stevenson, H.W. and Lee, S.Y. (1990) Contexts for achievement, *Monographs of the Society for Research in Child Development,* Vol. 55, pp. 1–2.

Stow, M. (1989) *Managing Mathematics in the Primary School: A Practical Resource for the Co-ordinator,* NFER-Nelson, Windsor.

Straker, A. (1996) Raising expectations and achievement, *Child Education,* December, pp. 12–13.

Sutton, R. (1991) *Assessment: A Framework for Teachers,* Routledge, London.

Tann, C.S. (ed.) (1988) *Developing Topic Work in the Primary School,* Falmer Press, London.

Thomas, N. (1985) *Improving Primary Schools: A Report of the Committee on Primary Education,* ILEA, London.

Thornton, C.A., Tucker, B.F., Dossey, J.A. and Bazik, E.F. (1983) *Teaching Mathematics to Children with Special Needs,* Addison-Wesley, Menlo Park, Calif.

Vygotsky, L.S. (1962) *Thought and Language,* MIT Press, Cambridge, Mass.

Vygotksy, L.S. (1978) *Mind and Society: The Development of Higher Psychological Processes,* Harvard University Press, Cambridge, Mass.

Walden, R. and Walkerdine, V. (1982) *Girls and Mathematics: The Early Years. Bedford Way Papers 8,* University of London Institute of Education, London.

Wilson, S. (1997) Social gene 'for women only', *The Scotsman,* 12 June, p. 3.

Winteridge, D. (ed.) (1989) *A Handbook for Primary Mathematics Co-ordinators,* Paul Chapman Publishing, London.

Wolfendale, S. (1993) *Baseline Assessment: A Review of Practice, Issues and Strategies for Effective Implementation,* Trentham Books, Stoke-on-Trent.

Wood, D. (1988) *How Children Think and Learn,* Blackwell, Oxford.

Wood, E. and Attfield, J. (1996) *Play, Learning and the Early Childhood Curriculum,* Paul Chapman Publishing, London.

Wragg, E.C. (1993) *Class Management,* Routledge, London.

Index